Music in Medieval Rituals for the End of Life

Music in Medieval Rituals for the End of Life

ELAINE STRATTON HILD

OXFORD
UNIVERSITY PRESS

Oxford University Press is a department of the University of Oxford. It furthers
the University's objective of excellence in research, scholarship, and education
by publishing worldwide. Oxford is a registered trade mark of Oxford University
Press in the UK and certain other countries.

Published in the United States of America by Oxford University Press
198 Madison Avenue, New York, NY 10016, United States of America.

© Oxford University Press 2024

All rights reserved. No part of this publication may be reproduced, stored in
a retrieval system, or transmitted, in any form or by any means, without the
prior permission in writing of Oxford University Press, or as expressly permitted
by law, by license, or under terms agreed with the appropriate reproduction
rights organization. Inquiries concerning reproduction outside the scope of the
above should be sent to the Rights Department, Oxford University Press, at the
address above.

You must not circulate this work in any other form
and you must impose this same condition on any acquirer.

Library of Congress Cataloging-in-Publication Data
Names: Hild, Elaine Stratton, author.
Title: Music in medieval rituals for the end of life / Elaine Stratton Hild.
Description: [First edition]. | New York, NY : Oxford University Press, 2024. |
Includes bibliographical references and index.
Identifiers: LCCN 2023042133 (print) | LCCN 2023042134 (ebook) |
ISBN 9780197685914 (hardback) | ISBN 9780197685921 (epub) |
ISBN 9780197685938 (ebook) | ISBN 9780197685945 (ebook)
Subjects: LCSH: Gregorian chants—History and criticism. | Death—Religious
aspects—Christianity—History—To 1500. | Death—Social
aspects—Europe—History—To 1500. | Funeral rites and ceremonies,
Medieval—Europe—History.
Classification: LCC ML3082.H52 2023 (print) | LCC ML3082 (ebook) |
DDC 781.5/880902—dc23/eng/20230922
LC record available at https://lccn.loc.gov/2023042133
LC ebook record available at https://lccn.loc.gov/2023042134

DOI: 10.1093/oso/9780197685914.001.0001

Printed by Integrated Books International, United States of America

The Press is grateful to Notengrafik Berlin for the creation of
custom music examples for this book.

Images of Biblioteca Apostolica Vaticana, Arch. Cap. S. Pietro F 11 pt. A
are reproduced by permission of the Vatican Apostolic
Library, all rights reserved.

for Florian

Contents

Acknowledgments ix
Editorial Symbols Used in Music Transcriptions xi

Introduction: Contemporary Approaches to Medieval Rituals
for the Dying   1

1. Religious Elites: Rome, "Old Roman" Tradition   14

    Manuscript Source: Vatican, Biblioteca Apostolica Vaticana,
    Arch. Cap. S. Pietro F 11 pt. A (SP F 11)

2. Political and Religious Leaders: Sens, Cathedral of Saint Stephen   59

    Manuscript Source: Paris, Bibliothèque nationale de France,
    lat. 934 (Paris 934)

3. With the Laity: Orsières, Switzerland   83

    Manuscript Source: Bourg-Saint-Pierre, Hospice du
    Grand-Saint-Bernard, ms. 3 (ancien 10091) (GSB 3)

4. Among Women: Abbey of Saint Mary the Virgin and
Saint Francis without Aldgate (England)   110

    Manuscript Source: Reigate (Surrey), Parish Church of St Mary
    Magdalene, Cranston Library, Ms. 2322 (Cranston 2322)

5. Analysis: Variation and Continuity within the Liturgical
Tradition   137

Final Considerations: Why Sing?   167

Appendix: Contents of Individual Rituals   175
Bibliography   193
Index: Manuscripts Cited (with Abbreviations)   211
Index: Chants and Other Items in Rituals   215
Index: General   221

Acknowledgments

Undertaking this research project has been possible because of the eleven years (and counting) that I have been a part of *Corpus monodicum*, a long-term scholarly program housed at the Universität Würzburg and dedicated to producing editions of previously unpublished medieval plainchant. It has been a privilege to learn the intricacies of medieval notations and scribal practices from leading scholars and from countless hours working with medieval manuscripts. My gratitude goes to my colleagues and mentors, most particularly Wulf Arlt, Charles Atkinson, Gunilla Björkvall, David Catalunya, Andreas Haug, Felix Heinzer, Gunilla Iversen, Ritva Maria Jacobsson, Isabel Kraft, Lori Kruckenberg, Michael Norton, Nils Holger Petersen, Andreas Pfisterer, Susan Rankin, Konstantin Voigt, and Hanna Zühlke, for the standards you have modeled and the collegial co-learning.

Completing this research project has been possible because of the support I received from the University of Notre Dame's Institute for Advanced Study, including the institute's leadership—Brad Gregory, Carolyn Sherman, and Donald Stelluto—as well as Harvey Brown, J. Patout Burns, Eric Chaisson, Francis X. Clooney, Xinyu Dong, Daniel Hinshaw, Luc Jaeger, Jarek Jankowski, Robin Jensen, Claire Taylor Jones, Henrike Lange, Yutong Liu, Janice Gunther Martin, Tom McLeish, and Finola Prendergast. During my semester in residence, the wider Notre Dame community provided a rich environment for study and conversation, and I am thankful to Lacey Ahern, Kimberly Belcher, Philip Bess, Jeffrey Bishop, Calvin Bower, Thomas Burman, Michael Driscoll, Margot Fassler, Jonathan Hehn, Daniel and Halle Hobbins, Peter Jeffery, Patrick Kronner, Stephen Little, Timothy O'Malley, Andrea Riedl, Artur Rosman, and Julia Schneider for their insights and encouragement.

This publication has benefited from presentations and discussions in several additional academic communities: North American Academy of Liturgy, particularly the Issues in Medieval Liturgy Seminar; Kenyon College, with Benjamin Locke and Lucy Barnhouse; IMS study group Cantus planus meeting in Växjö, Sweden, with Joseph Dyer, Luisa Nardini, and Rebecca Maloy; University of Saint Thomas (Houston), with Randall Smith and Tamara

Nicholl-Smith; Loveland Classical Schools, with Ian Stout, Rebecca Faust-Frodl, and Timothy Smith; Universität Freiburg, with Konstantin Voigt, Janine Droese, and Konrad Küster; Colorado State University, with Joel Bacon; the University of Colorado at Boulder, during Patrick Geary's visit and lecture; and in my own neighborhood, during long walks with the ever-curious and thoughtful Tobias Hild.

Katarina Ster, Lori Jones, and Nükhet Varlık supported my initial publications on medieval liturgies for the dying with their editorial guidance. I am also indebted to Miklós István Földváry (Eötvös Loránd University, Budapest) for generously allowing use of the Usuarium database to locate manuscript sources. Timothy Smith offered expert feedback on Latin translations, and my invaluable colleague Andreas Pfisterer reviewed the book's music transcriptions and appendix. The music transcriptions were typeset by Thomas Weber of Notengrafik Berlin using customized engraving software.

Manuscript images and permissions were provided by Biblioteca Apostolica Vaticana, Bibliothèque nationale de France, and Jean-Pierre Voutaz of the Archives du Gd-St-Bernard (facilitated by Alexis Deforge and Bryan Smith). I am also indebted to Anne Bagnall Yardley for facilitating access to images of the Cranston 2322 manuscript.

Norman Hirschy and Rachel Ruisard of Oxford University Press have offered skillful and timely editorial support, and I am also grateful to the anonymous reviewers of this book's earlier drafts. Their careful readings and thorough responses greatly improved the work.

Unfailing encouragement and good guidance from my academic mentors, Rebecca Maloy and Elissa Guralnick, and friends and family members Florian and Tobias Hild, Bryan and Allyson Smith, Arlene Seeber, Timothy and Delia Smith and Kathryn Harrison, John and Dorothy Stratton, and Catherine Stratton Treadway have nurtured the project from beginning to end.

My sincerest thanks and gratitude to each of you.

Editorial Symbols Used in Music Transcriptions

⟨ ⟩   Text within brackets has been supplied by the editor.

...   Editorial omission.

| Line change in manuscript source.

‖   Folio change in manuscript source.

⌒   Pitches under a bracket are graphically combined in the manuscript source.

⌒   A smaller notehead indicates a liquescent pitch.[1]

¶   A descending liquescence for which the scribe did not indicate pitch content.

♭   B-flats are the only accidentals that appear in the source material of the edited repertory. Their positions in the music transcriptions reflect their positions in the medieval notation. In certain contexts (for example, where a pitch "b" follows closely after an "f"), it seems likely that a "b-flat" would have been sung in order to avoid a tritone, although no flat is notated. In an effort to accurately reflect the scribal work, flats have not been added in these contexts.

---

[1] Hiley offers an overview of medieval liquescent signs and possible performative meanings in *Western Plainchant*, 357–358.

Introduction
Contemporary Approaches to Medieval Rituals for the Dying

"We study the past for the ways it can shock us."[1] Caroline Walker Bynum's words resonate as I remember the beginnings of this research project. Shock—even disbelief—formed my first reaction when I learned of the medieval practice of singing for a person at the moment of death. The contrast with our contemporary end-of-life care, with its focus on technology, medications, and medical professionals, amazed me.

Yet extant manuscripts reveal clearly that for centuries of European history, a sung liturgy was considered the exemplary accompaniment to a life's ending.[2] Rituals for the dying were well developed, practiced widely, and thoroughly integrated with music. Indeed, through these rituals, music held a privileged position at the time of death. Melody was, ideally, the final sensation of a human life. It is this music—the chants intended to accompany the final agony and the final breath—that forms the subject of the following study. Through detailed investigations of liturgical manuscripts, this book examines and recovers, to the extent possible, the music sung at the end of an individual's life during the Middle Ages.

---

[1] "[W]e study the past for the ways it can shock us into diagnosing what is oddest, most perplexing, and yet most glorious and enduring in our own situation," Caroline Walker Bynum, *The Resurrection of the Body in Western Christianity, 200–1336* (New York: Columbia University Press, 2019), xxvii.

[2] I use the term "liturgy" as is common in musicological scholarship: to indicate a series of items (often prayers, chants, and gestures) conducted or "performed" as a religious ceremony. The term "liturgy" implies both a prescription by an institutional authority and an expectation that the items will be performed in a largely predetermined way. As Dyer puts it: "approved by competent ecclesiastical authorities, international, national, or local" and with "a certain level of structural or verbal fixity" (Joseph Dyer, Kenneth Levy, and Dimitri Conomos, "Liturgy and Liturgical Books," in *Oxford Music Online: Grove Music Online* [2001], https://www-oxfordmusiconline-com.proxy.library.nd.edu/grovemusic/). Booth and Tingle offer additional, succinct terminology to describe end-of-life liturgies: "the institutional framework established for the consolation of the dying." Philip Booth and Elizabeth C. Tingle, eds., *A Companion to Death, Burial, and Remembrance in Late Medieval and Early Modern Europe, c. 1300–1700* (Leiden: Brill, 2021), 2.

Medieval deathbed liturgies have been the subject of academic research, but previous publications have focused on aspects of the rituals apart from their music. Fundamental questions remain. Which melodies were sung at the time of death? Were these chants taken from other liturgies, or did they form a unique repertory, created specifically for the end of life? To what extent did the people of different geographic areas and religious institutions maintain their own, "local" versions of deathbed rituals and chants? Amid the diversity of rituals for the dying evident in medieval manuscripts, one commonality is the use of song. Why was music given such a prominent position within these liturgies? What functions did the chants perform? In other words: why did communities gather and sing when a loved one was dying?

The robust, high-quality corpus of scholarship on the rituals' texts enables this study of their music. Frederick Paxton's pivotal publication *Christianizing Death* traces the development of European deathbed rites from late Antiquity through the Carolingian era, when their overall structures became largely fixed.[3] His work reveals significant innovations that occurred during the late eighth and ninth centuries in Frankish regions. Damien Sicard examined rituals in 139 manuscript sources, documenting the transmission patterns of individual prayers and chant texts and assessing the likelihood of their Roman origins.[4] Andrieu's earlier edition of a medieval rite for the death of an individual (which he termed *Ordo XLIX*) provided an important impulse for Sicard's work.[5] The extensive source base used by Sicard (which includes manuscripts from religious institutions and orders throughout Western Europe, dating into the seventeenth century) reveals the geographic breadth and longevity of the liturgical tradition. Early sources without music notation containing liturgical material for an individual's death have been edited by Férotin, Chavasse, Mohlberg, Frank, Deshusses, Dumas, and Heiming, among others.[6] (Most of these early sources are sacramentaries; some are

---

[3] Frederick S. Paxton, *Christianizing Death: The Creation of a Ritual Process in Early Medieval Europe* (Ithaca, NY: Cornell University Press, 1990).

[4] Damien Sicard, *La liturgie de la mort dans l'église latine des origines à la réforme carolingienne* (Münster, Westfalen: Aschendorffsche Verlagsbuchhandlung, 1978).

[5] Michel Andrieu, *Les Ordines Romani du haut moyen âge: Les Textes; Ordines XXXV–XLIX* (Louvain: Spicilegium Sacrum Lovaniense, 1956), 523–530. Andrieu edited *Ordo XLIX* from the eleventh-century manuscript Vatican, Biblioteca Apostolica Vaticana, Ott. lat. 312 (hereafter referred to as Vatican 312).

[6] Paxton provides a bibliography of editions of these early sources in *Christianizing Death*, 211–213. Some of the most significant are: Marius Férotin, ed., *Le liber ordinum en usage dans l'église wisigothique et mozarabe d'Espagne du cinquième au onzième siècle* (Rome: Centro Liturgico Vincenziano Edizioni Liturgiche, 1996); Antoine Chavasse, ed., *La Sacramentaire Gélasien (Vaticanus Reginensis 316): sacramentaire presbytéral en usage dans les titres romains au VIIe siècle* (Tournai: Desclée, 1958); Leo Cunibert Mohlberg, ed., *Liber sacramentorum romanae aeclesiae*

fragmentary *libelli*.) Van Dijk's work establishes the earliest versions of the deathbed rituals of the Franciscan Order, and Donohue considers several medieval rites as sources for the ritual published by the Roman Catholic Church in the early 1980s.[7] Most recently, Paxton has produced an edition and in-depth analysis of the medieval rites for the dying from the abbey of Cluny, France, and Susan Boynton has done the same for the abbey of Farfa.[8] By identifying manuscript sources and establishing textual readings and transmission patterns, these publications provide a foundation from which to investigate and secure the rituals' extant melodic content.[9]

Like many of the contributions cited above, this study limits itself to the European, Christian liturgical tradition that existed prior to the *Ars moriendi*

---

ordinis anni circuli (Cod. Vat. Reg. lat. 316/Paris Bibl. Nat. 7193, 41/56; *Sacramentarium Gelasianum*) (Rome: Casa editrice Herder, 1960); Hieronymus Frank, "Der älteste erhaltene Ordo defunctorum der römischen Liturgie und sein Fortleben in Totenagenden des frühen Mittelalters," *Archiv für Liturgiewissenschaft* 7 (1962): 360–415; Jean Deshusses, ed., *Le sacramentaire grégorien* (Fribourg [CH]: Éditions universitaires, 1971–1982); Antoine Dumas, ed., *Liber sacramentorum Gellonensis* (Turnhout: Brepols, 1981); and Odilo Heiming, ed., *Liber sacramentorum augustodunensis* (Turnhout: Brepols, 1984).

[7] S. J. P. Van Dijk and J. Hazelden Walker, *The Origins of the Modern Roman Liturgy: The Liturgy of the Papal Court and the Franciscan Order in the Thirteenth Century* (London: Darton, Longman & Todd, 1960), 280–291. A critical edition of the ritual is provided by: S. J. P. van Dijk, *Sources of the Modern Roman Liturgy: The Ordinals by Haymo of Faversham and Related Documents* (Leiden: E. J. Brill, 1963), 2:390–392. James Michael Donohue, "The Rite for the Commendation of the Dying in the 1983 *Pastoral Care of the Sick: Rites of Anointing and Viaticum*: A Study through a Comparison with Its Counterparts in the 1614 *Rituale Romanum* and in the 1972 editio typica of *Ordo unctionis infirmorum eorumque pastoralis curae*" (PhD diss., Catholic University of America, 2000).

[8] Frederick S. Paxton, "Death by Customary at Eleventh-Century Cluny," in *From Dead of Night to End of Day: The Medieval Customs of Cluny*, ed. S. Boynton and I. Cochelin (Turnhout: Brepols, 2005), 297–318; Frederick S. Paxton, *The Death Ritual at Cluny in the Central Middle Ages* (Turnhout: Brepols, 2013); Susan Boynton, "A Monastic Death Ritual from the Imperial Abbey of Farfa," *Traditio* 64 (2009): 57–84; Susan Boynton, *Shaping a Monastic Identity: Liturgy & History at the Imperial Abbey of Farfa, 1000–1125* (Ithaca, NY: Cornell University Press, 2006). Paxton's most recent overview of medieval liturgies for the dying will be published as "Sickness, Death, Burial," in *Brill Handbook of Medieval Latin Liturgy*, ed. Daniel DiCenso and Andrew Irving (Leiden: Brill, forthcoming). On the Sarum rite, see J. Wickham Legg, ed., *The Sarum Missal: Edited from Three Early Manuscripts* (Oxford: Clarendon Press, 1916); Matthew Cheung Salisbury, *The Secular Liturgical Office in Late Medieval England* (Turnhout: Brepols, 2015); and Madeleine Gray, "Deathbed and Burial Rituals in Late Medieval Catholic Europe," in *A Companion to Death, Burial, and Remembrance in Late Medieval and Early Modern Europe, c. 1300–1700*, ed. Philip Booth and Elizabeth C. Tingle (Leiden: Brill, 2021), 106–131. Osten-Hoschek has completed a new study on the Dominican rites for the dying: Andrea Osten-Hoschek, *Reform und Liturgie im Nürnberger Katharinenkloster: Die Sterbe- und Begräbnisliturgie des 15. Jahrhunderts; Edition und Kommentar* (Berlin: De Gruyter, 2023).

[9] These textual editions and analyses are referenced throughout the following discussions. Research on death and dying in the Middle Ages using other types of source material "has produced an enormous body of scholarship over the last thirty years and remains vigorous" (Booth and Tingle, *A Companion to Death, Burial, and Remembrance*, 1); these editors provide an extensive overview and evaluation of such scholarship, 3–30. See also Caroline Walker Bynum and Paul Freedman, eds., *Last Things: Death and the Apocalypse in the Middle Ages* (Philadelphia: University of Pennsylvania Press, 2000), 2–10.

publications of the fifteenth century; prior to the development of rites in vernacular languages prompted by the sixteenth-century reformation; and prior to the publication of the Rituale of 1614 by the Roman Catholic Church, which standardized deathbed liturgies and replaced local versions.[10] The liturgical tradition studied in this book is also distinguishable from the meditations on death and the afterlife prescribed by theologians during the Middle Ages.[11]

One further limitation of this study concerns the amount of material contained in the medieval sources. The manuscripts often present an extended series of items intended for the entirety of a life's ending: the final agony, death, the washing and preparation of the body, transporting the body to church, the vigil with the body, the funeral Mass, transportation to the grave, and burial, as well as commemorative services. Rubrics frequently coordinate sections of this material to specific moments in the progression from sickbed to grave, but the different sections seem to have been understood as parts of a whole. A single liturgy accompanied the soul from its residence in a human body to its residence in the heavenly community, and this same liturgy guided the human community through the loss of a member and the appropriate handling of the corpse. This study focuses on the liturgical items prescribed specifically for the gathering at the deathbed and the time period immediately following death,[12] rather than the services held in the church between death and burial or the items that accompanied the procession to the grave and the burial. The music indicated for this particular use—as an accompaniment to the final moments of life and the first moments after life—is least known in scholarship, having never been the subject of a

---

[10] For a comprehensive examination of the seventeenth-century Roman Catholic version of the rite (as well as the earlier sources from which it drew), see Donohue, "The Rite."

[11] See particularly Mark Chinca, *Meditating Death in Medieval and Early Modern Devotional Writing: From Bonaventure to Luther* (Oxford: Oxford University Press, 2020).

[12] The "rites of separation," in the terminology developed by Arnold van Gennep and systematically applied to the medieval deathbed rituals of Western Europe by Fredrick Paxton and Paul Binski. Arnold van Gennep, *Les rites de passage; étude systématique des rites de la porte et du seuil, de l'hospitalité, de l'adoption, de la grossesse et de l'accouchement, de la naissance, de l'enfance, de la puberté, de l'initiation, de l'ordination, du couronnement des fiançailles et du mariage, des funérailles, des saisons, etc.* (Paris: E. Nourry, 1909). Translated as *The Rites of Passage* (Chicago: University of Chicago Press, 1960). See also Paxton, *Christianizing Death*, 5–7; and Paul Binski, *Medieval Death: Ritual and Representation* (Ithaca, NY: Cornell University Press, 1996), particularly 29–30. On the subsequent reception and re-evaluation of van Gennep's work, see the dedicated issue of the *Journal of Classical Sociology*, which includes Nicole Hochner, "On Social Rhythm: A Renewed Assessment of Van Gennep's Rites of Passage," *Journal of Classical Sociology* 18, no. 4 (November 2018): 299–312.

dedicated study.[13] It also holds special interest, since it fulfilled additional functions than did the music of the Mass, Office, and processions. This music served not only as part of a liturgy, but also as a type of aid to a suffering person and the attending community.

As a musicological project, this study breaks new ground. With good reasons, chant scholars have focused primarily on the music sung at the liturgies of the Mass, Office, and processions. The music sung outside of these liturgies, and the music of liturgies sung outside of church buildings, is largely uncharted territory.[14] This book attempts to gain a more comprehensive understanding of the historic deathbed rituals by integrating one of their essential elements—music. But it also brings a previously undiscussed repertory of medieval plainchant into scholarly discourse and provides editions of previously unedited and unanalyzed chants. For these reasons, I hope it provides a beginning for scholarly conversations and an impetus for further studies.

The good reasons that have confined musicologists to the study of the Mass, Office, and processions point to the difficulties of investigating the music in deathbed liturgies. While copious numbers of manuscript sources survive for the Mass, Office, and processional liturgies, the same is not the case for the deathbed rites. These rituals were often recorded in portable, unbound *libelli*, meant to be carried to the bedsides of the dying. Such documents survive in smaller numbers than bound manuscripts that were housed and protected in churches and libraries. In many instances, particularly with the laity, practices

---

[13] Ottosen investigates related material—the chants of the Office of the Dead—in Knud Ottosen, *The Responsories and Versicles of the Latin Office of the Dead* (Aarhus, Denmark: Aarhus University Press, 1993); see also Michel Huglo, "Remarques sur les mélodies des répons de l'Office des Morts," *Nordisk Kollokvium IV i Latinsk Liturgiforskning* 4 (1978): 118–125. Rutherford offers a comprehensive study of postmortem liturgies: Richard Rutherford, *The Death of a Christian: The Rite of Funerals* (New York: Pueblo Publishing Company, 1980). See also Karen B. Westerfield Tucker, "Christian Rituals Surrounding Death," in *Life Cycles in Jewish and Christian Worship*, ed. Paul F. Bradshaw and Lawrence A. Hoffman (Notre Dame, IN: University of Notre Dame Press, 1996), 196–213. Engels investigates chants in Mass and Office liturgies that deal with the topics of death and the apocalypse: Stefan Engels, "Dies irae, dies illa," in *Krisen, Kriege, Katastrophen*, ed. Christain Rohr, Ursula Bieber, and Katharina Zeppezauer-Wachauer (Heidelberg: Universitätsverlag, 2018), 379–460.

[14] Exceptions are Richard Rastall's work on the music of medieval "plays" (*The Heaven Singing: Music in Early English Religious Drama I* [Cambridge: D. S. Brewer, 1996] and *Minstrels Playing: Music in Early English Religious Drama II* [Cambridge: D. S. Brewer, 2001]), and the pioneering study on music sung in medieval refectories by Tova Leigh-Choate ("Singing for their Supper: Chant in the Medieval Refectory" [Paper presented at the international conference of Cantus Planus, Dublin, 2–7 August 2016]). Courtly music, sung in the vernacular, has also been a focus of study for medieval musicologists. Two contributions in *The Cambridge History of Medieval Music*, ed. Mark Everist and Thomas Forrest Kelly (Cambridge: Cambridge University Press, 2018), provide recent surveys of scholarship: Elizabeth Aubrey, "Vernacular Song I: Lyric," 382–427; and Anne Ibos-Augé, "Vernacular Song II: Romance," 428–450.

at the deathbed likely went entirely unrecorded. Surviving documentation of deathbed rites proves to be the exception, not the norm. Three of the four manuscripts used in this study (SP F 11 in Chapter 1, Paris 934 in Chapter 2, and GSB 3 in Chapter 3) preserve the deathbed rites in a book type referred to as a "ritual" (a manuscript containing liturgies performed by a priest away from the altar). The Augustinian canonry of Klosterneuburg recorded its rites for the sick and dying in similar collections.[15] The women's community of Aldgate preserved its deathbed rites in a book intended for the use of a *cantrix*, the woman responsible for leading liturgical chant. (Manuscript Cranston 2322 is investigated in Chapter 4.) The rites for the sick and dying promulgated by the Franciscan Order were included in breviaries, in order to allow the friars to travel and maintain their own devotions, while also being ready to minister to the needy.[16] Convenience for each book's intended user was likely the motivating impulse for including the deathbed rituals within these manuscripts. But the rituals' incorporation into larger, bound collections of material also led to their preservation in these instances.

Although melody was an essential part of the deathbed rituals, the surviving sources often contain no music notation, or notation that provides only a partial representation of the melodies. These documents tended to be created and notated pragmatically. Scribes generally included only what a celebrant was expected to need in order to conduct the ritual successfully. If the melodies were considered well-known, a scribe did not need to include them. Such documents rarely provide descriptive information for someone unfamiliar with the rituals and their chants. The relatively late development of pitch-specific notation places an additional constraint on the available source material: only with documents created after the mid-eleventh century can one expect to find music notation that indicates the specific pitches of melodies, and is thus transcribable into contemporary notation.[17] These conditions greatly reduce the source material available for a study of the

---

[15] Klosterneuburg, Augustiner-Chorherrenstift, Cod. 628, 629, 1022A, and 1022B, examined in Elaine Stratton Hild, "Rites for the Sick and Dying in Sources from Klosterneuburg," *De musica disserenda* 14, no. 2 (2018): 7–24.

[16] Van Dijk and Donohue connect the innovative book type—a breviary with rites for the sick and dying—with the itinerant ideals and ministries of the Franciscans: "The new combination . . . is typical of the apostolic and itinerant life of the Order" (Van Dijk, *Sources*, 138). "The Franciscans' need for a portable Office book in the thirteenth century was the chief reason why the breviary, rather than the missal, became connected with 'going out' and the former became the logical book to contain a ritual for the last sacraments" (Donohue, "The Rite," 201).

[17] Rankin provides a history of the development of music writing in Western Europe: Susan Rankin, *Writing Sounds in Carolingian Europe: The Invention of Musical Notation* (Cambridge: Cambridge University Press, 2018).

deathbed rituals' music. From a small pool of eligible sources, I have chosen four of the earliest available that represent a diverse range of communities within the liturgical tradition.

Structure of the Book

Close readings of the deathbed rituals in these four manuscripts provide the foundation for the following study. The book is structured to offer a view of a repertory—the chants of the medieval deathbed liturgies—through the sources of individual institutions. The first four chapters thus contain a series of "case studies": analyses of single rituals, each as it appears in a single source. The rituals' chants are transcribed into modern notation and analyzed, both for their relationships between text and melody and for their functions within the rituals. Rather than conflating multiple manuscript versions into critical editions, I have chosen to edit chant texts and melodies as they appear in these single sources.[18] Each manuscript's idiosyncrasies of melody and textual orthography are preserved in the transcriptions and discussions. (Standardized spellings are used in discussions of a chant's broader transmission patterns.) This approach seems necessary and preferable for several reasons. The rituals for the time of death, along with their constituent chants, differ substantially from one another. Even when the same chant text is found in multiple manuscripts, the melodic contents of the different versions vary significantly. Yet each deathbed liturgy, and each chant, functioned as a coherent whole for the scribe who recorded them and the community that used them. Investigating each ritual and chant as an entity in its own right provides the greatest insight into the liturgical ideals—and possibly the liturgical practices—of individual communities.

The deathbed rituals have nothing to do with the precise boundaries separating our contemporary academic disciplines; they fall within the interest and purview of many fields of study. For this reason, I have tried to keep specialized musicological vocabulary to a minimum, without sacrificing the detailed observations necessary for credible argument and insight. Parenthetical comments supply basic definitions for the few musicological

---

[18] In creating a "source edition," I follow the editorial principles of Corpus monodicum, a long-term research and editorial project housed at the Universität Würzburg (Germany) and sponsored by the Akademie der Wissenschaften und der Literatur, Mainz. A description of the project is available at https://www.musikwissenschaft.uni-wuerzburg.de/forschung/corpus-monodicum/.

terms that appear; footnotes cite reference works that can give interested readers more information on musical topics. An appendix at the end of the volume provides a concise overview of each ritual: an inventory of contents, including rubrics, individual items, and the positions where music notation appears.

Each of the sources examined in Chapters 1 to 4 presents a different vantage point from which to observe medieval chants for the dying. Chapter 1 focuses on a manuscript connected with the most elite practitioners of medieval Christianity: Vatican, Biblioteca Apostolica Vaticana, Arch. Cap. S. Pietro F 11 pt. A (SP F 11). The twelfth-century manuscript is considered to be a witness to the "Old Roman" tradition (associated with the most prominent religious institutions in Rome), and it contains a unique ritual. It shares none of its chant melodies and only one of its chant texts with other deathbed liturgies.[19]

Chapter 2 examines the deathbed ritual in a late twelfth-century manuscript from the cathedral of Sens (Paris 934). It is the earliest manuscript I have found that preserves the melodies for the chants of the *Ordo XLIX* tradition.[20] The chants of this widespread and influential tradition are evident in manuscripts from the late eighth century, but in these older sources, only the chants' texts were recorded. With its clear, pitch-specific notation, Paris 934 is an important witness to the chants' melodies.

The manuscript studied in Chapter 3 (GSB 3) contains no music notation with its deathbed ritual, but it provides significant insight into the practices of a lay community far from urban centers. Scholars associate the manuscript with Orsières, a small village located in the Swiss Alps near the pass of Grand-Saint-Bernard. Coming from a small, rural community, the manuscript gives substantive evidence for a topic of great interest to historians: whether a gap existed between the religious practices and understandings of elite practitioners (educated clerics and monastics of major religious institutions) and those of the laity (particularly those who were less educated). Manuscript GSB 3 indicates that the practices of the "folk" shared many essentials with the practices of the "elites": their respective rituals share individual items, images of the afterlife, and tasks for the gathered community.

---

[19] See Chapter 1 for scholars' considerations on the specific Roman institutions that might have made use of the manuscript. Chapter 5 provides a detailed analysis of the chants' transmission patterns.

[20] The deathbed ritual known in scholarship as *Ordo XLIX* is discussed in Chapters 2 and 5.

The deathbed ritual from a community of women—the Franciscan convent of Aldgate, England—forms the focus of Chapter 4. Manuscript Cranston 2322 contains a version of the thirteenth-century deathbed ritual promulgated by the Franciscan Order, complete with notated chants. This thirteenth-century Franciscan version became widely known throughout Europe—through the work of the friars—and later served as a source for the seventeenth-century version disseminated by the Roman Catholic Church. Cranston 2322 not only offers a detailed look at this influential ritual, it also provides an opportunity to see the adaptations made to it by a community of women. As contemporary scholars consider instances of autonomy practiced by women in the Middle Ages, the deathbed ritual in Cranston 2322 gives specific, credible insights.

Coming from such diverse communities, the four deathbed rituals studied in this book present an opportunity to observe liturgical similarities and differences among a variety of institutional types and societal groups. Created for the powerful and the poor, the educated and the uneducated, women and men, monastics, clerics, and laity, the rituals in these four manuscripts offer a glimpse into the religious practices that both distinguished communities from one another and bound them together within a single tradition.

Chapter 5 takes a broader analytical perspective, using the material and insights from the four case studies of Chapters 1 to 4 to consider questions that arise when comparing the rituals of individual communities. Did commonalities exist? To what extent did specific geographical areas and institutions maintain their own versions of the deathbed rituals? Conversely, to what extent did standardization occur?

The chapter also uses evidence provided by the musical material to revisit questions that scholars have previously posed to the deathbed rituals. To what extent is it possible to determine the practice (or practices) of the medieval Roman church? Is there a particular ritual (and accompanying chant repertory) that seems to have originated in Rome? Were the chants prescribed in the rituals for the dying borrowed from other liturgies, or were they created specifically for the time of an individual's death?

Additionally, Chapter 5 considers the ways in which the deathbed rituals intersect with queries of current interest in scholarly discourse. As one example, the rituals allow for investigations into medieval conceptions of the afterlife. In their texts, the deathbed liturgies convey depictions—"imaginative structures"—of the soul's experiences following the death of the body.[21] Ottosen, in particular, has considered the extent to which sung liturgical texts can be used as sources for understanding the multiple, changing conceptions of the afterlife that existed in the Middle Ages.[22] While Ottosen's work focuses on chant texts in the Office of the Dead, the rituals for the dying also provide insights. As discussed in Chapter 5, this study shows that the chants of the deathbed liturgies continued to convey older, positive images of the afterlife, even when conceptions of purgatory and particular judgment had become widespread.

Furthermore, the chants of the deathbed rites have much to contribute to a topic of perennial interest for musicologists: the relationships between melody and text in medieval plainchant, specifically, the ways in which melodic material articulates sung words.[23] Singing is a performance of a text, and a melody tightly controls the manner in which a text is delivered. Musicologists consider which textual aspects a melody orients itself toward and thus, underscores, in performance. As one example, musical settings can articulate individual syllables of words. When a melody emphasizes the syllables typically accented in a spoken performance, it creates a speech-like declamation of a text (promoting its comprehensibility during the sung performance). Melodic elements can also emphasize meaningful groups of words—a text's syntactic units, such as clauses and sentences. With poetic texts, melodies can articulate aspects of verse structure, such as line endings, rhymes, or internal caesurae. It is also possible for plainchant melodies to

---

[21] The term "imaginative structures" is from Peter Brown, "The Decline of the Empire of God: Amnesty, Penance, and the Afterlife from Late Antiquity to the Middle Ages," in *Last Things: Death and the Apocalypse in the Middle Ages*, ed. Caroline Walker Bynum and Paul Freedman (Philadelphia: University of Pennsylvania Press, 2000), 41–59.

[22] Ottosen used the texts of responsories and versicles in the Office of the Dead to refine Le Goff's understanding of the development of the conception of purgatory: Ottosen, *Responsories* and "Liturgy as a Theological Place: Possibilities and Limitations in Interpreting Liturgical Texts as Seen for Instance in the Office of the Dead," in *Liturgy and the Arts in the Middle Ages*, ed. Eva Louise Lillie and Nils Holger Petersen (Copenhagen: Museum Tusculanum Press University of Copenhagen, 1996), 168–180; Jacques Le Goff, *La naissance du purgatoire* (Paris: Gallimard, 1981), translated as *The Birth of Purgatory* by Arthur Goldhammer (London: Scolar Press, 1984). Isabel Moreira focuses on earlier sources, particularly from the seventh and eighth centuries, in *Heaven's Purge: Purgation in Late Antiquity* (Oxford: Oxford University Press, 2010) and "Visions and the Afterlife," in *The Oxford Handbook of the Merovingian World*, ed. Bonnie Effros and Isabel Moreira (New York: Oxford University Press, 2020), 988–1011. See also Bynum and Freedman, *Last Things*. These collected essays (including Brown's, cited above) explore the interrelated medieval depictions of the experiences of the soul after an individual's death, the collective resurrection of bodies, and apocalyptic end times.

[23] This topic has stimulated research for generations of plainchant scholars and has produced a body of publications too extensive to cite here. Please see DiCenso for a recent literature review and a thoughtful analysis of scholarly tendencies: Daniel J. DiCenso, "Moved by Music: Problems in Approaching Emotional Expression in Gregorian Chant," in *Emotion and Medieval Textual Media*, ed. Mary C. Flannery (Turnhout: Brepols, 2018), 19–50.

orient themselves toward the semantic contents of words. A melody can even create a "mimetic" relationship by sonically imitating an aspect of a textual image. (This is sometimes referred to as "word painting.")

Indeed, the musical layer of a chant forms a dynamic and prominent element that decisively influences a text's performance, including which words, images, and ideas are emphasized. Musical settings have multiple ways of creating emphasis:

1. The number of pitches conveying syllables. If a syllable is conveyed with multiple pitches, while the surrounding syllables are conveyed with single pitches, the syllable sung with multiple pitches gains prominence in performance. (The term *melisma* refers to the multiple pitches that convey a single syllable.)
2. Melodic movement. The progressions between notes (technically termed *intervals*) can consist of steps or leaps, and leaps—particularly large ones—are attention-getters in performance, emphasizing the words they convey.
3. Relative pitch content. Each note in the melody is either higher, lower, or the same as those that precede and follow. A melody draws attention to syllables conveyed with relatively high or low pitches. Such micro-level changes in pitch content—particularly changes to higher pitches—can underscore syllables and words in performance.
4. Relative pitch content, large-scale changes. The pitch content of a musical setting can engage in macro-level changes as well. A melody can inhabit one area of pitch content—a particular range of pitches—to convey one portion of a text, and then make a large-scale change to convey the next portion of text with an area of pitch content that is relatively higher or lower. Such shifts in pitch content can create distinctive sonic "spaces" in the performance, providing audibly different conveyances for different portions of the text. (The term *ambitus* refers to the range of pitches presented in a chant.)
5. Musical endings. Each genre of music—including the medieval plainchant examined in this study—has characteristic gestures that appear at the endings of sections. (These are often referred to as *cadential gestures*). Where such gestures occur, they create a type of musical ending, lending a sense of finality and closure to the words they convey.
6. Repetition. Repeated musical gestures can create connections between words. By conveying different words with the same (or similar) music,

the melody relates the words to one another in performance and creates an impulse for listeners to consider their connections.

With all these musical elements, it is important to note that scholarly analysis of medieval plainchant focuses solely on the music reflected in a manuscript's notation. The analyses in the following chapters are not assumptions about how a chant was actually sung, but rather observations on a written record. The notation for each chant documents only one performance: that which occurred when the scribe wrote the melody on the page.[24] Determining if any particular chant was actually performed by a community and determining the extent to which those performances resembled the written record are separate considerations, which usually fall outside of the boundaries of possible historical inquiry. (Some manuscripts in this study do show specific signs of use, and these are noted in the following chapters.) This study examines each liturgical source as a reflection of possible practices at the deathbed, but the performance being analyzed—by necessity—is the performance depicted in the manuscript.

Even with these inherent limitations, an analysis of the music notation in the deathbed rituals yields clear findings. Far from being an incidental or neutral component, music shaped the performance of each text—and consequently, each ritual—in substantial ways. Occasionally, a musical setting prioritizes the comprehensibility of a text by rendering it more speech-like (with relatively high and low pitches emphasizing the syllables accented in spoken performance, and with cadential gestures and melismas articulating the endings of a text's syntactic units). But most often, the melodies are strikingly oriented toward the sung words' semantic contents. The melodies of the deathbed rituals promote specific interpretations of their sung texts. They emphasize individual words and draw connections between words with melodic repetition. Melodic movement sometimes mimics the movement depicted in a textual image, as when an ascending musical gesture conveys a portrayal of the soul ascending to God. The music of the deathbed rituals intrigues, not only because of the circumstances in which the chants were sung, and not only because the repertory is unknown to chant scholars, but also because the melodies form an active, interpretive element of the chants, articulating and emphasizing specific images and theological understandings.

---

[24] Leo Treitler describes the act of writing a chant as a "vicarious performance" in "Observations on the Transmission of Some Aquitanian Tropes," *Forum musicologicum* 3 (1982): 11–60, esp. 48. (Reprinted with additional commentary in *With Voice and Pen*, 252–297. The term cited here occurs on page 287.)

In their nuanced conveyances of texts, the melodies promote reassurance. Merciful images of God and serene depictions of the soul's afterlife are musically underscored. As I will argue in the following chapters, the melodies of the deathbed rituals seem to have served the functions of comforting the dying and promoting encouraging theological understandings of the afterlife. Paxton has already noted that the deathbed rituals show a care for the dying as much as a concern with the afterlife of the soul. Beginning with the late eighth-century rituals, Paxton observes a "change of emphasis from the exclusive concern with the fate of the soul to the needs of the dying person."[25] Eschatological affairs are interwoven with expressions of comfort. The following study shows that the rituals' chants served as vehicles for offering consolation. The chants' texts convey reassuring, peaceful images of the afterlife; the chants' music underscores the peaceful images. In studying the music of the rituals, we study beauty offered to console the dying and the bereaved.

We also glimpse how communities of that time "enacted, asserted, confronted, lived, and gave meaning to" the awful and awe-filled moment when a body fails, a life ends, a loved one dies.[26] We "encounter people who struggle as we struggle" with one fact that we cannot change: my life, and the life of each person I love, will end.[27] We are finally impotent when faced with death. I value the study of the medieval deathbed rituals not only as part of an academic discourse with its own inherent value, but also because these rituals show us how others chose to fight the losing fight. They show us how others engaged with death—the opponent that eventually, inevitably, wins. Singing a deathbed liturgy was an action undertaken by communities whom we might consider (mistakenly?) to have been powerless, since they lacked meaningful medical capabilities. Yet in these liturgies, the medieval sources reveal people who gathered, rather than staying away; people who acknowledged the end of life, rather than denying it; people who found the breath to sing at the very moment of loss. Even as we wield the astonishing resources of contemporary medical technology, the image of those people, gathering and singing at the deathbed, humbles and fascinates.

---

[25] Paxton, *Christianizing Death*, 205–206.
[26] "What religion does (and one must therefore define the phenomenon of religion very broadly) is to enact, assert, confront, live, and give meaning to such irresolvable contradictions [such as life and death]" (Bynum, *Resurrection of the Body*, xix–xx).
[27] In her call for a sophisticated and nuanced approach to studying the Middle Ages—an approach that neither demonizes nor idolizes the time and its sources—Bynum states: "If we are committed to encountering as full a range of medieval theory and practice as we can discover in our sources, then we will encounter people who struggle as we struggle" (Bynum, *Resurrection of the Body*, xv–xvi).

1

Religious Elites

Rome, "Old Roman" Tradition

Manuscript Source: Vatican, Biblioteca Apostolica Vaticana,
Arch. Cap. S. Pietro F 11 pt. A
(SP F 11)

Death was not private. According to a manuscript used by some of the most elite religious practitioners of medieval Europe, a dying member of the community became the focal point of a liturgical gathering. The twelfth-century manuscript Archivio del Capitolo di San Pietro F 11 pt. A (hereafter SP F 11) is understood by most scholars to have been used at Saint Peter's Basilica at the Vatican; a recent study suggests that it may instead have been used at a different Roman institution, possibly the church dedicated to Saints Cyrus and John in the Via Biberatica.[1] At either institution, the manuscript served a

[1] Boe's careful work reveals discrepancies between the feast days represented in the collects of SP F 11 and the feast days understood to have been celebrated at Saint Peter's Basilica in the twelfth century (John Boe, "Votive-Mass Chants in Florence, Biblioteca Riccardiana, MSS 299 and 300 and Vatican City, Biblioteca Apostolica Vaticana, Archivio San Pietro F 11: A Source Study," in *Western Plainchant in the First Millennium: Studies in the Medieval Liturgy and Its Music*, ed. Sean Gallagher, James Haar, John Nádas, and Timothy Striplin [Bookshelf.vitalsource.com: Routledge, 2017], 259–316). Boe cautiously suggests the church of Saints Cyrus and John *de Militiis* as an alternative place of origin and usage for the manuscript, based on what he calls the "flimsy" evidence of the use of capital letters in the rubric and collect for the feast day of Saints Cyrus and John ("Votive-Mass Chants," 280). He further suggests that an investigation of the Office of the Dead within the manuscript might offer better indications of an alternative place where the manuscript was used. Yet the most complete investigation of the Office of the Dead in SP F 11 (conducted by Ottosen, *Responsories*) points back to Saint Peter's Basilica at the Vatican. Based on the particular characteristics of its Office of the Dead, Ottosen includes SP F 11 in a category with other manuscripts of the Old Roman tradition, including the antiphoner from Saint Peter's Basilica (Vatican, Biblioteca Apostolica Vaticana, Arch. Cap. S. Pietro B 79, see especially *Responsories*, 325–328); he even suggests that the papal influence of Stephen IX can be seen in the readings chosen for the Office of the Dead in SP F 11 (*Responsories*, 83). These two credible studies—each focusing on different parts of the manuscript—counter each other, and the scholarly discussion regarding SP F 11's specific place of origin and usage stands unresolved. This present study makes use only of conclusions that have maintained a scholarly consensus: All investigations, including Boe's, posit an elite institution of Rome as the place where SP F 11 was used, and all agree that the manuscript's material represents the Old Roman tradition. Future research might offer possible explanations for why a manuscript created and used at Saint Peter's contains collects for a calendar of feast days that differs from those found in other manuscripts from the institution. Alternatively, future investigations might reveal additional indications of a place of origin and usage different from Saint Peter's Basilica.

liturgically sophisticated and skilled community. SP F 11 was created as a resource for priests: in addition to the deathbed ritual examined in this chapter, the manuscript contains items for the Mass, baptismal rites, and rites for anointing the sick. Yet a close examination indicates that the liturgy for the dying was not designed for a single officiant to perform by himself. Instead, the deathbed ritual prescribes an active role for additional participants; it assumes that the officiant will be joined at the bedside by others. If used by the community of Saint Peter's Basilica, the participants likely included clerics and ecclesiastical officials residing in the Vatican. (The presence of scholars and apprentices within the Vatican leaves open the possibility that these young men also participated.[2]) For the community using the manuscript—at Saint Peter's Basilica or the church of Saints Cyrus and John—the deathbed temporarily superseded the altar as a gathering place and center for liturgical activity.

Concerning the manuscript's dating, Ottosen considers SP F 11 to have been created between 1100 and 1130 (*Responsories*, 172); Cutter also considers the manuscript to have been created at the beginning of the twelfth century (Paul F. Cutter, *Musical Sources of the Old-Roman Mass: An Inventory of MS Rome, St. Cecilia Gradual 1071; MS Rome, Vaticanum latinum 5319; MSS Rome, San Pietro F 22 and F 11* [Neuhausen-Stuttgart: American Institute of Musicology, Hänssler Verlag, 1979], 14–15). Boe prefers a slightly later date of the mid-twelfth century ("Votive-Mass Chants," 270). Sicard (*Liturgie*, xviii) incorporates the manuscript as *Ro*; Klaus Gamber, *Codices liturgici latini antiquiores* (Freiburg Schweiz: Universitätsverlag Freiburg Schweiz, 1968), as number 1540. See also Pierre Salmon, *Les manuscrits liturgiques latins de la Bibliothèque vaticane* (Vatican City: Biblioteca Apostolica Vaticana, 1968–1972), 1:75, II:4, III:88; Michel Huglo, "Le chant 'vieux romain': Liste des manuscrits et témoins indirects," *Sacris Erudiri* 6 (1954): 101 and 113–114; Pierre-Marie Gy, "Collectaire, rituel, processional," *Revue des sciences philosophiques et théologiques* 44, no. 3 (July 1960): 441–469; here, 454. Digital images of the manuscript are provided by the Biblioteca Vaticana, "DigiVatLib: Manoscritto Arch.Cap.S.Pietro.F.11.pt.A," https://digi.vatlib.it/view/MSS_Arch.Cap.S.Pietro.F.11.pt.A. The library also provides digital images of Stornajolo's handwritten manuscript description: Cosimo Stornajolo, "*Inventarium codicum manuscriptorum Archivii Sancti Petri, tomus II, litterae E-H*" (unpublished manuscript, early 20th century), accessed July 9, 2023, at "DigiVatLib: Arch.Cap.S.Pietro.H.100," https://digi.vatlib.it/mss/detail/Arch.Cap.S.Pietro.H.100), f. 445. Stornajolo's and Salmon's findings concerning the manuscript are summarized at: OpacVatLib, "Manuscripts: Arch.Cap.S.Pietro.F.11.pt.A," https://opac.vatlib.it/mss/detail/228024 accessed February 6, 2021. On the history and liturgy of Saint Peter's, see Rosamond McKitterick, John Osborne, Carol M. Richardson, and Joanna Story, eds., *Old Saint Peter's, Rome* (Cambridge: Cambridge University Press, 2013), particularly Peter Jeffery, "The Early Liturgy of Saint Peter's and the Roman Liturgical Year," 157–176. Boe offers a succinct documentation of the changing status of the church of Saints Cyrus and John *de Militiis* in "Votive-Mass Chants," 269.

[2] On the inclusion of boys in the *Schola cantorum* (in preparation for clerical careers), see Joseph Dyer, "Boy Singers of the Roman Schola Cantorum," in *Young Choristers*, ed. Susan Boynton and Eric Rice (Woodbridge: Boydell Press, 2008), 19–36. See also Dyer, "The Schola Cantorum and Its Roman Milieu in the Early Middle Ages," in *De musica et cantu: Studien zur Geschichte der Kirchenmusik und der Oper: Helmut Hucke zum 60. Geburtstag*, ed. P. Cahn and A.-K. Heimer (Hildesheim: Olms, 1993), 19–40; and Andreas Pfisterer, "Origins and Transmission of Franco-Roman Chant," in *The Cambridge History of Medieval Music*, ed. Mark Everist and Thomas Forrest Kelly (Cambridge: Cambridge University Press, 2018), 69–91 (here, 72–75).

The ritual for the dying preserved in SP F 11—along with its distinctive and rich chant repertory—has no duplicate among the surviving sources of the Middle Ages. Musicologists recognize the manuscript as a witness to the "Old Roman" chant tradition; it appears to be the only surviving source representing this tradition that contains a deathbed ritual.[3] One notable feature of this deathbed liturgy is the foundational role given to music. The ritual prescribes singing as one of the primary tasks for the gathered community. In addition to psalms and a litany, which were conveyed with simple, formulaic melodies, the ritual contains thirteen chants with distinctive texts and melodic content. (The Appendix contains an inventory of the ritual's contents; Chapter 5 contains documentation and discussion of the chants' transmission patterns.)

Why gather and sing for a person suffering through the death agony? The following discussion offers a close reading of the ritual, in order to consider both the functions performed by the community and the functions performed by the melodies themselves, as they conveyed—and interpreted—the ritual's texts. What responsibilities did the community take on during the ritual for the end of life? And why sing, rather than speak?

An analysis reveals that the liturgy offered a formalized structure with which participants could support the dying person in specific ways. In singing the seven penitential psalms, the gathered community openly acknowledged the dying person's suffering and asserted trust in a God who could relieve it. In the litany, the participants petitioned the heavenly community for assistance on the dying person's behalf. Taken together, the ritual's components provided a comprehensive, vivid understanding of death by describing the journey of the soul, its heavenly protectors, and its destination in the afterlife.

An analysis also reveals the significant functions of music within the ritual. In the repertory of thirteen chants, musical settings sometimes prioritize their texts' comprehensibility (by articulating accented syllables and

---

[3] Pivotal contributions to scholarly discourse on the Old Roman tradition are compiled in Thomas Forrest Kelly, ed., *Chant and Its Origins* (Farnham, Surrey: Ashgate, 2009); see particularly Andreas Pfisterer, "Origins and Transmission," 82–88; and Joseph Dyer, "Sources of Romano-Frankish Liturgy and Music," 92–122, particularly 113–116. See also Edward Nowacki, "Studies on the Office Antiphons of the Old Roman Manuscripts" (PhD diss., Brandeis University, 1980); and Andreas Pfisterer, *Cantilena Romana: Untersuchungen zur Überlieferung des gregorianischen Chorals* (Paderborn: Ferdinand Schöningh, 2002). Maloy provides a succinct overview of musicological considerations on the Old Roman chant tradition in *Inside the Offertory: Aspects of Chronology and Transmission* (Oxford: Oxford University Press, 2011), especially 3–12. Please see Chapter 5 for an extended discussion of what might have constituted "Roman" practices of deathbed liturgies.

syntactic units). But more frequently, the melodies seem attuned to the words' semantic contents. Using multiple means of creating emphasis, the melodies promote specific interpretations of the texts, often underscoring comforting images of a God who is able and willing to relieve the suffering of humans. The chants are permeated with audible images of answered prayers.

The Penitential Psalms: Acknowledging Suffering

| In primis dicantur VII psalmi speciales cum letania | First are sung the seven penitential psalms with the litany |

The ritual's succinct opening rubric, prescribing the seven penitential psalms, seems ambiguous regarding some fundamental questions:

1. Who participated in the ritual? One cleric, or multiple participants?
2. How was the material performed? *Dicantur* is a neutral verb—in this context, does it indicate singing, speaking, or something in between?
3. When did the "commendation of the soul" begin? In other words, how was the ritual coordinated to the dying process?

Considering the rubric in the context of other liturgical manuscripts and our knowledge of customary performance practices allows for specific inferences.

Although this rubric does not explicitly coordinate the ritual's opening to a precise moment in the dying process, it seems likely that the liturgy began during the final moments of life. The next rubric in the ritual that offers a point of orientation reads Antiphona per uiam ("Antiphon for the way"), indicating a time after death had occurred, when the body was moved from its place of cleansing and preparation to the place of the funeral service. Between these two rubrics, an extensive amount of material appears. This material could potentially have been considered appropriate not only for the final agony, but also for the moment of death, as well as the washing and preparation of the body. However, the material's content (which takes on the voice of a suffering person and encourages the soul to depart) combined with its quantity (seven psalms, a litany, as well as a substantial collection of prayers) suggests that it was intended to accompany the potentially long death agony. The lack of further specificity indicating the coordination of the material with the dying process might have provided latitude for participants to adapt the progression of the ritual to the unpredictable timing of an individual's death.

How were the psalms to be performed? The verb used in the rubric to indicate performance, *dicantur*, can be understood and translated with a fairly wide variety of meanings, ranging from speaking and singing to articulating, affirming, and pronouncing. But within the more limited context of medieval liturgical manuscripts, the verb is often used immediately prior to (and referring to the performance of) material that was undoubtedly sung—chants written with music notation. In liturgical material such as the deathbed ritual of SP F 11, scribes commonly used the verb to refer to singing. Given that psalms were customarily sung in other liturgical contexts, the most plausible understanding of this rubric is that it indicates singing, not speaking.

Many portions of the ritual suggest the participation of multiple people, not simply a single officiant, and this is true of the ritual's opening. Psalms provided the primary substance of a religious community's regularly occurring Office liturgies. The performance of the psalms during the deathbed ritual probably followed the manner in which they were typically performed in the Office services: participants formed two groups, with one group singing a psalm verse and then listening while the other group responded with the next verse. Thus, although it is brief, the ritual's opening rubric probably offered clear indications to the community that used the manuscript. The penitential psalms prescribed by the ritual's opening were likely sung by multiple people, gathered at the bedside when death seemed imminent.

In singing the seven penitential psalms, the community would have listed a veritable catalog of physical, emotional, mental, and spiritual pain, narrated in the voice of a suffering person.[4] The performance of these psalms would have offered those gathered at the bedside a way of acknowledging and articulating the distress that can come with the end of life. Physical suffering is among the primary types detailed in the penitential psalms. Psalm 6 states, for example, "My limbs are stricken ... I weary in my sighing. I make my bed swim every night, with my tears I water my couch." Likewise, Psalm

---

[4] On the penitential psalms (Psalms 6, 31, 37, 50, 101, 129, and 142), see especially Michael Driscoll, "The Seven Penitential Psalms: Their Designation and Usages from the Middle Ages Onwards," *Ecclesia orans* 17 (2000): 153–201. All translations used in the following discussion are drawn from Robert Alter, *The Hebrew Bible: A Translation with Commentary* (New York: W. W. Norton, 2019), in which the psalm numbering follows that of the Hebrew Bible.

37: "There is no whole place in my flesh. . . . My sores make a stench," and Psalm 101: "My bones are scorched like a hearth." The narrative voices of the penitential psalms—like the dying person—experience the demise of the body. These psalms also describe the distress of isolation: "My friends and companions stand off from my plight and my kinsmen stand far away" (Psalm 37). Images from nature vividly describe the sense of separation: "I become like the owl of the ruins. I lie awake and become like a lonely bird on a roof" (Psalm 101). Additionally, these psalms give voice to the suffering of shame, caused by one's own errors: "For my crimes I know, and my offense is before me always" (Psalm 50). "My crimes have welled over my head, like a heavy burden, too heavy for me" (Psalm 37).

Yet the entirety of this extreme and varied suffering occurs in an orientation toward God—an all-powerful God, capable of relieving pain and offering consolation. Even the most agonizing assertions of the narrative voices intertwine with an expectation of divine assistance. As one example, Psalm 6 moves in a progression from petition to relief. While the opening verses appeal: "Have mercy on me, Lord, for I am wretched. Heal me, for my limbs are stricken"; the final verses triumph: "Turn from me, all you wrongdoers, for the Lord hears the sound of my weeping. The Lord hears my plea, the Lord will take my prayer." For the narrative voice of Psalm 31, need leads directly to a petition of the divine: "You are a shelter for me. From the foe You keep me." This intimacy and trust in God remains steadfast, even with the psalmist's understanding that God could be the very cause of the suffering. "Your arrows have come down upon me, and upon me has come down Your hand. There is no whole place in my flesh through Your rage" (Psalm 37). The God of the penitential psalms is the sole, trustworthy source of comfort for the distressed person.

In singing these psalms, then, the gathered community articulated both the suffering and the hope of the person in the deathbed. Those gathered took on the voice—and thus, to an extent, the identity—of the dying person. Rather than drawing sharp distinctions between the one who was actively dying and those who were not, the ritual defines suffering and mortality as common features of humanity. The performance of the penitential psalms at the deathbed would have blurred the distinction between the living and the dying.

Psalm 129 (the sixth of the penitential psalms) begins, "From the depths I called You, Lord," and these words summarize the function of the psalms within the ritual. Singing the penitential texts required the gathered community to call out human suffering—suffering that was happening in their sight—and to join the extremity of distress with trust in a God capable of offering relief. The essence of the penitential psalms lies in the word "yet"—"I am suffering, yet I trust in you, Lord." The word "yet" expresses the pivotal moment of faith heard in the psalmists' voices as well as the driving force of the ritual. The narrative voices of the psalms suffer, but they also anticipate relief. Just as relief does not always follow immediately in the psalms, it likely did not always occur quickly during the course of a performance of the ritual. The waiting in suffering, the suffering in the waiting, forms the tension of both the penitential psalms and the moments for which the deathbed ritual was constructed.

By beginning with these psalms, the ritual directs the gathered community to first acknowledge the dying person's distress—and hope. This beginning also reveals an understanding that the process of death followed a specific trajectory: the suffering person moved from pain to relief, from danger to safety, from anguish to consolation. The penitential psalms defined the starting point of the process, the depths from which the ascent to the afterlife began.

The Litany: Calling for Assistance

The litany following the penitential psalms expands the focus of the gathered community beyond the suffering individual to those who were considered able to help. The specific chant referenced by this rubric is not preserved. The manuscript's scribe included the indication to sing a litany, but not the litany itself. (This omission might indicate the expertise of the community—that the litany was known without written assistance—or, alternatively, that the litany was available in a separate but readily accessible document.) Yet litanies had common features that allow us to understand the contribution this chant would have made to the ritual. Medieval litanies typically begin with a repetition of the *Kyrie eleison*, a sung prayer requesting mercy from God and Christ. They continue by naming individuals in the heavenly community in a hierarchical order—beginning with Mary and moving to the angels, the apostles, and other venerated saints—and asking each for intercessory prayers. For the ritual's participants, the litany evoked a crowd of unseen but able protectors; it appealed for assistance in leading the dying person from suffering to relief.

Like the psalms, the performance of the litany likely would have involved all gathered individuals. Litanies were typically sung responsorially, in a call-and-response pattern. The name of each personage in the heavenly community was sung by one participant—a cantor or celebrant—with other participants responding with a repeated request. In this ritual, the response was most likely, "Pray for him."[5] With the psalms, the ritual's participants sang from the suffering person's perspective; with the litany, they sang on his behalf. The focus of the ritual now encompassed both the dying person and the heavenly community. In the trajectory described by the ritual—the journey from earthly suffering to an afterlife of peace—the litany engaged the companions who would accompany the soul on its way.

Kyrie eleison, Pater noster, and *Capitulum*: Asserting Relationships

The ritual then directs the community, together, to articulate a connection between the lowest point in the trajectory—the person suffering the death agony—and the highest point—God. The *Kyrie* immediately following the litany invokes a relationship, through mercy, between the suffering person and the divine power that relieves. The subsequent prayer, the *Pater noster*, asserts a more intimate relationship: one of family. According to Augustine's understanding, expressed and widely transmitted in a sermon to those preparing for baptism, this prayer had much relevance for the time of death. In saying the words, "Our Father," the ritual's participants were invited to claim a relationship of siblinghood with Christ. "He's the only Son, and he didn't want to be the one and only; he thought it proper to have brothers and sisters."[6] The offer is both expansive and sufficient: "the only Son has innumerable brothers and sisters, who can say, *Our Father, who art in heaven*." Performed at the deathbed, the first two words of the prayer would have asserted a connection between each of the ritual's participants—including the dying person—and the summit of the heavenly hierarchy. In consequence, those saying the prayer defined themselves as a community, in their

---

[5] As in the Cluniac ritual for the dying (Paxton, *The Death Ritual at Cluny*, 94–101).
[6] The sermon appears in Jacques-Paul Migne, ed., *Patrologiae cursus completus, Series latina* (Paris: Migne, 1844–1891), 38:386–393. All translations in the following discussion are drawn from Edmund Hill's work with "Sermon 57" in Augustine, *Sermons: Vol. III (51–94) on the New Testament* (Brooklyn: New City Press, 1991), 109–110.

shared relationship with God.[7] The prayer's manner of performance—the collective recitation—would have highlighted this understanding. The *Pater noster* invited those reciting it to think of themselves in familial relationship with one another and God.

The prayer also references—according to Augustine—the successful end to the dying process: "We all had our fathers and mothers on earth, of whom we were born to a life of toil and ultimately death; we have found other parents, God our Father and the Church our mother, of whom we may be born to eternal life." Given Augustine's understanding, the *Pater noster* was appropriate for the end of life, in its confirmation of the connections existing among humans and God.

The ritual then engages the gathered participants in a series of statements concerning the dying person, beginning with Psalm 111:7. "The just will be in eternal remembrance" could be understood from the perspective of those who remain alive and remember the one who dies. It might also have been understood as an expression of the faithfulness of Christ, who will not forget or abandon the human, in life or in death. The second statement—"On hearing evil he will not be afraid"—attributes courage to the dying person in the face of threats, and reveals an understanding that dangerous encounters could arise in the process of dying and transitioning to the afterlife. The final statements refer to an existential hazard and ask for the best possible outcome: "From the gate of hell, rescue his soul, O Lord. May he rest in peace."[8]

The scribal work directs the gathered participants to recite these statements responsively. As seen in Figure 1.1, the scribe used the color red (with the rubric Cap\<itulum\> and the first letter of the psalm verse) to indicate the beginning of the new item. The rubric "R" before "Ab auditu" indicates the participants' response (R\<esponsum\>). The distinctively colored rubrics and initials continue to indicate the alternation between the celebrant and other participants. Together, their statements form a coherent and complete petition. This portion of the ritual concludes with an entreaty from Psalm 101: "Lord, hear my prayer, and let my cry come before you." This psalm verse—also spoken in alternation, with the celebrant articulating the

---

[7] Buc describes this conception of *religiones*: "They are ceremonies that happen to manifest the presence of a consensual community of human beings because they demonstrate the existence of a vertical bond tying these humans to God" (Philippe Buc, *The Dangers of Ritual* [Princeton, NJ: Princeton University Press, 2001], 21).

[8] Translations from Paxton, *The Death Ritual at Cluny*, 107 and 167.

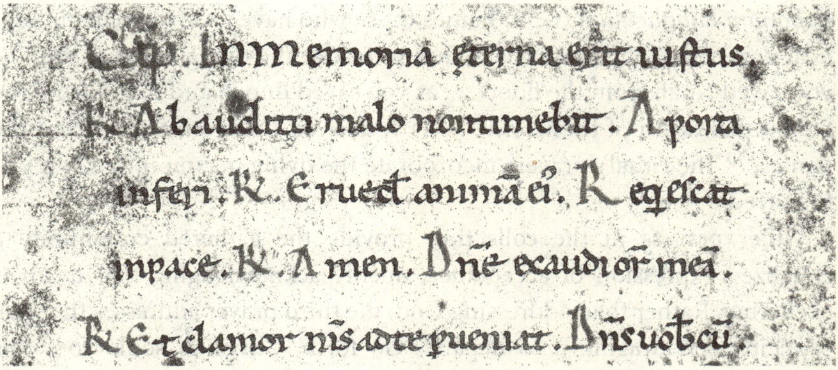

Figure 1.1 Capitulum, with rubrics indicating the alternation between the celebrant and other participants (SP F 11, f. 33v). Image © 2024 Vatican Apostolic Library. Reproduced by permission of the Vatican Apostolic Library, all rights reserved.

first clause and the other participants the second—served as both a conclusion to the capitulum and a transition to the following prayers.

Prayers: Depicting the Journey

The collection of fourteen prayers depicts the soul's experiences with vivid images and metaphors. In doing so, the prayers continue to define death as a journey—from danger to safety—that the soul travels with the assistance of the heavenly community. Like the litany, these prayers assert a connection between the dying person and heavenly companions and helpers: "We commend to you, Lord, the soul of your servant, in the hands of the patriarchs Abraham, Isaac, and Jacob. . . . We commend to you, Lord, the soul of your servant, in the hands of the prophets Isaiah, Ezechiel, and Daniel. . . . We commend to you, Lord, the soul of your servant, in the hands of the apostles Peter, Paul, Andrew, Jacob, John, and all the apostles."[9] Another prayer in the collection, *O anima tibi dico*, addresses its litany directly to the soul of the dying person: "O soul, I say to you . . . through the intercession of the saint and always virgin Mary, and Saint Michael, archangel, and through the intercession of the blessed Peter, leader of the apostles . . . may you be absolved from the chains of sins." The prayer *Svscipe domine seruum tuum*

---

[9] The prayer *Commendamus tibi domine animam famuli tui* appears on folio 36v.

in bonum habitaculum (f. 39) names those who have received relief in biblical narratives. The prayer asks God to rescue the dying person's soul "as you saved Noah from the flood . . . as you saved Enoch and Elijah from the communal death of the world . . . as you saved Lot from Sodom and the flames."[10] The ritual's prayers incorporate the dying person into a litany of the saved.

Other prayers in the collection provide the gathered community a ritualized expression of acceptance, openly acknowledging that death is occurring. Rather than addressing God, the third prayer addresses the soul, explicitly encouraging it to depart. "Go forth, Christian soul, from this world."[11] The prayer is, in effect, a litany-like blessing for the journey. "Go forth, Christian soul, from this world, in the name of the Lord father omnipotent, who created you; in the name of Jesus Christ, living son of God, who died for you; in the name of the Holy Spirit, who is poured out in you; in the name of angels and archangels."[12] In this prayer, the community articulates an understanding that the soul departs in illustrious companionship.

The prayers also describe the goal of the soul's journey, echoing metaphors from earlier centuries. One image recalls the parable of Luke 16, in which the destitute Lazarus dies and is carried by angels to rest on the bosom of Abraham.[13] Other prayers in the ritual of SP F 11 include requests of God

---

[10] Paxton characterizes the prayer as a "prose litany" in *Christianizing Death*, 118.

[11] *Proficiscere anima Christiana* appears on folio 34v.

[12] The text of the prayer in SP F 11 conforms to the edition in Paxton, *Christianizing Death*, 118, n. 77, with omission of "in nomine omnis humanu generis quod a deo susceptus est" and additions of Michael, all angels, Peter and Paul, John the evangelist, and the elect. The prayer is discussed in Paxton, *Christianizing Death*, 117. On the historical uses of the prayer, see also John S. Lampard, *Go Forth, Christian Soul: The Biography of a Prayer* (Peterborough: Epworth, 2005).

[13] This image is found in the ritual for the dying in the late eighth-century manuscript Berlin 1667. On the visual depictions of the bosom of Abraham in the Middle Ages, see Maria R. Grasso, "The Ambiguity in Medieval Depictions of Abraham's Bosom in the Areas and Spaces of the Christian Afterlife," in *Place and Space in the Medieval World*, ed. Meg Boulton, Jane Hawkes, and Heidi Stoner (Milton: Taylor & Francis Group, 2018), 103–113; and Stephen Bates, "Preparations for a Christian Death: The Later Middle Ages," in *A Companion to Death, Burial, and Remembrance in Late Medieval and Early Modern Europe, c. 1300–1700*, ed. Philip Booth and Elizabeth C. Tingle (Leiden: Brill, 2021), 72–105. Harrison notes the prevalence of metaphors of rest to describe the afterlife in Bernard of Clairvaux's sermons: Anna Harrison, "Community among the Saintly Dead: Bernard of Clairvaux's Sermons for the Feast of All Saints," in *Last Things: Death and the Apocalypse in the Middle Ages*, ed. Caroline Walker Bynum and Paul Freedman (Philadelphia: University of Pennsylvania Press, 2000), 191–204. For the appearance of the image of the bosom of Abraham in Merovingian sources, see Moreira, "Visions and the Afterlife," in *The Oxford Handbook of the Merovingian World*, ed. Bonnie Effros and Isabel Moreira (New York: Oxford University Press, 2020), 988–1011. Lester notes how the image was used to form understandings of the afterlife of lepers: Anne E. Lester, *Creating Cistercian Nuns: The Women's Religious Movement and Its Reform in Thirteenth-Century Champagne* (Ithaca, NY: Cornell University Press, 2011), 136.

to "place the soul in the bosom of the patriarchs" and for the soul to be embraced in blessed peace "in the bosom of the patriarchs."[14] Another prayer uses the image of the heavenly city to reassure the dying person: "Today is made in peace your place and your dwelling in the heavenly Jerusalem."[15] The biblical, poetic images envisage realms of the afterlife for the ritual's participants.

Yet the prayers also imply that dangers stood between the soul and its peaceful destination. The texts name threats that the dying person, and his soul, needed to be rescued from: the stain of sin, the chain of wrongdoings, enemies, Satan and his companions, as well as legions of the infernal regions and ministers of Satan.[16] One prayer references "all that trembles in darkness, that cracks in the flames, that crucifies in torment."[17] Terrifying as these lists are, they occur within the context of requests for protection, and they are far outnumbered by references to the soul's destination—the place of peace and rest. The dangers appear as part of a journey that ends in relief. In these ways, the prayers concretize and define the dying process for the ritual's participants, envisioning it as a journey of the soul—a journey with distressing hazards, but also powerful companions and a sublime destination.

Antiphons: Melodies Conveying and Interpreting Texts

Following the prayers, the ritual includes a collection of thirteen antiphons (a chant genre used in Mass and Office liturgies and typically sung in conjunction with psalms) for the time period immediately after death had occurred, while the body was moved to the church; these thirteen chants contain substantive and distinct melodic content that both conveys and interprets the sung texts. The scribe did not include music notation with previous portions of the ritual, most likely because the psalms, litany, and prayers made use of simple, formulaic melodies that would have been known to the rituals' participants without written indications. In contrast, with the collection of

---

[14] The prayers containing these images are *Commendamus tibi domine animam famuli tui* (f. 37–37v) and *Commendamus te omnipotenti deo* (f. 37v–38).
[15] *Hodie factus est in pace locus tuus et habitatio tua in Hirusalem celestem* (f. 34v–35r).
[16] *peccati macula* (f. 33v); *delictorum catena* (f. 34); *inimici* (f. 38); *Satanas cum satellitibus* (f. 38); *Tartareę legiones et ministri Satanę* (f. 38v).
[17] *omne quod horret in tenebris, quod stridet in flammis, quod cruciat in tormentis* (f. 38).

antiphons the scribe used detailed notation—notation that reveals complex and individual melodies. As the following analyses indicate, these melodies partner equally with the texts they convey. They promote particular interpretations of the texts by emphasizing individual words (with relatively high pitches or extended melodic gestures). The melodies also control the pacing of each text's delivery by varying the number of pitches for individual syllables. (Syllables conveyed with many pitches extend longer in performance—and gain more prominence—than those conveyed with only one or two pitches.) Through the use of repeated musical gestures, the melodies associate individual words with one another, drawing connections that are not immediately evident in the texts alone. At times, the melodies even offer their own depictions of textual images and actions. Rather than conveying the antiphons' words neutrally, then, the melodies offer layers of nuance and meaning.

Each antiphon is individual: the contents of their texts and the interpretive acts of their melodies vary. Yet as a whole, the melodies point toward hope. They tend to deliver the sung texts in ways that emphasize their most reassuring aspects, conveying empathy for the person whose life was ending, hope for his future, and images of a powerful and loving God. The melodies themselves seem to have been intended to offer comfort, perhaps even a type of pastoral care, both to the person (and soul) experiencing the end of life, as well as to the attending community.

Although this material is indicated for the time period immediately following death, it shows much continuity with previous portions of the ritual. The antiphons depict the person experiencing the end of life in a manner similar to the penitential psalms and litany—as someone who is in close relationship with God and who fervently needs (and expects) divine assistance. In singing the antiphons, the ritual's participants continue to take on the voice of the person experiencing the end of life, and the distinctions between the living and dead continue to blur. The person who has just died is still in need of God and the liturgical efforts of the community; those who sing the liturgy will also die and have the same needs.

Antiphon 1: *Dirige domine* (Music Transcription 1.1)

Dirige domine deus meus	Direct, Lord, my God	
in conspectu tuo uias mea\<s\>	in your sight my paths	cf. Psalm 5:9

Music Transcription 1.1 *Dirige domine* (SP F 11, f. 40v)

In the context of moving the corpse, the psalm verse that serves as the first antiphon's text gains a very specific meaning. The narrative voice becomes associated with the person whose life has just ended, and the paths he asks God to direct are the paths that lead through death to the afterlife. The antiphon's melodic setting underscores this prayer, heard in the text, and offers a reassuring image: a powerful God capable of guiding the narrator's future. The melody also affirms a close connection between the recently deceased person and God. It does so by emphasizing the words that assert a relationship between the narrative voice and the God who can save.

The chant's beginning strongly articulates the narrator's plea to God. The opening musical gesture conveys the directive "Lead, Lord" (*Dirige domine*) as one complete, melodic unit. With these words, the melody creates an arch-shape (one of the most common contours for complete musical gestures in medieval plainchant) beginning with the first pitch of "c," peaking on "f" with the final syllable of *dirige*, and then descending back to "c" for the final syllables of *domine*. The repetition of the pitch "c" with the syllables -*mi* and -*ne* contributes to the sense of completeness and finality, since repeating pitches often occur within cadential gestures. Using these means, the melody conveys the chant's opening two words—the narrative voice's essential request of God—as a complete utterance. The cry for help is articulated emphatically in performance.

In calling to "my God" (*deus meus*), the narrative voice of the chant asserts a relationship with the divine helper. The chant's setting lends emphasis—perhaps even credibility—to this assertion. The words *deus meus* are given prominence by their musical setting, which conveys these words differently than those that preceded. The melody with the second syllable of *deus* fluctuates between "d" and "c," and the first syllable of *meus* is conveyed by twelve pitches—a highly ornamented contrast to the melodic material that preceded it. The expansive, twelve-pitch musical gesture draws attention to the word it conveys; by articulating *meus*, it emphasizes the possessive element of the phrase *deus meus*, as well as the narrative voice's understanding of his close relationship with the divine: *my* God. Also with the words *deus meus*, the melody descends a fourth and explores a new territory of pitch content. Both the ornate setting and the melodic descent beyond the range of the chant's opening lend emphasis to the words declaring a relationship between the person in need and the divine helper.

The chant contains two other melismas (groupings of multiple pitches conveying a single syllable), and their placement continues to underscore the relationship with the divine asserted by the narrative voice. The melismas in this chant occur only with possessive pronouns—*my* God, *your* sight, *my* paths. Taken together, these word pairs, emphasized by melismas, summarize and convey the essential request of the chant's text.

As the chant continues, its melody creates a distinction that is only implicit in the words: the great contrast between God and the suffering human. The melodic pitch content conveying the words *meus* and *mea<s>*, which reference the human, occupy the lower part of the chant's ambitus, while the pitch content conveying the word "your" (*tuo*), which references the divine, rises to encompass the most elevated notes of the setting. This differing pitch content creates a contrast between the self-references of the narrative voice and the reference to the divine. In performance, one hears two registers: the lower one associated with the words referring to the human, and the lofty one, associated with the word referring to God. In this way, the chant subtly implies that the narrative voice perceives a great contrast between God and himself. Emphasized by its pitch content, the chant depicts the outer points of the ritual's trajectory: the depths of the suffering person and the heights of the divine, who embodies relief and peace.

The chant's musical setting portrays God as one whose view is broad, extending widely enough to encompass the human's paths. The words "your sight" (*conspectu tuo*) are conveyed with the broadest ambitus of any musical gesture within the chant. The first syllable (*con-*) is articulated with the setting's lowest pitch ("f"); the melody then ascends directly up an octave, so that the final syllable of *tuo* is conveyed with the setting's highest pitch (the "f" an octave above). While other melodic gestures in the chant change direction and circulate around single pitches, the melodic movement with "your sight" (*conspectu tuo*) climbs unswervingly higher. The extreme ends of the gesture not only touch the lowest and highest pitches of the chant (the lower and upper "f"), they also extend beyond the ambitus of the melody with the following words, "my paths" (*uias mea<s>*). The melodic setting thus conveys the understanding that the sight of God extends beyond the paths of the human. God is portrayed as capable of seeing the paths of the sufferer, and thus, as capable of answering the narrator's plea.

The chant contains a subtle repetition that associates the opening plea—"Lead, Lord" (*dirige domine*)—with the sight of God (*conspectu tuo*). In both of these positions the words are conveyed with a melodic gesture that contains the highest pitch of the chant (the high "f") followed by a scalar descent. The pitch content of the melodic gesture conveying the words "your sight" (*conspectu tuo*) is more ornate and extended, and it encompasses the melody of the opening plea "Lead, Lord" (*dirige domine*). In this way, the music again conveys the understanding that the divine sight encompasses and embraces the needs of the suffering one.

At its beginning, the setting emphasizes the plea of the narrative voice and the assertions of relationship between the human and the divine helper. At its conclusion, the melody offers reassurance that the plea can be answered—that God's vision takes in the person and his paths; that God is capable of directing the human's journey through death. The melody thus offers an additional, comforting layer of meaning: as the narrative voice asks God for guidance, the melody assures that God is able.

Antiphon 2: *Secundum magnam* (Music Transcription 1.2)

Secundum magnam	In accordance with your great	
misericordiam tuam domine	mercy, Lord	
miserere mei	have compassion for me	
et exultabunt ossa humiliata	and the humbled bones will exult	Psalm 50:3, 10

Music Transcription 1.2 *Secundum magnam* (SP F 11, f. 40v)

The setting of *Secundum magnam* offers a musical depiction of an answered prayer. The narrative voice of the text cries out for God's compassion, and the melodic setting suggests he will receive it. The chant conveys this reassuring understanding by several musical means. First, the melody emphasizes the words describing the characteristics of God that prompt compassion: the words "great mercy" (*magnam misericordiam*) are conveyed in an ornate and distinctive manner. The setting's first prominent ascension occurs with the word *magnam*: the first pitch with this word ("f") rises a third above the previous note, and it is followed by an ascent of a fourth, to the highest pitch of the setting thus far ("b-flat"). The melody conveying the rest of the word *magnam* continues to fill out this higher range, reaching the "b-flat" twice more, for a total of three times within the two syllables. A second, even more striking ascent occurs with the following word, *misericordiam*. The syllable emphasized in spoken pronunciation (-*cor*-) is conveyed musically by an upward leap of a fourth (from "g" to "c"), reaching the highest pitch of the entire setting. In a chant whose melody moves primarily by small steps, the placement of a large, upward leap creates emphasis. With these musical means, the words describing God's mercy—*magnam misericordiam*—become a focal point in performance.

The setting then offers a contrasting depiction of the narrative voice. The two words *miserere mei* ("have compassion for me") are conveyed with the most modest melodic gesture of the chant, suggesting the humble and reduced perspective of the suffering one, as well as the difference in power between the petitioner and the one being petitioned. While conveying the words *miserere mei*, the melody stays within an ambitus of a minor third, expanding this narrow range only slightly (to a fourth) with the descent to "d" on the final syllable. Apart from two, small leaps (of a minor third), the melodic motion is by step. The pitches conveying these words occupy the middle range of the setting, touching neither extreme of high nor low. While the melody conveyed the previous words—the words referencing the great mercy of God—with leaps and expansive ranges, the direct request from the sufferer to the divine is articulated quietly and unassumingly.

After conveying the words referring to the mercy of God and the words referring to the narrative voice in such different manners, the musical setting then draws connections between the two. The chant's final words—"humbled bones" (*ossa humiliata*)—reference the suffering of the narrator. Yet rather than continuing the modest, restricted musical conveyance heard with the previous words referring to the narrator (*miserere mei*), the setting uses the more expansive leaps and higher pitch content previously heard with the words referencing God's "great mercy" (*magnam misericordiam*). The highest pitch of this chant's setting ("c") occurs with only two words: mercy (*misericordiam*) and humbled (*humiliata*). In both positions, the high pitch is preceded by a melodic descent (from "a" down to "g").[18] From the "g," an upward leap of a fourth is required to sing the "c." The highest pitch of the setting and the marked approach to it strongly articulate the word *humiliata* and draw a vivid connection to the word *misericordiam* ("mercy"). By using the same, striking gesture to convey these two words, the melody draws together the mercy of God and the suffering human. The prayer of the text is that God's compassion will reach the sufferer; the music portrays such a connection.

---

[18] The scribe corrected an error in the notation (regarding the placement of the clef) with the word *ossa*: "a-g" replaces "f-e."

It is also worth noting which words and images are *not* emphasized by the musical setting. The word that refers to the future exaltation and relief of the suffering person, *exultabunt*, receives an appropriate and sensitive setting, but not the attention-grabbing extravagance of the words referring to God's mercy and the human's suffering. The melody conveying the word *exultabunt* rises: it begins with the lowest pitch of the chant ("c") and moves upward—primarily stepwise—through a seventh to "b-flat." Yet it is not the word *exultabunt* that receives the highest pitch of the setting. Neither is this word conveyed with leaps or melismatic gestures; such ornate musical means are reserved for the words referencing suffering—*ossa humiliata*—and the words referencing the characteristic that will cause God to respond to the suffering: *magnam misericordiam*. In this chant, it is not the future relief that receives attention, but rather the present, distressed situation and the characteristic of mercy in the one who can offer relief. The chant's setting creates a musical depiction of the mercy of God being applied to the humbled bones. As the text articulates a prayer, the melody depicts the answer.

Antiphon 3: *Domine deus* (Music Transcription 1.3)

Domine deus	Lord God	
in multitudine misericordie tue speraui	in the multitude of your mercies I have hoped	
deduc me in tua iustitia in eternum	lead me in your justice in eternity	cf. Psalm 5:8–9

The melodic setting of *Domine deus* emphatically articulates the statement of hope that forms the third antiphon's text. The melody is notable for its efficiency: most syllables (thirty of thirty-six) are conveyed with three or fewer pitches. This minimalistic tendency highlights the few words that receive more elaborate settings. Six syllables of the text are conveyed with melismas: the final syllable of *deus* is conveyed with eleven pitches; the final syllable of *speraui* ("hoped") with twelve; the final syllable of *deduc* ("lead") with four; *me* with seven; the final syllable of *iustitia* ("justice") with eight; and the second syllable of *eternum* ("eternity") with five. The contrast between the sparse settings for the majority of the text and the ornate settings for these few syllables gives great prominence to the words that form the core of the text's pronouncement.

Music Transcription 1.3 *Domine deus* (SP F 11, f. 40v)

The vital words of the text are emphasized in other ways as well. Although the melody remains in an extremely narrow ambitus, these words stand out by being conveyed with the highest and lowest pitches of the chant. The settings of *speraui* ("hoped") and *iustitia* ("justice") reach the chant's lowest pitch, "c"; the setting of the word *me* reaches the chant's highest pitch, "a." Additionally, the settings of these words are distinctive in their melodic motion. While the chant's melody tends to circulate around single pitches in the middle of the range, rarely moving in the same direction for multiple pitches, in five positions the melody creates extended, linear motion (moving stepwise in the same direction through the interval of a fourth): with the word *deus*, twice with the final syllable of *speraui*, as well as with *me* and the final syllable of *iustitia*. The combination of these musical means—melismatic settings, relatively high and low pitches, and unusually linear melodic motion—conveys these words in a distinctive manner.

These distinctive settings also convey the text with maximum comprehensibility. The words *deus*, *speraui*, *me*, and *eternum* not only communicate the text's vital concepts, they also end the text's syntactic units. Articulating their final syllables with lengthy melismas delays the conveyance of further text and thus creates a type of division in performance. The melodic setting thus partitions the text into meaningful units; the endings of each syntactic unit are marked with an extended, melismatic performance and pitches reaching the highest and lowest extremes of the chant's ambitus. In these ways, the setting prioritizes a clear, comprehensible conveyance of the text. The hope and prayer heard in the narrative voice are delivered emphatically, with clear divisions between syntactic units and with emphasis on essential words.

Antiphon 4: *Conuertere domine* (Music Transcription 1.4)

Conuertere domine et eripe animam meam	Turn, Lord, and snatch my soul	
quia non est in morte	because there is no one in death	
q<ui> memor sit tui	who may be mindful of you	Psalm 6:5–6

Music Transcription 1.4 *Conuertere domine* (SP F 11, f. 41)

The setting of the fourth antiphon, *Conuertere domine*, creates musical depictions of two possible futures awaiting the soul of the person whose life has ended. The first possibility appears in the text's beginning: the soul could be taken hold of by God, as the narrative voice requests ("Turn, Lord, and snatch my soul"). The melody mirrors these words. With the final syllables of "turn" (*conuertere*), the melody descends, but then immediately begins to rise with the word *domine*; as the narrative voice asks God to turn, the melody itself does so. After this change of direction, the melody continues to ascend. With the third syllable of *domine*, the melody has risen to a "c" (a fourth above the chant's first pitch and a full seventh above the final pitch conveying *conuertere*). The melody continues to inhabit this upper area of the chant's ambitus while conveying the words *eripe animam meam*, so that as the narrative voice asks God snatch his soul, the melody depicts an ascension. This portion of the chant creates a sustained rising motion that arrives at and then dwells in a higher place. The melodic motion traces a contour illustrating the hope expressed by the narrative voice.

The following portion of the chant's text relates a contrasting possibility: the soul confronts the danger of death. A close reading indicates that this danger is not the death of the body (physical death is assumed in the context of this ritual) but rather the death of the soul, a separation from God following physical death. The explicit mention of this possibility makes the chant's text extremely unusual in the ritual. While some chants convey images of suffering, only one other (the following antiphon, *Nequando rapiat*) suggests that the soul might be separated from God after the death of the body. *Conuertere domine* describes a moment of risk, when the soul teeters on the edge of danger.

The musical setting conveys this distressing image in a distinctive manner, one that contrasts with the chant's opening. The melody with the words *quia non* strongly delivers the negative "no one" by peaking with the highest pitch of the chant ("d") while conveying the word *non*. Following this emphatic moment, the melody descends with the word "death" (*morte*). This word receives emphasis in performance, given that its two syllables are conveyed with twelve pitches—the most ornate, melismatic conveyance of any word in the chant. The words relating the image of God snatching and rescuing the soul were conveyed with pitch content in the chant's upper ambitus (touching the high "c" four times), while the melodic setting for the words relating the possibility of the soul's death inhabit the lower end of the ambitus, descending to the low "f" and finally to the low "d" with the word *qui*.

In these ways, the chant associates the differing possibilities for the soul with distinctive melodic settings: the ascending melodic line and higher ambitus depict the positive fate—God's capture of the soul—while the descending melodic line and lower ambitus depict the danger—the soul's death. The image of the soul being rescued by God and the image of the soul experiencing death sound different in performance. As the chant musically reflects the images in the text, the possible fates of the soul are available not only in the chant's words (for the ritual's participants to understand intellectually), but also as musical illustrations (for the participants to experience with the senses). The chant's melody creates contrasting aural spaces to portray the contrasting possibilities for the soul.

Antiphon 5: *Nequando rapiat* (Music Transcription 1.5)

Nequando rapiat ut leo anima\<m\> mea\<m\>	May he never ravage like a lion my soul
dum non est qui redimat	while there is no one who redeems
neque qui saluum faciat	and no one who salvation brings Psalm 7:3

Music Transcription 1.5 *Nequando rapiat* (SP F 11, f. 41)

The antiphon *Nequando rapiat* displays an empathy for the dying person; both the text and its musical setting articulate the fear and loneliness that are possible at the end of life. The narrative voice states what he is afraid of: an enemy with the power to despoil his soul, an isolation that leaves him vulnerable to this destruction. The chant's melodic component conveys the words describing these dangers with forceful precision and emphasis. The first named danger is that the enemy might "ravage my soul like a lion," and the words *rapiat ut leo anima<m>* are given a distinct articulation—one that greatly contrasts with the preceding material of the chant's opening. The melody conveys the first words of the chant melismatically, and these multiple-note gestures meander through a fairly wide ambitus (of a sixth, from "d" to "b-flat"), changing direction five times while conveying the first three syllables *Nequando*. The setting then changes starkly. Beginning with the word *rapiat* ("ravage"), the melody closely follows the patterns of spoken language, providing listeners a speech-like declamation of the words *rapiat ut leo anima<m>* that prioritizes comprehensibility. Syllables are conveyed with single pitches, and the syllables that receive emphasis when spoken (the first syllables of *rapiat*, *leo*, and *anima<m>*) are emphasized by the melody with relatively high pitches (higher than those preceding and following). The wider ambitus heard in the chant's opening narrows in this position; the melody moves tersely by step, rather than by leap. By conveying the words *rapiat ut leo anima<m>* in this assertive and direct manner, the musical performance clearly and urgently states the danger feared by the narrative voice.

Also articulated in performance is the speaker's fear of isolation. The word *non* ("no one") provides the moment of greatest intensity within the setting. Conveyed with the highest pitch ("c"), which is heard only this one time in the chant and is further emphasized by its approach by leap, the word *non* rings out like a bell of urgency. This moment forms the chant's peak, to which the previous material leads, and from which the following material descends. The melody creates a focal point of the words expressing the narrator's fear of isolation.

To a greater extent than other antiphons in the collection, this chant expresses a worst-case scenario—the dangers and fears faced at the end of life. Rather than diminishing or distracting from the words conveying these fears, the musical setting openly displays the emotional state revealed in the text, and in doing so, opens the possibility for empathy with the sufferer.

Antiphon 6: *Dextera tua* (Music Transcription 1.6)

Dextera tua domine suscepit me	Your right hand, Lord, sustained me	
disciplina tua ipsa me docebit	your own teaching will instruct me	cf. Psalm
anima mea deo uiuit	my soul lives by God,	17:36
qui non auertit faciem suam a me	who does not turn his face from me	

Music Transcription 1.6 *Dextera tua* (SP F 11, f. 41)

The narrative voice of *Dextera tua* claims a closeness with God, and the chant's musical setting expresses this understanding melodically. In the text, the narrative voice speaks of having experienced God's presence in the past (he has been sustained by God); he also speaks of his expectation of future guidance (God will instruct him). The following words intensify the portrayal of dependence: the narrative voice says that God gives his soul life. The final words express trust, since the God on whom the narrator so profoundly relies "does not turn his face from me." Thus, the chant's text conveys the narrator's understanding that God has been—and will continue to be—a constant, reliable source of support.

The musical setting reflects this portrayal of dependence and closeness. Even in the conveyance of the first line of text, the melody creates associations between God and the narrator; melodic repetition draws connections between the first words referring to God (*dextera tua*, "your right hand"), and the first word referring to the narrator (*me*, "me"). The melody rises with the words *dextera tua*: while the first pitch of the chant is a low "c"—the lowest of the entire setting—the melody immediately begins to ascend, until it has reached "b-flat" (a seventh above the chant's first pitch and the highest pitch of the setting) with the final syllable of *tua*. These higher pitches give the word *tua* prominence in performance. The word is also emphasized by the number of pitches conveying it. While the three syllables of *dextera* receive only four pitches, the two syllables of *tua* are conveyed with twelve. This melismatic setting extends the word's performance, creating a focal point of *tua*, a word that both refers to God and—as a second-person pronoun—does so with an understanding of connection between the speaker and the addressee. The narrative voice speaks directly to God, and this direct address is emphasized in performance.

The setting conveys the first reference to the narrator in a similarly emphatic way. The melismatic setting of the word *me*, with pitch content in the upper part of the chant's ambitus, would be enough to emphasize it in performance, yet the setting does more. The melisma conveying this word is an exact repetition of the one conveying the final syllable of *tua*. The distinctive and extended melodic gesture, repeated with the first references to God and the narrator, draws an audible connection between the two, and underscores the narrator's claim of closeness with God.

The setting further underlines this claim with an additional use of the melismatic gesture. It occurs once more in the setting, in a slightly varied form, with the word *uiuit* ("lives"), as the narrative voice claims, "My soul lives by God" (*anima mea deo uiuit*). The three melismas conveying the words *tua*, *me*, and *uiuit* contain the setting's only instances of "b-flat," the highest pitch of the chant. The repeated, distinctive pitch content and similar melodic contours draw connections among the words referring to God, the narrator, and the narrator's soul.

This melodic repetition musically depicts the narrator's claim of dependence on God. The word referring to the soul's life (*uiuit*) is conveyed by a melodic gesture extremely similar to the one associated with God (*dextera tua*). At the chant's musical level, then, "soul" is dependent on the melody of "God's right hand" for its audible manifestation—its existence—in performance, much as the narrator claims that his soul depends upon God for its life. With these musical means, the antiphon *Dextera tua*—in both text and melody—asserts the narrator's reliance on God. To the ritual for the end of life, the chant contributes a portrayal of intimacy and trust in the divine.

Antiphon 7: *Dominus suscepit me* (Music Transcription 1.7)

Dominus suscepit me	The Lord sustained me	cf. Psalm 117:13
quia ego credidi uidere bona	because I trusted to see the good of	cf. Psalm 26:13
domini in terra uiuentium	the Lord in the land of the living	

Music Transcription 1.7 *Dominus suscepit me* (SP F 11, f. 41v)

Even the restrained musical gestures of the antiphon *Dominus suscepit me* provide a delivery and interpretation of the text appropriate for the time of death. The text pivots on the word *credidi*—"I trusted." For the narrator, all else depends on this action. He claims that his trust led to the life-giving support he received: "Because I trusted, God sustained me." The musical setting creates an audible focal point with this pivotal word. The chant's overall range is narrow: from its lowest to its highest pitch, the melody spans only the distance of a perfect fifth (from "c" to "g"), and the majority inhabits only a minor third (between "d" and "f"). The restricted range provides for an exceptional moment. When the melody ascends to a "g"—and this happens only one time in the setting—the pitch stands out as a high point, and the word conveyed with this pitch—*credidi*—is emphasized.

Along with the setting's highest pitch, *credidi* receives additional musical attention. While almost all other words in the chant are conveyed with only one or two notes, *credidi* is conveyed with three. In such a tightly conscribed setting, even the small melisma of three pitches stands out; the musical delivery lingers on the decisive word "trusted." The ritual's listeners and participants might have considered the word to have particular importance, given that the ability to trust might have been the only action available to a person at the end of life.

One other word stands out in the performance of the chant. Of the twelve words in the text, only *credidi* and *me* have syllables conveyed with more than two pitches. Indeed, its melismatic conveyance with seven pitches distinguishes *me* from all other words in the setting. Such a prominent performance of the first-person pronoun—the narrator's self-reference—places the focus on the suffering person: the one on whose behalf, and in whose voice, the community sings.

Apart from these moments of emphasis, the chant's musical setting prioritizes a performance of the text that aids comprehension. The musical setting mimics a spoken delivery, in that the syllables accented when speaking are given a type of musical accent. Six of the chant's twelve words have their accented syllables articulated by relatively low pitches; three additional words have their accented syllables articulated by pitches that are relatively high. The musical setting's imitation of the accent patterns used in speech facilitates the text's intelligibility in a sung performance.

Additionally, the musical setting marks the beginnings of the text's two primary syntactic units. An arch-shaped musical gesture (with the pitch content "c-d-f-e-d") conveys the initial syllables of the first syntactic unit (*Dominus sus<cepit>*) as well the initial syllables of the second (*quia ego cre<didi>*). This melodic gesture returns to mark the initial syllables of the significant phrase *terra uiuentium* ("the land of the living"). With this musical repetition, the setting creates a pattern of sound associated with the beginnings of textual units. Meaningful groups of words are clearly and audibly defined.

In sum, the setting prioritizes the text's clarity in performance, both by emphasizing the syllables accented in speech (with relatively high and low pitches), and also by defining the beginnings of the text's syntactic units and significant phrases (with melodic repetition). *Dominus suscepit me* offers the ritual a statement of trust in the divine, presented in a manner that facilitated its comprehension.

Antiphon 8: *Redemisti me* (Music Transcription 1.8)

Redemisti me domine deus ueritatis	You have redeemed me, Lord, God of truth	
in manus tua\<s\> domine commendo spiritum meum	into your hands, Lord, I commend my spirit	Psalm 30:6 Luke 23:46

Music Transcription 1.8 *Redemisti me* (SP F 11, f. 41v)

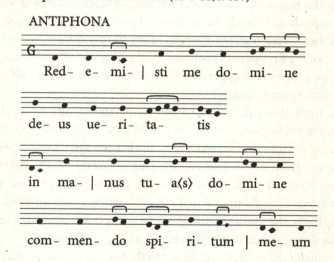

The antiphon *Redemisti me* creates a powerful theological image by associating the recently deceased person with Christ. In using the words attributed to Jesus on the cross (in the gospel account of Luke), the antiphon draws a connection between the experiences of the human and the passion of the Christ. This chant positions the person whose life is ending—and the act of dying—in the center of the Christian narrative of salvation.

The antiphon's musical setting offers these words a clear and poignant vehicle. The melody prioritizes an easily intelligible conveyance of the text by articulating the beginnings of important word groupings; where the text is divided into two complete sentences, melodic repetition reflects the beginning of each. Similar pitch content ("d," followed by a descent to "c" and an upward leap) conveys both the text's opening—the beginning of the first sentence—and the beginning of the second sentence (*in manus tua<s>*, "into your hands"). The melody also articulates an additional division in the first five words of text. The chant's first sentence could well be considered complete with the words *redemisti me domine* ("You have redeemed me, Lord"), but the sentence is extended with an appositive that renames the prayer's addressee "Lord" as *deus ueritatis* ("God of truth"). The musical setting marks the beginning of the appositive with a shift in melodic direction. While the melody with the first three words ascends, the beginning of the appositive (the first syllable of the word *deus*) is conveyed with the highest pitch of the chant ("b" or "b-flat"); the melody then traces a descent throughout the word *ueritatis* (with an ornamental embellishment on the syllable -*ta*). The two parts of the sentence are thus distinguished in performance by contrasting melodic directions; the first sentence, as a whole, is delineated in performance with an arch-shaped gesture. The musical setting provides a clear structure articulating the beginnings and endings of the text's major syntactic units.

That this particular melody would be oriented toward the text's syntactic structures is not surprising. It is one of the "completely stereotyped" melodies found with multiple texts in the "Old Roman" Office antiphon repertory.[19] (Nowacki classifies the melody in the D2 series i category; it is found in existing sources with over twenty-five texts.) Such formulaic melodies are adapted to texts of differing lengths by coordinating melodic gestures with the first and final syllables of a text's syntactic units. Aligning musical gestures—particularly repeating musical gestures—with syntactic divisions delineates the word groupings in performance.

Formulaic as the melody is, it interacts with this specific text in a poignant way. The narrative voice commends his soul "into God's hands" (*in manus tua<s>*), offering an image of movement away from the human body. The melodic motion seems to reflect this image. In performance, the first syllable of *manus* is melodically approached by leap—and not simply the smaller

---

[19] Nowacki, "Studies on the Office Antiphons," 1:165–166. The Old Roman repertory, of which SP F 11 is a witness, is discussed more extensively in Chapter 5.

leaps (of a third) found several times in the setting, or the larger leap (of a fourth) found in the melody's opening, but an unusually wide leap of a perfect fifth. Singers performing this chant feel the upward motion within the vocal apparatus as they sing the words "into your hands." As the narrator speaks of committing his soul to God, the melody creates a leaping, upward motion, ascending as one might imagine a soul spanning the distance from the human body to the awaiting hands.

Together, these musical details create a balanced, graceful vehicle for the words attributed to Jesus as he died. Other rituals for the dying reveal a similar desire to associate the end of life with the passion of the Christ; a manuscript from the second half of the ninth century, for example, includes directions to read gospel accounts of the crucifixion "until the soul leaves the body."[20] For the Roman community that used SP F 11, though, the pivotal words of the narrative were not simply read, but sung; and not simply sung, but conveyed in a melodic framework of extraordinary symmetry and beauty.

Antiphon 9: *Animam eius (Ad dominum)*
(Music Transcription 1.9)

Animam eius quam creasti domine	His soul, that you created, Lord
suscipe eam in regno tuo	take it into your kingdom
et in sinu Habrahę collocari iubeas	and in the bosom of Abraham command it to be established
ut cum beato Lazaro portionem accipiat	so that with blessed Lazarus he might his portion receive
PSALMUS Ad dominum dum tribularer	PSALM To the LORD when I was in straits ... Psalm 119[22]
<Gloria ... seculorum amen>[21]	<Glory ... of ages amen>

---

[20] *Quousque egrediatur anima de corpore* (in manuscript Vatican, Pal. lat. 485). See Sicard, *Liturgie*, 22–25; Paxton, "Bonus Liber: A Late Carolingian Clerical Manual from Lorsch," in *The Two Laws: Studies in Medieval Legal History Dedicated to Stephan Kuttner*, ed. Laurent Mayali and Stephanie A. J. Tibbetts (Washington, DC: Catholic University of America Press, 1990), 1–30; and Paxton, *Christianizing Death*, 186–192.

[21] The scribe included indications for the doxology's melody with music notation above the words *dum tribularer*.

[22] Translations of the psalm here and in the following discussion follow Alter, *The Hebrew Bible*, 3:291 (as Psalm 120).

Music Transcription 1.9 *Animam eius* (SP F 11, f. 41v)

With both text and melody, *Animam eius* depicts the movement of the soul from the human realm to a place of divine peace. As the text describes the soul's destination with metaphors—the kingdom of God, the bosom of Abraham, the company of the blessed Lazarus—the melody creates distinctive, sonic spaces for these images. The setting associates specific sounds—particularly lower pitch content—with images of the afterlife. Unusually for this repertory, the melody of *Animam eius* begins in the higher part of its ambitus: The chant's first pitch ("e") turns out to be a full sixth above the final pitch ("g"). The melody conveying the first line of text remains in the higher part of this range, occupying only the span of a major third (from "e" down to "c"). This high, restricted ambitus provides a foil for the following expansion. While conveying the words *in regno tuo* ("into your kingdom"), the melody opens a new area of pitch content, descending a full fourth and cadencing on a repetition of the pitch "g," the lowest pitch heard in the setting until this point.[23] The text speaks of entering a new realm, and the melody itself enters a new area of sound.

The chant engages this sonic territory only one other time, also in a position that conveys an image of the afterlife. The final request heard in the antiphon's text is that the soul might "receive its portion." The word *accipiat* ("receive") ends the chant and forms a point of culmination, since it completes the image of the soul being fully rooted in the place of peace. By this point in the text, not only has the soul entered the kingdom and been established in the bosom of Abraham, it has also reached the ultimate stage of receiving its reward. While conveying the final word *accipiat*, the musical setting moves again into the lower area of pitch content ("c" down to "g") heard only one time before, with the words *in regno tuo*. Thus, as the image of the soul becoming completely established in the peaceful afterlife unfolds in performance, it is musically overlaid with the sounds that previously conveyed the words "your kingdom." The distinctively low range becomes associated with images of the soul being welcomed into the place of relief.

Another image of the afterlife receives a different type of musical emphasis. The chant's melodic setting conveys each syllable of text with only one or two pitches—with a single exception: the name "Habrahę" (in the metaphor "the bosom of Abraham") has its final syllable conveyed with seven pitches. Within this sparse setting, the melisma provides great prominence—even more so because the melismatic gesture contains the setting's highest pitch. Given this distinctive melodic conveyance, the name "Abraham" (and the image of the afterlife as "the bosom of Abraham") becomes a central focus of the performance.

---

[23] The descent most likely begins with the second syllable of *eam*, although the music notation contains ambiguity in this position. The scribe included both the pitch "b" and "c" above the second syllable of *eam*. It seems most likely that the scribe inadvertently continued writing the pitch "c" one syllable further than he intended, and then, realizing the error, corrected it to the pitch "b," without erasure.

Strikingly, this particular chant does not finish by returning to its melodic starting point (the pitch "e" in the higher octave). Instead, the melody leaves its listeners in the area of sound associated with the place of repose—the audible space first established with the image of "your kingdom." Like the soul depicted in the chant, listeners have been brought to, and left resting in, a new place.

The antiphon *Animam eius* focuses on the soul's imagined, desirable future in the afterlife. This is not the case for the psalm paired with the antiphon in performance. Psalm 119 focuses on the soul's surroundings in the human realm—a place of distress, suffering, and war, a place with "lying lips" and "a tongue of deceit." Because antiphons were typically performed both before and after their accompanying psalms, the peaceful images of *Animam eius* would have encompassed the descriptions of suffering found in Psalm 119. The narrative voice of the psalm cries out, "LORD, save my life," and the antiphon offers a close description of deliverance. The narrative voice of the psalm states, "To the LORD when I was in straits I called out and He answered me"; the accompanying antiphon details the divine answer. In the performance of *Animam eius* and Psalm 119, suffering is acknowledged, but it is not the final word.

Antiphon 10: *Leto animo (De profundis)*
(Music Transcription 1.10)

Leto animo pergo ad te	With a joyful soul I hurry to you	
suscipe me domine	take me up, Lord	
quia de limo terre plasmasti me	because from the mud of the earth you molded me	cf. Genesis 2:7
spiritus de celo introiuit in me	spirit of Heaven enter into me	
iussio tua uenit	by your order it comes	
vt commendes terre corpus meum	to commend my body to the earth	
animam quam dedisti	the soul which you gave,	
suscipe illam deus	take it up, God	
PSALMUS De profundis	PSALM From the depths...	Psalm 129
<Gloria...seculorum amen>[24]	<Glory...of ages amen>	

---

[24] The scribe included indications for the doxology's melody with music notation above the final syllable of *profundis*.

Music Transcription 1.10 *Leto animo* (SP F 11, f. 42)

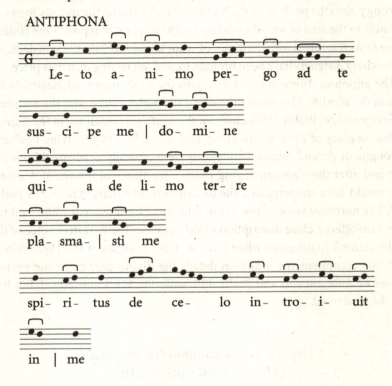

The antiphon *Leto animo*, with its paired psalm, offers a portrayal of trust and joy. The first word of the text names an emotion not mentioned before in the ritual (*leto* can be translated as joy, happiness, or gladness) as the narrative voice eagerly anticipates encountering God. God is portrayed as being intimately involved in the processes of life and death: God gives life ("from the mud of the earth you molded me"); directs death ("by your order [the spirit of heaven] comes to commend my body to the earth"); and receives the soul when death occurs ("take it up, Lord"). Performed immediately after the antiphon, Psalm 129 continues this portrayal of trust and dependence: "My soul hoped in the Lord... because with the Lord there is mercy." The narrative voice of the psalm hopes in God while waiting in a place where God's relief is not yet evident (*de profundis*; "the depths"). The narrator trusts in expected consolations.

The chant's melody contributes to this portrayal of eager anticipation by emphasizing the phrases "with joyful soul" (*leto animo*) and "I hurry to you" (*pergo ad te*). Throughout the setting, two cadential gestures systematically convey the endings of syntactic units; these gestures help to divide the lengthy

RELIGIOUS ELITES 49

Music Transcription 1.10 (cont.)

text in performance and deliver it in a comprehensible manner.[25] (The first cadential gesture contains the pitch content "e-d-d," sometimes ornamented as "e-d-c-d-d"; the second contains the pitch content "a-g-g.") Unusually, both of these cadential gestures appear with the first line of text: the first conveys the second word of the chant, *animo*; the second conveys the final syllables of the following word grouping, *pergo ad te*. Musical gestures with this sense of finality normally appear with the endings of syntactic units. In this chant, however, they convey the text's first words. The eager anticipation of meeting

[25] With seventy syllables, *Leto animo* contains the longest text in the collection of antiphons. The melody uses repeated cadential gestures to partition the text along its syntactical divisions. As one example, the first syntactic unit ends with the words *ad te* ("to you"); the melody conveys these words with a pattern of pitches often seen at musical endings ("g-a-g g"). This pattern repeats later in the chant while conveying the end of another syntactic unit: *uenit*. A slightly shortened form of the gesture ("a-g g") appears with other endings: *plasmasti me* and *illam deus*. A transposed version of the same gesture ("d-e-d d") conveys two others: *introiuit in me* and *meum*. Altogether, this gesture conveys the endings of six of the text's seven syntactical units. A different cadential gesture—a repeated "d" approached by a second below—conveys the remaining ending (*domine* of Line 2). These musical gestures segment the melody and convey the text's syntactical units as distinct entities, allowing for easier comprehension in performance.

God, and the happiness of the soul about to find relief, are emphasized in performance with this striking use of cadential gestures.

The chant's musical setting also emphasizes the narrator's understanding that God controls the process of dying. The words *iussio* ("by your order") and *suscipe* ("take up," in the antiphon's final line) are conveyed with a repeated, distinctively shaped melisma. The melisma's distinguishing contours trace a directly descending scale (from "e" down to "g") and then immediately ascend (from "g" back to "c"). With both *iussio* and *suscipe*, this gesture is identically distributed across the three-syllable words. The musical emphasis of these words, and the connection created between them with musical repetition, articulates the narrator's understanding that God directs the end of life and takes up the soul in death.

As the narrative voice petitions God to receive the soul, the melodic setting depicts an answer to the prayer. Perhaps the most idiosyncratic musical gesture of the chant conveys both the words *de celo* ("[spirit] of heaven") and *animam* ("soul," in the antiphon's penultimate line). The melodic gesture stands out because of its successive melismas—syllables receive three and four pitches—and because it contains the highest pitch of the chant (the "g" an octave above the final). Through this musical repetition and relatively high pitch content, the words *spiritus de celo* and *animam* emerge from the surrounding material and become associated with each other in performance. By connecting these words, the setting reflects the desire of the narrative voice—and the ritual as a whole—to bring the departing soul into close association with God.

This desire has even more poignancy when expressed in the medium of song. Singing requires the controlled use of breath, and breath is associated not only with its physical source in the human body, but also—through the creation story of Genesis referenced in the chant—with the spirit of God.[26] With the understanding that the spirit of God—the breath of God—animates humans, the act of singing the chant reflects what the narrative voice of the text requests: "spirit of God, enter into me" (*spiritus de celo, introiuit in me*). In singing this chant, the gathered community used their God-given breath to petition God's breath, on behalf of the person for whom breathing had ceased.

---

[26] Gen 2:7. Hart draws attention to a related association between the creation story and the New Testament "Letter of James." In his commentary on the statement, "For just as the body without spirit is dead," Hart writes: "James apparently uses *pnevma* for the principle of corporeal life, almost certainly as the Greek equivalent of the *neshamah* ("breath," "spirit") that God breathed into Adam in Genesis 2: 7." David Bentley Hart, *The New Testament* (New Haven, CT: Yale University Press, 2017), 459. Additional associations between "pneuma" and sung medieval liturgies are considered in Bissera V. Pentcheva, "Performative Liturgies and Cosmic Sound in the Exultet Liturgy of Southern Italy," *Speculum* 95, no. 2 (April 2020): 396–466.

Antiphon 11: *Qui cognoscis (Secundum magnam)*
(Music Transcription 1.11)

Qui cognoscis omnia[27] occulta	You who know all hidden things	
a delicto meo munda me	from my crimes cleanse me	cf. Psalm 18:13
tempus michi concede	give me time	
vt repenitens clamem	so that I can cry out, repentant:	
peccaui tibi	I have sinned against you	
miserere mei deus	have mercy on me, God	
PSALMUS Secundum magnam	PSALM According to <your> great <mercy>...	Psalm 50
<Gloria... seculorum amen>[28]	<Glory... of ages amen>	

The eleventh antiphon of the collection, *Qui cognoscis*, gives voice to an expression of repentance. In this, it resembles Psalm 50, with which it is paired. King David of the Hebrew Bible was traditionally understood to be the narrative voice of Psalm 50; the psalm was read as David's prayer of contrition when the prophet Nathan confronted him with his transgressions of adultery and murder. In both the antiphon and the psalm, narrative voices confess wrongdoing, articulate regret, and plead to God for cleansing. In closely mirroring the expressions and emotions of the psalm, the antiphon's text associates the person at the center of the ritual with the biblical figure of David, who successfully achieved reconciliation with God.

The chant's musical setting also draws a connection between the recently deceased person and the repentant David. As seen in the music notation (Figure 1.2), the performance seamlessly joins the antiphon and the psalm by creating a type of elision. The final words of the antiphon, *miserere mei deus*, are also the first of the psalm; the words marked in the manuscript as beginning the psalm, *Secundum magnam*, are actually a continuation of it. The melody itself, in its pitch content, further blurs the division between the antiphon and the psalm. What sounds like the ending of the antiphon—the words *miserere mei deus*, conveyed with a cadential gesture—are actually the first words of the psalm; the psalm's simple melody (technically termed the *psalm tone*) begins with the psalm's continuation, the words *secundum*

---

[27] omnia] manuscript: omniu.
[28] The scribe included indications for the doxology's melody with music notation above the word *magnam*. The notation in this position includes one superfluous "c," which is excluded from Music Transcription 1.11.

Music Transcription 1.11 *Qui cognoscis* (SP F 11, f. 42)

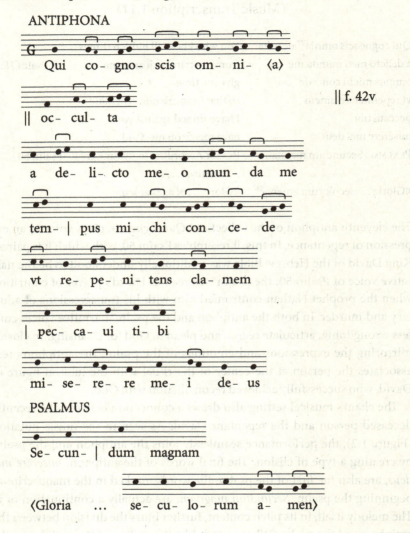

magnam. Additionally, the musical transition between the antiphon melody and the psalm tone is unusually smooth. With other pairs of antiphons and psalms in the ritual, the musical notation reveals large leaps (of a perfect fifth) between the final pitch of the antiphon melody and the first of the psalm tone. In *Qui cognoscis*, however, the same pitch ("g") ends the antiphon's melody and begins the melody of the psalm. Musically, then, as well as textually, the narrative voice of the chant—associated with the person whose life

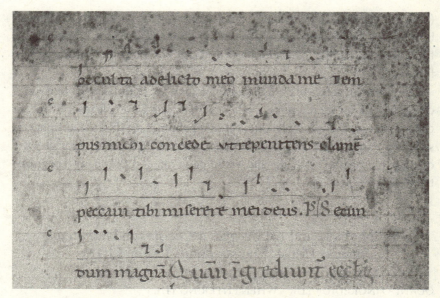

Figure 1.2 The ending of *Qui cognoscis* and the beginning of Psalm 50 (SP F 11, f. 42v). Image © 2024 Vatican Apostolic Library.

is ending—is brought into close connection with the narrative voice of the psalm—associated with David, a model of successful repentance.

Yet the antiphon distinguishes itself from the psalm in one particular position, and in a way that seems appropriate for the end of life. The antiphon's text contains a plea that is not present in the psalm, or in the biblical story of David's repentance: *tempus michi concede* ("give me time"). The antiphon's melody conveys this plea with particular urgency. The pitches that articulate these three words leap above those that came before: the pitches conveying the first syllable of *tempus* are approached by an interval of a fourth (the setting's largest leap) and are conveyed with a gesture that rises even further, from "c" to "d" (the setting's highest pitch). This new, higher pitch content emphasizes the plea for time. A distinctive cadential gesture gives the words even more prominence in performance: while the melodic gestures that convey all other endings of the text's syntactic units have typical, falling contours, the melodic gesture that conveys the final syllable of the plea for time (the last syllable of *concede*, "give") traces an unusual ascension. These distinctive musical characteristics—relatively high pitch content and a rising cadential gesture—are even more noticeable, given that the words immediately prior to *tempus michi concede* are conveyed with a cadential gesture (which could well have been performed with a slowing pace, or even followed by a pause). The melody creates an ending immediately prior to the plea for time, and this ending lends emphasis to the new, articulated beginning that follows.

The narrative voices of both the antiphon and the psalm confess to wrongdoing and ask for mercy, but only the text of the antiphon pleads for time, in order to successfully complete the act of repentance. In this, the antiphon is suited to—and adapts the psalm to—the end of life. The psalm associates the dying person with David, the successful penitent, and the chant recognizes the distinctive need for time.

Antiphons 12 and 13: *Svscipiat te Christus* and *Induc eum domine* (Music Transcriptions 1.12 and 1.13)

QUANDO INGREDIUNTUR ECCLESIAM	WHEN ENTERING THE CHURCH
ANTIPHONA	ANTIPHON
Svscipiat te Christus	May Christ receive you
qui uocauit te	who called you
et in sinu Habrahę	and to the bosom of Abraham
angeli deducant te	may angels lead you cf. Luke 16:22
ANTIPHONA	ANTIPHON
Induc eum domine	Lead him, Lord
in montem hereditatis tue	to the mountain of your inheritance
et in sanctuarium	and to the sanctuary
quod preparauerunt manus tue domine	that you have prepared with your hands, Lord cf. Exodus 15:17

The ritual uses the chants *Svscipiat te Christus* and *Induc eum domine* to distinguish and bring associative meaning to the moment when the corpse was carried into the church. The text of *Svscipiat te Christus* offers an explicitly Christian blessing to the person whose life has ended, referencing Christ and a depiction of the afterlife—the bosom of Abraham—from the gospel account of Jesus's sayings. At the moment when the community brought the

Music Transcription 1.12 *Svscipiat te Christus* (SP F 11, f. 42v)

QUANDO INGREDIUNTUR ECCLESIAM
ANTIPHONA

Svscipiat te Christus qui uocauit te et in sinu Habrahę angeli deducant te

Music Transcription 1.13 *Induc eum domine* (SP F 11, f. 42v)

ANTIPHONA

Induc eum domine in montem hereditatis tue et in sanctuarium quod preparauerunt manus tue domine

body of the deceased person into the church building, the words of the chant depicted the person being brought into the presence of Christ and Abraham. The human activity of moving the body echoed the images of activities in the afterlife.

Similarly, the text of the antiphon *Induc eum domine* draws a connection between the body's entrance into the church and the person's entrance to the afterlife. While the corpse is brought into the earthly sanctuary, the singers pray that the person (as a soul) might be brought into the sanctuary prepared by the Lord, "the mountain of inheritance." The chant also draws connections between the experience of dying and the experience of being freed from captivity. The antiphon's text references the words attributed to Moses after the Israelites have been decisively rescued from slavery (Exodus 15). The journey of the Israelites is brought into association with the deceased person and offered as a metaphor for the journey of the soul away from the human body, into the afterlife. As the community brought the corpse into church, they sang of the person being brought into a place of freedom.

Although these melodies begin with gestures found in other antiphons in the Old Roman repertory,[29] they articulate the specific texts of *Svscipiat te Christus* and *Induc eum domine* in meaningful ways. Because the melodies are generally restrained (in the two chants, only six syllables are conveyed with more than two pitches), the syllables conveyed with three or more pitches receive strong articulation in performance. Most notable are the repetitions of the word *te* ("you") in *Svscipiat te Christus*. The eight-syllable melisma that conveys these words makes the direct address of the recently deceased person quite prominent. The musical setting draws attention to the fact that the community still addresses the person as one who can be spoken to—and blessed—directly. In singing these chants, the deceased person was envisioned as being present to the community, and the community was understood to have the ability—perhaps the responsibility—to pray on his behalf.

Conclusion: The Functions of Community and Melody

The ritual for the end of life in SP F 11 requires an engaged presence, with specific, substantive tasks assigned to the dying person's community. Psalms,

---

[29] Nowacki classifies the opening gesture seen in each chant as the intonation for Type D 2 series ii ("Studies on the Office Antiphons," 138–176).

litanies, versicles with responses, and antiphons—which together form a large portion of the ritual—were customarily performed collaboratively; prayers are formulated as "we," with first-person, plural pronouns. The ritual assumes that the community—not simply a single officiant—will gather.

The community gathered to attend to the dying person during the final agony and to provide assistance—through the liturgy—to the departing soul. Each portion of the ritual offered its own type of support, not only to the dying person and his soul, but also to the ritual's participants. In singing the penitential psalms, those gathered at the bedside acknowledged and gave voice to the suffering of the dying person, even while articulating a trust in and an orientation toward God. Images of a merciful, all-powerful God provided boundaries to the distress, contextualizing and containing the suffering by offering a vision of both future relief and the ever-present reliever. In singing the litany, the community called upon God, angels, and saints to provide assistance and protection. The ritual's prayers required those gathered to articulate an acceptance of the death that was occurring, even to the point of encouraging the soul to "go forth from this world." Singing the antiphons allowed the community to further articulate the suffering that occurred at the end of life, and even—with *Redemisti me*—to associate the dying person's experiences with those of Jesus on the cross.

The ritual as an entirety provided a coherent understanding of the dying process. It presents death as a journey the soul travels from earthly suffering to heavenly rest; it presents God as omniscient and capable of relieving suffering; it presents the dying person as being in intimate relationship with this capable God. The ritual also provides evocative descriptions of the soul's destination. The image of the heavenly Jerusalem depicts a place of peace, the bosom of Abraham a place of rest. Through the ritual and its images, the community shared a comprehensive conceptualization of the dying process, complete with powerful companions and a beautiful destination for the soul.

As people gathered at the bedside, the liturgy drew them into further collaboration with its performance requirements. Participating in the ritual structured the actions, the speech, and—in singing—even the breath of those gathered. The psalms, litany, versicles with responses, and antiphons required coordination of listening and responding, of rhythm and pacing, of inhalation and exhalation. In these very tangible ways, the ritual provided a structure to accompany the changeability of a life's ending. The progression of liturgical prayers and chants moved the community through unpredictable situations in a coordinated, disciplined way. Singing shaped the experience of the ritual's participants.

The melodies shaped the understandings of the chant's texts. Most often, they provide interpretations resonating with empathy and reassurance. When the narrative voice of *Dirige domine* entreats God for guidance, the melody conveys the words with a perfectly symmetrical and self-sufficient gesture, giving the impression that the plea itself is sufficient and acceptable. In *Qui cognoscis*, the melody joins the narrative voice of the dying person to the voice of David, reconciled with God. The antiphons' melodies sometimes even trace the movements asked for in the sung texts. When the narrator of *Conuertere domine* asks God to turn, the melody itself changes direction. When the text of *Redemisti me* speaks of the suffering human placing his soul into God's hands, the melody leaps up, as if to bridge the distance.

The music creates aural depictions of the soul's destination. The narrator of *Animam eius* asks God to take the departing soul into his kingdom, and the melody soars into a new range as it conveys the words "in the bosom of Abraham." While the narrative voice of *Conuertere domine* asks God to "snatch my soul," the melody rises above the previous pitches, leading listeners into an elevated aural space. The texts of the ritual's chants characterize God as being merciful and just, and the melodies emphasize these characterizations. The melody of *Secundum magnam* provides great prominence to the word "mercy"; the melismas of *Domine deus* underscore the words "eternal justice."

The melodies, along with the texts, depict a close connection between the suffering person and God. In *Secundum magnam*, the striking melodic gesture conveying the word "mercy" (of God) is echoed in the melodic gesture with "humiliated bones" (of the dying person). In *Leto animo*, when the narrative voice asks the spirit of heaven to enter into him, the music offers a depiction of this union: the same, distinctive musical gesture conveys the words "spirit of heaven" and "soul."

Indeed, the beauty of the music itself adds meaning to the texts and to the ritual as a whole. A plea for assistance, conveyed by a symmetrical, balanced melody, sounds like a prayer about to be fulfilled. A cry of repentance, musically associated with the psalm of David, carries the assurance of forgiveness. A request to God to establish the departing soul in the bosom of Abraham, when conveyed by a melody soaring to new heights, sounds as though the soul will soon be in that place of peace. The chants of SP F 11 infuse the gathering at the bedside with expressions of peace and reassurance.

2
Political and Religious Leaders

Sens, Cathedral of Saint Stephen

Manuscript Source: Paris, Bibliothèque nationale de France, lat. 934 (Paris 934)

The liturgy for the dying in Paris 934, a manuscript from the cathedral of Sens, shows the persistence of a local tradition. Paris 934 contains a late twelfth-century version of a deathbed ritual developed around 300 years earlier at the abbey of St-Amand and distributed at that time to both the abbey of St-Denis and to Sens.[1] Yet this "local" ritual, maintained for centuries in Sens, was itself an eclectic creation. As it is recorded in the ninth-century sources, as well as in Paris 934, the ritual reveals a confluence of diverse practices: the interest in supporting an individual in the moments prior to death can be traced back

---

[1] Paris, Bibliothèque nationale de France, lat. 934 is dated to the late twelfth or thirteenth century. Images are available at Bibliothèque nationale de France, "Gallica: Pontificale Senonense," at https://gallica.bnf.fr/ark:/12148/btv1b8432295p.r=934?rk=21459;2. The manuscript's contents—particularly its litany and ritual for consecrating an abbot—indicate its use in Sens: Victor Leroquais, *Les pontificaux manuscrits des bibliothèques publiques de France* (Ligugé: Bibliothèque de l'abbaye Saint-Martin Ligugé, 1937), 2:1–5; Philippe Lauer, *Catalogue général des manuscrits latins* (Paris: Bibliothèque nationale, 1939), 1:331; Océane Boudeau, "Manuscrits notés en neumes en Occident (MANNO): Paris, Bibliothèque nationale de France Latin 934," available at https://manno.saprat.fr/sites/default/files/manno/notice/Latin%20934_1.pdf (accessed July 9, 2023). The ninth-century sacramentary created by St-Amand for the abbey of Saint-Denis is manuscript Paris, Bibliothèque nationale de France, lat. 2290; its rites for the dying are discussed in Paxton, *Christianizing Death*, 173–179. Sicard includes the manuscript as Den (*Liturgie*, xi); Gamber, *CLLA*, as number 760; Deshusses as R (*Le sacramentaire grégorien*, 3:34–35). The ninth-century sacramentary created by St-Amand for the cathedral community of Sens is held as Stockholm, Kungliga biblioteket, Holm. A 136; Paxton's discussion appears in *Christianizing Death*, 179–185; Sicard includes the manuscript as Ad (*Liturgie*, xi); Gamber, *CLLA*, as number 763; Deshusses, *Le sacramentaire grégorien*, as T4 (3:41–43). For the historical, liturgical, and political context in which these sacramentaries were created, see Yitzhak Hen, "When Liturgy Gets out of Hand," in *Writing the Early Medieval West: Studies in Honour of Rosamond McKitterick*, ed. Elina Screen and Charles West (Cambridge: Cambridge University Press, 2018), 203–212. Robertson offers a study of the surviving liturgical documents from St-Denis: Anne Walters Robertson, *The Service-Books of the Royal Abbey of Saint-Denis: Images of Ritual and Music in the Middle Ages* (Oxford: Clarendon Press, 1991); Grier considers the interplay among the liturgies of medieval monastic institutions and the "larger secular and ecclesiastical worlds": James Grier, "Musical and Liturgical Practice," in *The Oxford Handbook of Christian Monasticism*, ed. Bernice M. Kaczynski (Oxford: Oxford University Press, 2020), 333–348.

to late eighth-century Francia; the ritual's chants are part of the *Ordo XLIX* tradition, attributed to the Roman church prior to the Carolingian era; and the ritual also contains prayers compiled by Benedict of Aniane in the early ninth century.[2]

From these varied traditions, it is more often the items conveying benevolent, hopeful images of the dying process that appear in Paris 934 for the portion of the ritual conducted at the bedside. For the dying person, the ritual portrayed death as a migration, rather than a judgment. Even at a time when the concept of purgatory was gaining specificity and acceptance, and images of a judicial God were widely established, the ritual for the time of death in Paris 934 retained a hopeful focus.[3] The multitude of positive texts and metaphors within the ritual suggests an intention to comfort: in the final moments of life, the dying person was surrounded with vivid images of a peaceful future. The deathbed ritual of Paris 934 shows a persistent impulse toward reassurance.

Paris 934 also shows the persistence of a particular chant repertory—the chants and psalms edited by Andrieu as part of *Ordo XLIX*.[4] Andrieu's edition drew from an eleventh-century manuscript source (Vatican 312), but the chants and psalms prescribed in Paris 934 and Vatican 312 for the time of death are also present in one of the oldest extant documents containing a deathbed ritual, a late eighth-century manuscript from Autun (now housed in Berlin as Staatsbibliothek zu Berlin–Preußischer Kulturbesitz, Ms. Phil. 1667).[5] Moreover, these same chants and psalms are often seen in the

---

[2] As Paxton has noted, the rite in the ninth-century sacramentaries of St-Denis and Sens "synthesized the Frankish rite for the agony with the prayers of Benedict's Supplement and the psalmody of the old Roman ordo" (*Christianizing Death*, 179–180). Paxton provides the most comprehensive narrative of the late eighth-century development of rites for the time period immediately preceding death. See especially *Christianizing Death*, 114–127. The chants in the deathbed ritual of Paris 934 are understood by scholars to be part of an older, Roman rite, which Andrieu edited as *Ordo XLIX* (from the eleventh-century manuscript Vatican 312): Andrieu, *Les ordines*, 523–530. Please see Chapter 5 for considerations on the possible Roman origins of *Ordo XLIX*. Benedict of Aniane compiled prayers for the time of death as part of the *Hucusque* supplement to the Gregorian sacramentary, edited by Jean Deshusses in *Le sacramentaire grégorien*, 1:457–463. Deshusses also identified Benedict of Aniane as the author of the supplement: "Le 'supplément' au sacramentaire grégorien: Alcuin ou Saint Benoît d'Aniane?" *Archiv für Liturgiewissenschaft* 9 (1965): 48–71; see also *Le sacramentaire grégorien*, 1:66–70 and 3:66–75. On Benedict's "unenviable task" of supplementing the Roman materials, see Daniel Joseph DiCenso, "Sacramentary-Antiphoners as Sources of Gregorian Chant in the Eighth and Ninth Centuries" (PhD diss., University of Cambridge, 2011). For an extended discussion of Benedict of Aniane's work with the rites for the sick and dying, see Paxton, *Christianizing Death*, 131–161. Ottosen, *Responsories*, 32–33 and 42, considers Benedict of Aniane's contribution to the development of liturgical commemorations of the dead in his role as abbot of Aniane.

[3] Please see Chapter 5 for a discussion of the prevalent medieval images of the afterlife and their relationships to the images found in deathbed liturgies.

[4] Andrieu, *Les ordines*, 523–530.

[5] Berlin 1667. This earlier manuscript contains no music notation, meaning that the melodic continuity of the chants between the eighth and twelfth centuries can neither be established nor denied.

deathbed rituals of manuscripts created after Paris 934. In medieval liturgies for the dying, they are the most commonly prescribed. That part of this repertory also surfaces in Dante's *Divine Comedy* (written in the early fourteenth century) further suggests that it was part of a widespread and long-lasting liturgical tradition. As a witness to this sung material, Paris 934 forms a point of connection with both earlier and later rituals.

Indeed, Paris 934 provides an extraordinary opportunity to examine this widespread repertory. In earlier manuscripts, the chants appear in abbreviated form—without music notation, and with only their first words written. In contrast, the melodies in Paris 934 were recorded with a precise use of staff notation, providing clear indications of their pitch content and text underlay. To my knowledge, Paris 934 offers the earliest extant source of the chants of the *Ordo XLIX* tradition with pitch-specific music notation. The manuscript provides the oldest known rendering of the chants' melodies as part of a liturgy at the deathbed.[6]

The following analysis of the deathbed ritual in Paris 934—with its music notation—reveals that the chants play a substantial role in conveying the ritual's reassuring images. The chants' melodies shape the delivery of the sung texts in fundamental ways: emphasizing the words describing the soul's peaceful destination and using melodic ascension to underscore textual descriptions of the soul's ascension, away from the body. The chants' melodies also join two texts—portraying two different journeys—into one, unified performance: by musical association, the journey of the departing soul (portrayed in the antiphon *Suscipiat te Christus*) is equated with the Israelites' journey to freedom (the exodus narrative of the Hebrew Bible, presented in the ritual in Psalm 113).

Who might have benefited from these images and chants? On whose behalf might the ritual in Paris 934 have been conducted? The earlier manuscript sources from both Sens and St-Denis, as well as numerous later sources, indicate that the ritual had a broader transmission than is revealed in the

---

Paxton discusses the eighth-century manuscript (under its earlier shelfmark, Berlin Öffentliche Wissenschaftliche Bibliothek MS lat. 105 Phillipps 1667) in *Christianizing Death*, 106–109 and 119–122. Gamber, *CLLA*, includes the manuscript as number 853; Sicard, *Liturgie*, incorporates the manuscript as *Ph* and considers the chants of its deathbed ritual as part of the *Ordo XLIX* tradition.

[6] Two of the ritual's chants, *Suscipiat te Christus* and *Subuenite*, appear notated in a slightly earlier source (the early twelfth-century manuscript discussed in the previous chapter: SP F 11, f. 46) but assigned to different liturgical positions—during the procession that brought the body into the church and during the vigil with the corpse in the church prior to burial. Chapter 5 considers material that is shared among liturgies for the dying and liturgies conducted after an individual's death.

single manuscript witness of Paris 934. Yet focusing on the single manuscript gives a clear picture of the most likely celebrants and beneficiaries in twelfth-century Sens. Paris 934 seems to have been created for the archbishops of Sens, for whom the cathedral of Saint Stephen served as a seat (and the adjacent palace as a residence). In addition to the ritual for the dying, the manuscript contains material for ceremonies conducted by an archbishop, including the coronation of a king and queen and consecrations of bishops, abbots, and abbesses. The manuscript even contains professions of obedience to two successive archbishops of Sens, written by abbots and abbesses under their authority.[7] Given this context, it seems likely that the ritual for the dying within Paris 934 could have been conducted on behalf of these same people: the political and religious leaders in the diocese of Sens, including the archbishop, as well as bishops and clerics within his jurisdiction. As the following analysis shows, scribal work with the ritual's prayers indicates that the liturgy was considered appropriate for women, perhaps abbesses or female members of the royal family. Furthermore, the ritual's opening rubric indicates that laity might have been present in a gathering at the deathbed. A dying person's family and companions might well have been present.

The Opening Rubric: Indications for the Ritual's Performance

INCIPIT COMMENDATIO ANIME	THE COMMENDATION OF THE SOUL BEGINS
CUM IGITUR ANIMA IN AGONE SUI EXITUS	WHEN THEREFORE THE SOUL, IN THE STRUGGLE OF ITS EXIT,
DISSOLUTIONE CORPORIS UISA FUERIT LABORARE	IN THE DISSOLUTION OF THE BODY, HAS BEEN SEEN TO BE LABORING
CUM UENIRE STUDEBUNT FRATRES UEL CLERICI QUIQUE FIDELES	WHEN THE BROTHERS, OR CLERICS, ALL THE FAITHFUL EAGERLY STRIVE TO COME
ET AGATUR HOC MODO COMMENDATIO	AND IN THIS WAY THE COMMENDATION OUGHT TO BE CONDUCTED

The first rubric gives insight into the circumstances in which the ritual would be conducted and the expectations of who would participate. These opening words indicate that the liturgy was intended to begin as the body of the dying

---

[7] These professions are found in the manuscript on folios 1v–3.

person "falls apart" and the soul struggles to leave (*cum igitur anima in agone sui exitus dissolutione corporis*). With the individual so close to death, the rubric assumes that a gathering will occur: not simply a single priest, or religious professionals, but a more varied community, which could include monks, clerics, and laity (*fratres uel clerici quique fideles*).

This rubric also offers insight into the ritual's forerunners. Nearly identical wording appears in the ninth-century sacramentaries of Sens and St-Denis.[8] All versions of the ritual were intended to begin when the person was very near to death—what we might term "actively dying"—and all versions mention both monastic and lay participants as part of the gathering at the bedside.

Yet Paris 934 does not identically replicate the earlier, ninth-century versions of the ritual. The opening rubric in this later manuscript omits indications to sing the seven penitential psalms and a litany. These omissions create a shorter ritual; they also remove the focus on suffering and the expressions of guilt that are found in the penitential psalms. With these changes, the version in Paris 934 remains centered on the metaphor of death as a migration, and the ritual's chants—with their visions of a welcoming afterlife—take on more prominence.

Responsory and Verse: *Subuenite–Suscipiat* (Music Transcription 2.1)

Responsorium	Responsory
Subuenite sancti dei	Advance, saints of God
occurrite angeli domini	run, angels of the Lord
suscipientes animam[9] eius	taking his soul
offerentes eam in conspectu altisimi	offering it in the sight of the most high

---

[8] Paxton edits the first rubric in the ritual for the dying in Paris 2290 (the ninth-century sacramentary of St-Denis) in *Christianizing Death*, 175, note 36:

CUM ANIMA IN AGONE SUI EXITUS
DISSOLUTIONE CORPORIS SUI UISA FUERIT LABORARE
CONUENIRE STUDEBUNT FRATRES UEL CETERI QUIQUE FIDELES
ET CANENDI SUNT VII PAENITENTIAE PSALMI

Sicard provides a documentation of the rubric's broader transmission in "La mort du chrétien et sa communauté," *La Maison-Dieu: Revue de pastorale liturgique* 144 (1980): 59–64.

[9] An erased and illegible letter is visible prior to the word *animam*.

Versus	Verse	
Suscipiat eam Christus	May Christ receive it	
qui uocauit[10] <eam>	who called <it>	
et in sinu Habrahe angeli deducant <eam>	and to the bosom of Abraham may angels lead <it>	cf. Lk 16: 22
Offerentes...	Offering <it in the sight of the most high>	

The first of these chants, the responsory *Subuenite*, begins the ritual: appearing immediately after the first rubric, it is indicated as an accompaniment for the final moments of life—the moments when the soul "struggles to exit."[11] Singing *Subuenite* was the liturgical prescription for the critical moments when death seemed imminent.

The chant's text reflects the urgency and momentousness of these circumstances. The first word, *subuenite*, has militaristic connotations; it suggests "the advance of a military reserve."[12] The use of the verb in this context likens death to the high-stakes situation of a battle—and not just any battle, but one that has reached an advanced, critical point, when one side is depleted enough to require its reserve troops. The verb links the saints of God to an army, suggesting that they have the numbers, the training, the skill, and the courage of a military force. Asking the saints of God to "advance" or "reinforce" asks for the last, best hope—the ultimate rescue squad—to engage. The stakes are high, the need is great, but the forces are strong.

Along with this metaphor (which is briefly echoed at later points in the ritual in Psalms 113 and 117), the chant's text articulates an essential

---

[10] As seen in Music Transcription 2.1, the music notation stops in this position, perhaps because of the missing word. My thanks go to Andreas Pfisterer for this possible explanation (personal correspondence, September 20, 2022).

[11] The text of the chant is edited in Sicard, *Liturgie*, 66–68; Paxton, *Christianizing Death*, 39–40; Donohue, "The Rite," 124–125; René Jean Hesbert, *Corpus Antiphonalium Officii* (Rome: Herder, 1963–1979), as numbers 7716 and 7716v. Donohue's discussion of the chant as a response to death occurs in "The Rite," 164–169. Ottosen edits the responsory as number 90 and the verse as number 221 (*Responsories*, 228, 401, and 418). Paxton's edition and translation appear in *The Death Ritual at Cluny*, 114–115; see also 211.

[12] As defined in *A Latin Dictionary* by Lewis and Short (available online at Tufts University, "Perseus Digital Library: Latin Word Study Tool," Gregory R. Crane, editor-in-chief, accessed April 4, 2020, at http://www.perseus.tufts.edu/hopper/morph?l=subvenite&la=la#lexicon). My sincere thanks to the professors at the University of St. Thomas (Houston) for an informative discussion concerning the verb and its connotations. Rachel Fulton Brown considers the use of military metaphors in medieval descriptions of intercessory prayer: Rachel Fulton Brown, "Prayer," in *The Oxford Handbook of Christian Monasticism*, ed. Bernice M. Kaczynski (Oxford: Oxford University Press, 2020), 316–332.

Music Transcription 2.1 *Subuenite–Suscipiat* (Paris 934, f. 113v)

| et in sinu Habrahe angeli deducant ⟨eam⟩

Offerentes

understanding of death as a migration. In a successful death, the soul moves from its residence in the human body to the presence of God (*in conspectu altis<s>imi*); angels and saints assist with this journey.[13] The safe passage of the soul is the focus of the liturgy at the deathbed; the chant *Subuenite* describes both the journey and the soul's protectors.

The chant's melody mimics the movement of the soul depicted in the text. Even while conforming to the customary melodic characteristics for the responsory genre,[14] the musical setting conveys the text in a way that specifically reflects its semantic contents. As the words describe the soul's journey into "the sight of the most high," the musical setting creates patterns of ascension. With the first lines of text, the melody forms a series of short, arch-shaped gestures with rising pitch content. Arch-shaped gestures are typical—even characteristic—of plainchant melodies; yet in *Subuenite*, they are arranged in a distinctive way that reflects the metaphorical images of the sung text. The first such gesture (conveying the second syllable of *subuenite*) begins on the pitch "d," peaks a third higher on the pitch "f," and then descends back to "d." A second arch-shaped gesture occurs with the final syllable of *dei*, but it contains slightly higher pitch content: it begins on "e," and peaks with the pitch "g" before descending back to "e." The third and fourth arch-shaped gestures (conveying the first three syllables of *occurrite* and the final syllable of *occurrite* through the first two syllables of *angeli*) peak with the pitch "a"; the fifth such gesture (conveying the final syllable of *angeli*) peaks on "b-flat." In this way, the melodic content moves gradually higher, ascending a fourth from its first peak of "f" to the final peak of "b-flat." Gestures of ascension structure the melody's beginning.

---

[13] Reinhold Hammerstein documents uses of the metaphor in *Die Musik der Engel: Untersuchungen zur Musikanschauung des Mittelalters* (Bern: Francke, 1962), particularly 81–91. See also Janine Droese, *Die Musik der Engel in ihrer Bedeutung für Musik und Musikanschauung des 13.-16. Jahrhunderts* (Hildesheim: Olms, 2021).

[14] The genre's most notable melodic characteristics include 1. melismas conveying syllables near the endings of textual syntactic units and 2. the alternation of pitch content (between the final and non-final pitches of the mode) with the final syllables of syntactic units. These melodic tendencies, and others, have been analyzed by Peter Wagner, *Einführung in die gregorianischen Melodien: Ein Handbuch der Choralwissenschaft* (Hildesheim: Olms, 1962 [reprint edition]); Walter Howard Frere, *Antiphonale Sarisburiense: A Reproduction in Facsimile of a Manuscript of the Thirteenth Century* (London: Farnborough Gregg, 1901-1924); Andreas Pfisterer, "Skizzen zu einer gregorianischen Formenlehre," *Archiv für Musikwissenschaft* 63, no. 2 (2006): 145–161, especially 147–152; Katherine Eve Helsen, "The Great Responsories of the Divine Office: Aspects of Structure and Transmission" (PhD diss., University of Regensburg, 2008), 61ff.; and "The Use of Melodic Formulas in Responsories: Constancy and Variability in the Manuscript Tradition," *Plainsong and Medieval Music* 18, no. 1 (2009): 61–75.

As the text describes the soul reaching the apex of its journey—being "offered in the sight of the most high" (*offerentes eam in conspectu altis<s>imi*)—the musical ascension intensifies. With these words, the melody begins from a lower position (the pitches conveying *offerentes eam* are the lowest in the chant) and ascends in a compressed time-frame of ten syllables: the first melodic peak of "f" occurs with the word *offerentes*; the melody reaches a "g" with the final syllable of *conspectu*, and the highest pitch of the chant, "b-flat," occurs with the first syllable of *altis<s>imi*. Additionally, this is the only line of text that ends with a pitch higher than the one with which it began. Ascension permeates multiple aspects of the melody while conveying the words describing the summit of the soul's journey. The chant's music echoes the textual description of the soul rising toward God.

The melody uses additional means to emphasize the pivotal words *offerentes eam in conspectu altis<s>imi*. Of the entire chant, this line of text has the most syllables conveyed melismatically (with three or more pitches) and the most upward leaps: all but one of the chant's melodic leaps occur with this line of text. With this musical emphasis—and the pervasive ascension—the chant's melody offers an audible image of the essential movement hoped for in death: the soul's rising to God. Most poignantly, the chant offers this image at the time when the soul's movement is understood to be occurring. In the context of the ritual, the chant *Subuenite* both reflects and accompanies the journey.[15]

Oratio: *Tibi domine commendamus*

The prayer following *Subuenite* shows another strand of influence, with a tone quite different from the chant's benevolence. *Tibi domine commendamus* appears in the early ninth-century supplement to the Gregorian sacramentary (referred to as the "Hucusque") compiled by Benedict of Aniane.[16] (The prayer also appears in the ninth-century versions

---

[15] McCall's application of a "scholastic formula" seems apt here, as well: "[The liturgy] attempts... to accomplish what it represents," Richard D. McCall, *Do This: Liturgy as Performance* (Notre Dame, IN: University of Notre Dame Press, 2007), 57.

[16] The prayer is edited by Deshusses, *Le sacramentaire grégorien*, as number 1415; Paxton, *Christianizing Death*, 147, note 71; Sicard, *Liturgie*, 355–358; and Donohue, "The Rite," 229–230. Paxton's edition and translation also appears in *The Death Ritual at Cluny*, 158–159.

of the deathbed ritual and is most likely included in Paris 934 as part of this earlier transmission.) The language of sinfulness and guilt, along with images of death as a time of judgment, characterizes the work of Benedict of Aniane. In the ritual of Paris 934, the prayer *Tibi domine commendamus* is one of the few times when the dying person is named as one who has transgressed; sins are mentioned as part of a request to God to "wipe them away."[17] Benedict of Aniane's influence is kept to a minimum, however, both in the ninth-century versions of the ritual and in the later version in Paris 934. Of the seventeen prayers and one group of versicles and responses that Benedict included in the *Hucusque* for the death of an individual,[18] only this one is prescribed in Paris 934 at the bedside of the dying. Of Benedict's collection, it is fairly short and innocuous. The sinfulness of the dying person is mentioned—not expounded upon—and only in the context of a request for mercy. Benedict's images for the time of death receive only cursory appearances in the ritual from Sens.

Alia: *Misericordiam tuam domine*

Like the opening chant, *Subuenite*, the ritual's next prayer describes death as a journey, with the soul receiving protection and assistance on its way. *Misericordiam tuam domine* shows another instance in which the ritual avoids the language and images of Benedict of Aniane.[19] The prayer instead continues metaphors from older, more confident traditions by naming Michael (traditionally understood as a psychopomp, a member of the heavenly community who could accompany the soul in its journey to the afterlife) and by describing the peaceful, joyful place in which the soul will reside. Paxton notes that this prayer is new in the ninth-century version of the ritual found in the sacramentary of St-Denis; the creation of a new prayer using migratory images continued an impulse and a positive understanding of death evident in the older *Ordo XLIX* tradition.[20]

---

[17] Translation from Paxton, *Christianizing Death*, 147.
[18] These prayers and versicles with responses are edited in Deshusses, *Le sacramentaire grégorien* (1:457–463) and listed in Paxton (*Christianizing Death*, 141).
[19] The prayer is edited in Deshusses, *Le sacramentaire grégorien*, as number 4071; see Paxton, *Christianizing Death*, 175–178, for translation and discussion; also Sicard, *Liturgie*, 323–325.
[20] Paxton, *Christianizing Death*, 175–178.

Antiphon and Psalm: *Suscipiat te Christus–In exitu Israhel* (Music Transcription 2.2)

Suscipiat te Christus qui creauit te	May Christ receive you who created you	
et in sinu Habrahe angeli deducant te	and to the bosom of Abraham may angels lead you	cf. Luke 16: 22
<Gloria ... seculorum> amen[21]	<Glory ... of ages> amen	
In exitu Israhel	When Israel came out ...	Psalm 113[22]

The earlier, confident expressions of the *Ordo XLIX* tradition are again evident in the antiphon *Suscipiat te Christus*.[23] Performed together with Psalm 113, the chant continues the metaphor of death as a journey but also incorporates a more specific image: the Israelites' exodus from Egypt. *Suscipiat te Christus* describes the soul's journey when the body dies; Psalm 113, immediately following, describes the journey of the Israelites leaving Egyptian captivity. In performance, the juxtaposition of the antiphon and psalm implies that the soul's separation from the body resembles a miraculous release from slavery: just as the community of Israel was freed from bondage in Egypt, so is the soul freed from the body during death.

The proximity of these texts in performance invites comparisons between the individual soul and the Israelite community. Psalm 113 describes the Israelites as having an inseparable bond with God: "When Israel came out of Egypt ... Judah became His sanctuary, Israel His dominion." Including this psalm in the liturgy at the deathbed implies that the dying person enjoys a similarly close relationship and protection from God.

The antiphon and psalm together also suggest God's power over the natural processes of dying. The psalm describes God's domination of nature during the Israelites' exodus: "The sea saw and fled, Jordan turned back. The mountains danced like rams, hills like lambs of the flock." Sung at the deathbed,

---

[21] The scribe included indications for the doxology's melody with music notation above the word *amen*.

[22] The translation here and in the following discussion is from Alter, *The Hebrew Bible*, 3:270 (as Psalm 114).

[23] The chant's text is found in two of the earliest witnesses to the *Ordo XLIX* tradition: Berlin 1667 and Vatican, Biblioteca Apostolica Vaticana, Pal. lat. 485. (See Sicard, *Liturgie*, 75–76; Paxton, *Christianizing Death*, 39–40; and Donohue, "The Rite," 124–125.) Ottosen considers the text *Suscipiat* in a different liturgical position (as a responsory verse in the Office of the Dead, number 221, p. 418). See also Paxton's translation and discussion in *The Death Ritual at Cluny*, 114–115 and 210–211. *Suscipiat te Christus* is edited in Hesbert, *CAO*, as number 5092.

these words might have suggested to participants that the physical aspects of dying—unpredictable, uncontrollable, and potentially distressing as they may have been—were also within the realm of God's control. Compared with the command over nature depicted in Psalm 113, the salvation of a dying person might have seemed easily accomplished.

Most important, the inclusion of Psalm 113 in the liturgy for the dying suggested that the success of the exodus—the Israelites' decisive escape from their captors through the intervention of God—foreshadowed success for the dying person's soul. God's role in accompanying and protecting the Israelites, described in Psalm 113, is paralleled in *Suscipiat te Christus* by the angels, who lead the soul to the bosom of Abraham. Referencing the Israelites' escape from captivity and arrival at the promised land implies that the soul will also reach its desired destination. The jubilation heard in Psalm 113 becomes reassurance for the dying person.

Finally, the performance of Psalm 113 at the time of an individual's death suggests that release from bondage is a recurring experience for God's people. Sung at the deathbed, the psalm reframes the individual's experience into one shared by the community, both the community of the past (those who were rescued from slavery) and the contemporary community (those gathered at the bedside). All experience the same, if not simultaneously. For these reasons, Psalm 113 infuses the deathbed ritual with hope: in an all-powerful God who intervenes on behalf of humans; in the recurring evidence of the divine helper's faithfulness; and in an understanding of death as a release into freedom.

The inclusion of Psalm 113 in a deathbed ritual is not unique to this particular manuscript; Paris 934 represents a widespread practice, first evident in eighth-century sources and continuing even through the sixteenth century.[24] The psalm was also associated with the death and resurrection of Christ. In manuscripts from the cathedral of Civitale, for example, the psalm is assigned to the processions of Easter week: the chant *Venite et videte* ("Come and see <the place where the Lord was>") is followed by Psalm 113.[25]

---

[24] Sicard, *Liturgie*, 68–69 (as well as the unnumbered table in appendix) documents the early deathbed rituals that include the psalm. On the early use of the psalms in rituals for the time of death, see also Paxton, *Christianizing Death*, 40; Donohue, "The Rite," 124–125; and Richard Rutherford, "Psalm 113 (114–115) and Christian Burial," in *Studia Patristica* 12, ed. Elizabeth A. Livingstone (Berlin: Akademie Verlag, 1975), 391–395. For the psalm's inclusion in the rituals for the time of death at the abbey of Cluny, see Paxton, *The Death Ritual at Cluny*, 130–131.

[25] Cividale del Friuli, Museo Archeologico nazionale, Cod. CII, f. 42; and Cividale del Friuli, Museo Archeologico nazionale, Cod. CI, f. 39 (from the fourteenth and fifteenth centuries, respectively).

Yet Dante provides the best-known association of Psalm 113 with the time of death. In *The Divine Comedy*, the narrator (who is observing purgatory for the first time) sees a ship, steered by an angel and carrying the souls of individuals who have just died. They sail toward a mountain, where the souls will be purged and made worthy to enter heaven. As they travel, the angel and the souls sing Psalm 113. In Longfellow's translation:

> Upon the stern stood the Celestial Pilot;
> Beatitude seemed written in his face,
> And more than a hundred spirits sat within.
> "In exitu Israel de Aegypto!"
> They chanted all together in one voice,
> With whatso in that psalm is after written.
> Then made he sign of holy rood upon them,
> Whereat all cast themselves upon the shore,
> And he departed swiftly as he came.[26]

In this scene, Dante depicts the metaphor found in *Suscipiat te Christus*: death releases the soul from the body, and the soul travels to a new destination in angelic company. Although the "hundred spirits" in Dante's portrayal do not receive immediate entry into heaven—a time of purgation intervenes—death is understood as the catalyst that begins the journey and leads, eventually, to a place of rest. Following Vettori's reading, the use of Psalm 113 in Dante's work engages multiple meanings: "the allegorical one of Christ's redemption in the transition from death to resurrection; the moral or tropological one of the soul's conversion from the misery of sin to the state of grace; and the anagogical one of the soul's elevation from the slavery of worldly preoccupations to the freedom of everlasting glory."[27] Dante's work

---

The text of *Venite et videte* is edited by Hesbert in *CAO*, number 5352. In her reconstructions of Dante's liturgical contexts, Helena Phillips-Robins documents additional uses of the psalm during Easter week. See *Liturgical Song and Practice in Dante's Commedia* (Notre Dame, IN: University of Notre Dame Press, 2021), particularly 30–44.

[26] Dante Alighieri, "Digital Dante: The Divine Comedy; Purgatorio" (Columbia University and Columbia University Libraries, Teodolinda Barolini et al., eds.), Canto II:43–51, accessed September 15, 2020, at https://digitaldante.columbia.edu/dante/divine-comedy/.

[27] Along with these "poignant theological superimpositions," Vettori discusses possible personal associations for Dante. Alessandro Vettori, "Religion," in *The Oxford Handbook of Dante*, ed. Manuele Gragnolati, Elena Lombardi, and Francesca Southerden (Oxford: Oxford University Press, 2021), 302–317. Le Goff observes that "Dante integrates into his poem the liturgy that scholastics usually kept out of their writings" (Le Goff, *The Birth of Purgatory*, 349). Mulchahey

Music Transcription 2.2 *Suscipiat te Christus* (Paris 934, f. 114v)

reveals the multiple resonances that lent the psalm significance when it was sung in the deathbed rituals. The liturgy in Paris 934 is one representative of an apparently widespread practice—reflected in Dante—that incorporated Psalm 113 into deathbed rites, specifically, and, more broadly, described death using the metaphor of a journey.

In Paris 934, musical settings combine the antiphon *Suscipiat te Christus* and Psalm 113 into a single, cohesive performance, audibly underscoring the metaphor of an individual's death as an escape to freedom, similar to the

---

provides a summary of scholarship on Dante's possible educational and religious influences in Florence: M. Michèle Mulchahey, "Education in Dante's Florence Revisited: Remigio De' Girolami and the Schools of Santa Maria Novella," in *Medieval Education*, ed. Ronald B. Begley and Joseph W. Koterski (New York: Fordham University Press, 2005), 143–181. See also Nardini's considerations of other elements pointing to the "shared religious culture" evident in Dante's work and contemporaneous chant repertories. Luisa Nardini, "Allusioni liturgico-musicali in Dante attraverso un'analisi del manoscritto 13 dell'Harry Ransom Center," in *Nel 750° anniversario della nascita di Dante Alighieri: Letteratura e musica del Duecento e del Trecento. Atti del Convegno Internazionale Certaldo Alto, 17–18 Dicembre 2015*, ed. Paola Benigni, Stefano Campagnolo, Rino Caputo, Stefania Cori, and Agostino Ziino (Gesualdo: Fondazione Carlo Gesualdo, 2016), 131–139. Phillips-Robins, *Liturgical Song*, offers the most comprehensive considerations of Dante's incorporation of liturgical materials. She argues that Dante's inclusion of Psalm 113 "provides an opening for the reader herself to join the penitential community" (19).

Israelites' exodus. When sung according to the manuscript's notation, the text describing the journey of the soul (*Suscipiat te Christus*) leads seamlessly to the text describing the exodus of the Israelites (Psalm 113). The melodies of the antiphon and the psalm show many similarities. In fact, the simple melody of *Suscipiat te Christus* resembles the melodies with which psalms were typically sung (often referred to as *psalm tones*): almost every syllable is conveyed with a single pitch, the melodic motion is constrained to steps (with only occasional small leaps), and the total ambitus is limited.

Additionally, the antiphon's melody—like a psalm tone—prioritizes the clear declamation of the text. Word boundaries are defined in performance by pitch content, as the melody forms arch-shaped or inverted arch-shaped gestures whose beginnings and endings coincide with the beginnings and endings of words. (To name just a few examples, the word *suscipiat* is conveyed by an inverted arch-shape beginning and ending on "d" and descending to "b"; *Habrahe* is conveyed by an arch-shaped gesture that begins on "a," rises to "c," and falls to "b"; similar conveyances are seen with *creauit, angeli,* and *deducant*.)

Also assisting with the clear declamation of the text is the melodic reflection of syntactic units. The antiphon's melody articulates the beginnings of syntactic units with repetition: the first words of the chant, *Suscipiat te*, are conveyed with a reciting tone of "d" that integrates a downward leap of a third to "b"; the beginning of the second major syntactic unit (*et in sinu Habrahe*) repeats this melodic contour, with slightly different pitch content (the reciting tone of "c" integrates a downward leap of a third to "a"). The endings of the text's two major syntactic units (*creauit te* and *deducant te*) are articulated in performance with lower pitch content: they are both conveyed with cadential descents to "g," the lowest pitch of the chant. Thus, the beginnings of syntactic units are marked with relatively high pitch content and repeated melodic contours; the endings are marked with identical pitch content that is relatively low. With these musical means, the text's syntactic units are distinctly articulated in performance, facilitating a clear declamation, similar to that heard in the recitation of psalms. The melody creates a psalm-like performance of the antiphon's text. At the musical level, the depiction of the soul's journey (in the antiphon) and the depiction of the Israelites' journey (in the psalm) together form a single entity.

Unifying the musical settings of the antiphon and psalm seems to have been a high priority. Psalm 113—sung weekly as part of the Office liturgy—typically was conveyed with a different, distinctive melody called the *tonus peregrinus* ("pilgrim melody"). In fact, Hiley suggests that the "pilgrim melody" might have received its name through its association with Psalm 113, with its references to the Israelites' journey.[28] (An additional possibility for the melody's designation as *peregrinus* concerns its reciting tone: rather than conforming with a single mode, the *tonus peregrinus* "wanders" from a reciting pitch of "a" to a reciting pitch of "g.") Associated with the specific psalm text, as well as situations of travel and transition, the *tonus peregrinus* would seem to be appropriate for the liturgy at the deathbed, yet the scribal work in Paris 934 clearly indicates a different melody: one that fits comfortably in Mode 7 and strongly resembles the antiphon's musical setting. Musically integrating the antiphon and psalm in performance seems to have taken precedence over using the psalm's customary melody, although this customary melody contained appropriate connotations of journey, movement, and change.

Prayer: *Omnipotens sempiternę deus... letifica clementissime deus*

The prayer *Omnipotens sempiternę deus*, immediately following the chant and psalm, also presents death as the journey of a human soul toward God. Paxton considers it likely that the text's opening (a reworking of the positive images seen in earlier material) was a composition of the later ninth century, since it is first extant in the sacramentary of St-Denis.[29] Also at this point in the ritual, then, one encounters material that minimizes Benedict of Aniane's understanding of death as judgment and instead emphasizes an understanding of death as a journey of the soul, undertaken with the help of a protective and welcoming heavenly community.

The prayer's ending, *Letifica clementissime deus*, harmonizes with the forgiving tone of the previous material. While admitting human error, the text offers reasons for forgiveness and understanding, including the dying person's faith and baptism. ("Gladden the soul of your servant, most merciful God... although he sinned, he never denied you, but having been marked by the sign of faith... faithfully adored you."[30])

---

[28] David Hiley, *Western Plainchant: A Handbook* (Oxford: Clarendon Press, 1993), 64.

[29] Paxton, *Christianizing Death*, 176 and 178, note 39. The prayer is edited in its entirety by Deshusses, *Le sacramentaire grégorien* (as number 4077). Concerning the prayer's beginning, see also Sicard, *Liturgie*, 272–274 (where it appears as *Omnipotens aeterne Deus*).

[30] *Letifica clementissime deus animam serui tui... licet enim peccauerit tamen te non negauit sed signo fidei insignitus te... fideliter adorauit* (Paris 934, f. 115r–v).

> tam te non negauit s; signo fidei insigni-
> a ei
> tus te qui omnia et eum inter omnia

Figure 2.1 Scribal annotations providing alternative endings (Paris, Bibliothèque nationale de France, lat. 934, f. 115v). Image © BnF. Reproduced by permission of the Bibliothèque nationale de France.

The scribal work with this portion of the prayer shows an interest in making the text appropriate for women as well as men, and also for multiple recipients. As one example (seen in Figure 2.1), where the text reads *signo fidei insignitus*, annotations written in red ink directly above the final syllable of *insignitus* provide the alternative endings *a*, *e* (*ae*), and *i*, which make the participle suitable for an individual female, multiple females, or multiple males, respectively. The scribe seems to have worked with the understanding that the ritual—and particularly this text—would be used for men and women, and even for commemorations of multiple, deceased individuals.

Antiphon and Psalms: *Chorus angelorum–Dilexi quoniam–Ad dominum cum tribularer* (Music Transcription 2.3)

Chorus angelorum te suscipiat et in sinu[31] Habrahe ibi te collocet	May the choir of angels take you up and there, in the bosom of Abraham, establish you	cf. Luke 16:22
et cum Lazaro quondam paupere eternam habeas[32] requiem	and with Lazarus, once poor, may you have eternal rest	
PSALMUS Dilexi quoniam	PSALM I love the LORD, for ...	Psalm 114[33]
VSQUE Ad dominum cum tribularer	UNTIL To the LORD when I was in straits ...	Psalm 119

---

[31] Erasures are visible with the music notation above the word *sinu*. The pitches were changed from "d" to "c."
[32] An erasure of the pitch "f" is visible in the music notation above the final syllable of *habeas*.
[33] Translations from Alter, *The Hebrew Bible*, 3:273 and 291 (as Psalms 116 and 120).

Music Transcription 2.3 *Chorus angelorum* (Paris 934, f. 115v)

Following this prayer, the antiphon *Chorus angelorum* uses both text and melody to depict the soul's movement in death: ascension.[34] The antiphon's text addresses the soul of the dying person directly, with a hope that it be received and "taken up" by a choir of angels (*chorus angelorum te suscipiat*).[35]

---

[34] The chant is discussed in Sicard, *Liturgie*, 69–71, and Paxton, *Christianizing Death*, 39–40. Donohue considers the replacement of *Chorus angelorum* with *Requiem aeternam* in later sources ("The Rite," 176); Ottosen discusses the text's use in a different liturgical position (as a responsory verse in the Office of the Dead), *Responsories*, 228. Hesbert, *CAO*, edits the chant's text as number 1783.

[35] The word *suscipiat* refers to the action of lifting up an object or person; it can also carry connotations of acknowledging a person as a family member or citizen. Lewis and Short, *A Latin Dictionary*, accessed September 16, 2020, at Tufts University, "Perseus," http://www.perseus.tufts.edu/hopper/morph?l=suscipiat&la=la#lexicon.

The melody mirrors the textual image by conveying these words with ascending pitch content. With the chant's first two words, *chorus angelorum*, the melody inhabits a relatively low ambitus, from "f" to "a" (only once ascending to "c"). A contrast occurs with the following words, *te suscipiat*. The melody's ambitus rises to the pitches "b," "c," and "d" (descending only once to "a"). As the text describes the soul being taken up by angels, the melody itself ascends into a new realm.

Rather than a smooth, predictable rise, this melodic ascension is agile and vigorous, with leaps of thirds and fourths. In total, six melodic leaps occur with the first line of text (an upward leap of a fourth with the first syllable of *chorus*; a descending leap of a third on the first syllable of *angelorum*; an upward leap of a third to *te*; and a descending leap of a fourth followed by an upward leap of a third with the first two syllables of *suscipiat*). In contrast, the following, longer line of text is conveyed with only one leap (an ascending third with the word *ibi*). The animated melodic motion conveying the first line of text portrays the ascent of the soul and angels as one of energetic vitality.

As the text then describes the place to which the soul is brought, the melody offers its own depiction. The words *in sinu Habrahe* ("the bosom of Abraham") are conveyed with the most elevated and ornate music of the setting. The melody continues to inhabit the higher range gained with the chant's first line and ascends even further to the highest pitch of the chant, "e." The final syllable of *Habrahe* is conveyed with six pitches—twice as many as any other syllable of the chant. The melody lingers with these words, making them the primary focal point in the chant's performance and creating a distinctive, aural rendering of the textual image—the place to which the soul ascends.

While the chant's opening is thus marked by ascent and elevation, both in text and melody, the remainder of the chant is oriented toward a depiction of resting. After naming the bosom of Abraham, the text speaks of establishing and settling the soul in that place (*ibi te collocet*). The music reflects this change of image. With these words, the melody itself settles, descending from the higher pitch content to occupy a lower range. Particularly the word *collocet* is conveyed with finality and security. The melody immediately prior to the word descends in a scalar, stepwise fashion, creating a sense of predictability and inevitability. After falling to the pitch "g," the melody repeats it three times while conveying the word *collocet*. This is the first time in the chant that a single pitch is repeated three times in succession. The extraordinary, static gesture echoes the textual image of planting and establishing. The melody itself is established and unmoving, offering an audible reflection of the hope for the soul expressed in the text.

The musical setting then defines a contrasting aural space to convey an image of earthly poverty. As the text references Lazarus' life as a poor man, the melody descends further, to pitches not yet heard in the setting, reaching the chant's lowest pitch of "d" with the final syllable of Lazarus' name. No other line of this chant's text is conveyed with such a low range (with its highest pitch as an "a" and the lowest pitch as "d"). The reference to Lazarus' earlier poverty occupies a distinctively different melodic region than the reference to his after-worldly comfort in the bosom of Abraham (heard in the second line of the chant with the words *in sinu Habrahe*). The melody—as the text—creates a great contrast between the images of Lazarus' earthly destitution and his other-worldly blessedness.

The chant reaches its textual and musical culmination with the final word: rest (*requiem*). The melody moves in the lower range while conveying *eternam habeas requiem*, and finally settles on the pitch "e." The threefold repetition of this pitch provides a musical equivalent to the word "rest": the lack of motion in the melody echoes the understanding that all traveling has ceased; the melody itself rests on one pitch. (This melodic descent and repetition is even more notable, given that it establishes the melody within a different modal framework. While the antiphon began with musical gestures and an ambitus associated with Mode 8, the final repetition of the pitch "e" by the end of the chant is more typically associated with Mode 3.) This musical setting of *requiem* also recalls that of the word *collocet* ("establish"). The performance of *collocet* served as an end point for the chant's opening by creating a release from higher pitches and a cadential gesture with striking finality; the melodic descent with *eternam habeas* and the static final gesture with the word *requiem* create a similar effect. Just as the melody of the chant's opening reflected the image of ascension, the melody of the chant's ending echoes the depiction of rest. The melody soars and then settles as it traces the images described in the text.

With Psalms 114–119 (those designated for performance with *Chorus angelorum*), expressions of gratitude supplement the depictions of the soul's rest.[36] Psalm 114 describes a situation similar to the one the dying person inhabits: "The cords of death encircled me—and the straits of Sheol found

---

[36] Sicard discusses the use of these psalms in liturgies for the dying, *Liturgie*, 74–75. See also Paxton, *Christianizing Death*, 176–178, and Paxton, *The Death Ritual at Cluny*, 240–241, for the psalms' incorporation into Cluniac liturgies. All translations in the following section are from Alter, *The Hebrew Bible*, 3:273ff. (as Psalm 116).

me." Yet for the psalmist, this situation has passed: distress is narrated in the past tense; gratitude is the current reality. "[The LORD] has heard my voice, my supplications." The narrative voice of the psalm tells of the benevolent character of God: "Gracious the LORD and just, and our God shows mercy. The Lord protects the simple." The subsequent psalms continue this portrayal of a loving, steadfast God, ready and able to help a suffering human. These narrations of answered prayers add to the reassuring depictions in the antiphon *Chorus angelorum*. Within the framework of the psalms, the peaceful rest described in *Chorus angelorum* becomes one more reason to thank God.

The musical beginnings of the antiphon and Psalm 114 contribute to the understanding of continuity between the texts. The melodies of both the antiphon and the psalm convey their first words with a distinctive leap of a fourth, from "g" to "c" (associated with Mode 8 melodies), such that the performance of the psalm's opening recalls the beginning of *Chorus angelorum*. The antiphon's serene images of the soul's destination are joined in performance with the psalms' accounts of answered prayers. Together, they offer expressions of hope and reassurance as they portray death as a journey to a place of rest.

Prayer: *Diri uulneris nouitate*

The prayer following the antiphon and psalms gives another indication that the creators of the ritual bypassed the work of Benedict of Aniane in favor of older materials. Both Paxton and Sicard note the Gallican origins of the prayer.[37] Additionally, the scribal work with this prayer in Paris 934 indicates an expectation that it would be used with both men and women. The primary scribal hand wrote the words *animam cari nostri*—referring to the dying person—with masculine endings. Yet annotations made in red ink immediately above the words provide the feminine endings *e* (*car<a>e nostr<a>e*), indicating the appropriate modifications of the text for a female (Figure 2.2, final line). As with the prayer *Letifica clementissime deus*, scribal work suggests that the ritual was considered suitable for both men and women.

---

[37] Paxton, *Christianizing Death*, 64, 176–178; Sicard, *Liturgie*, 305–308. Deshusses, *Le sacramentaire grégorien*, edits the prayer as number 4059. See also Mohlberg, *Liber sacramentorum*, 234 (number 1608).

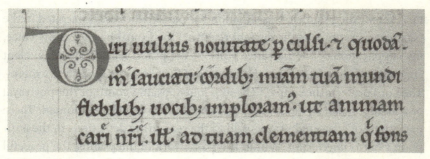

Figure 2.2 *Diri uulneris nouitate* with scribal annotations (Paris, Bibliothèque nationale de France, lat. 934, f. 115v). Image © BnF. Reproduced by permission of the Bibliothèque nationale de France.

Pater noster	Our father...	Matthew 6
Non intres in iudicium	Do not come into judgment...[38]	Psalm 142:2
A porta inferi	From the gate of hell...[39]	
Requiem eternam	Rest eternal...	cf. IV Esdras 2:34–35
Domine exaudi	Lord, hear...	Psalm 101:2
Dominus uobiscum	The Lord be with you...	
ORATIO	PRAYER	
Partem beatę resurrectionis	A part of the beautiful resurrection...	

Benedict of Aniane's influence is present in the series of versicles and responses following the *Pater noster*, which asks God for restraint from judgment and a rescue from "the gate of hell."[40] Yet this portion of the ritual (conducted at the bedside) closes with the prayer *Partem beatę resurrectionis*—a text that separates itself from the work of Benedict of Aniane.[41] Rather than emphasizing the unworthiness of the dying person, this prayer makes a confident claim: "A part of the blessed resurrection he [she] ought to have."[42] With the prayer, this portion of the ritual concludes as

---

[38] Translation from Alter, *The Hebrew Bible*, 3:324 (as Psalm 143).
[39] Translation from Paxton, *The Death Ritual at Cluny*, 107.
[40] The ritual from Cluny contains a similar series of versicles and responses. See Paxton, *The Death Ritual at Cluny*, 106–107 and 112–113 for editions and translations and 203–204 for a discussion; also Paxton, *Christianizing Death*, 146, esp. note 66. His analysis of *Requiem aeternam* supersedes Sicard's (*Liturgie*, 72–74 and 76–78).
[41] Following Paxton, the prayer is new to the ninth-century sacramentary of St-Denis (Paris 2290): *Christianizing Death*, 176–179; the prayer is edited in Deshusses, *Le sacramentaire grégorien*, as number 4072.
[42] *Partem beatę resurrectionis obtineat*... (f. 116).

it began—with expressions of hope, with images of a peaceful, joyful afterlife, and with confidence that the soul will be accepted by God.

Conclusion: A Local Practice

The ninth-century deathbed ritual that forms the basis of the version in Paris 934 partook of existing materials and images from different traditions to form an overwhelmingly comforting whole. The twelfth-century version in Paris 934 continued this trend and even intensified it by eliminating the penitential psalms that were included in the ritual's earlier versions. In studies of conceptions of the afterlife, scholars have traced broad changes that occurred during the medieval time period, including the development of the idea of purgatory.[43] In general, images of judgment at the time of an individual's death became more prevalent both during and after the Carolingian era; yet the deathbed ritual in Paris 934 shows how one specific community

---

[43] Major studies detailing the development of the concept of purgatory include Isabel Moreira, *Heaven's Purge: Purgatory in Late Antiquity* (Oxford: Oxford University Press, 2010), and Le Goff, *The Birth of Purgatory*. See also Tingle, "Changing Western European Visions of Christian Afterlives, 1350–1700: Heaven, Hell, and Purgatory," in *A Companion to Death, Burial, and Remembrance in Late Medieval and Early Modern Europe, c. 1300–1700*, ed. Philip Booth and Elizabeth C. Tingle (Leiden: Brill, 2021), 33–71; and Stephen Bates, "Preparations for a Christian Death: The Later Middle Ages," in *A Companion to Death, Burial, and Remembrance in Late Medieval and Early Modern Europe, c. 1300–1700*, ed. Philip Booth and Elizabeth C. Tingle (Leiden: Brill, 2021), 72–105. Ottosen analyzes the texts of liturgical items—primarily responsories and readings of the Office of the Dead—to trace changes in the conceptions of the afterlife in different areas of Europe. See Ottosen, *Responsories*, particularly 44–49 and 373–385, as well as his discussion on using liturgical documents as sources for such considerations: Knud Ottosen, "Liturgy as a Theological Place: Possibilities and Limitations in Interpreting Liturgical Texts as Seen for Instance in the Office of the Dead," in *Liturgy and the Arts in the Middle Ages*, ed. Eva Louise Lillie and Nils Holger Petersen (Copenhagen: Museum Tusculanum Press University of Copenhagen, 1996), 168–180. Booth and Tingle offer a review of scholarly findings on the changing (and persisting) conceptions of the afterlife (primarily from the thirteenth century and later) in *A Companion to Death, Burial, and Remembrance*, particularly 4–30. See also Bynum and Freedman, *Last Things*. The collected essays in Bynum and Freedman's volume explore the interrelated medieval conceptions of the possible fates awaiting an individual's soul at the moment of death, the collective resurrection of bodies, and apocalyptic end times. Peter Brown's essay, in particular, explores the changing conceptions of the afterlife and the multiplicity of "imaginative structures" within this conceptual nexus: Brown, "The Decline." Brown's earlier work traces the shifting understandings of the afterlife from 200 to 700: Peter Brown, *The Ransom of the Soul: Afterlife and Wealth in Early Western Christianity* (Cambridge, MA: Harvard University Press, 2015). Bonnie Effros discusses the changing portrayals of the afterlife in prayers for the deceased and funerary liturgies in the sixth through eighth centuries: *Caring for Body and Soul*, particularly 169–171. Bynum considers the relationships among body, soul, and identity in medieval understandings (Bynum, *The Resurrection of the Body*). See also Bruce Gordon and Peter Marshall, eds., *The Place of the Dead: Death and Remembrance in Late Medieval and Early Modern Europe* (Cambridge: Cambridge University Press, 2000). D. Vance Smith considers the metaphors and images used by medieval English writers to describe death and dying: *Arts of Dying: Literature and Finitude in Medieval England* (Chicago: University of Chicago Press, 2020).

interacted with—and resisted—these larger trends. With its preponderance of older chants and metaphors, its elimination of the penitential psalms, and its minimal use of the material compiled by Benedict of Aniane, the ritual in Paris 934 cultivated and propagated reassuring images of the soul's afterlife. While other rituals (e.g., the ones investigated in Chapters 3 and 4) show these same tendencies, the ritual of Paris 934 is notable for having emended the older version on which it is based to exclude the penitential psalms. The collection of material found in the manuscript's deathbed ritual most often portrays death as a soul's journey to God, accompanied and protected (in the chant *Subuenite*, militarily protected) by members of the heavenly community.

Additionally, the manuscript's music notation shows the significant role that melody played in conveying the ritual's benevolent conceptions of the dying process. The chants' melodies offer aural counterparts to textual images (such as the soul's ascension away from the body) and create distinct aural spaces when articulating textual depictions of the afterlife (such as Lazarus' repose in the bosom of Abraham). The ritual's performance, following the manuscript's music notation, underscores the idea that the soul's release from the body in death is a release from slavery to freedom, such as the Israelites experienced as they left Egypt. Through curated texts and music, then, the ritual of Paris 934 lead with reassurance, for the comfort and benefit of the men—and women—who experienced it.

3
With the Laity

Orsières, Switzerland

Manuscript Source: Bourg-Saint-Pierre, Hospice du
Grand-Saint-Bernard, ms. 3 (ancien 10091)
(GSB 3)

Wealth, education, religious expertise: all are evidenced in the manuscripts from Rome and Sens. And what if these were lacking? Were liturgies for the time of death also conducted for lay persons unassociated with large ecclesiastical institutions? If so, were these liturgies similar to those of cathedrals and monasteries? This chapter leaves behind the powerful, urban centers of Rome and Sens and moves to Orsières, a village isolated in the mountainous terrain of southwestern Switzerland (Canton Valais).

In a stroke of luck for historians, a manuscript associated with this small community survives from the fourteenth century (Bourg-Saint-Pierre, Hospice du Grand-Saint-Bernard 3, hereafter GSB 3).[1] Not only does this manuscript contain a ritual for the time of death, but the ritual also shows signs of having been used. Editorial corrections and annotations, as well as discoloration on the lower, right-hand margins of the folios, indicate that the manuscript was frequently opened to the rites for the sick and dying. For

---

[1] Manuscript images are provided by the Congrégation du Grand-Saint-Bernard, "Patrimoine culturel MS 3 (ancien 10091)," at https://gsbernard.ch/6/64/643-1/man03/index.html (accessed September 22, 2020). Manuscript descriptions and datings are from Josef Leisibach, "Grosser St. Bernhard," in *Scriptoria Medii Aevi Helvetica: Schreibstätten der Diözese Sitten; Denkmäler schweizerischer Schreibkunst des Mittelalters* 13, ed. Albert Bruckner (Genf: Roto-Sadag, 1973), 135–157; and Josef Leisibach and François Huot, *Die liturgischen Handschriften des Kantons Wallis (ohne Kapitelsarchiv Sitten)* (Freiburg, Switzerland: Universitätsbibliothek, 1984), 82–87. The manuscript gives few explicit indications of the place it was used. Leisibach concludes from the saints in the litanies that the document was created in western Switzerland ("Grosser St. Bernhard," 141); the addition of the name Pantaleon in litanies on folios 5 and 20 further suggests Orsières, where Pantaleon was a patron saint of the parish church (*Die liturgischen Handschriften*, 82 and 87). According to an annotation on the verso side of the manuscript's flyleaf, Orsières housed GSB 3 before it was transferred to the care of the provost of the Grand Saint Bernard community in the nineteenth century. (The annotation is edited by Leisibach, *Die liturgischen Handschriften*, 87.)

these reasons, GSB 3 offers an extraordinary opportunity to attempt a better understanding of the liturgical practices conducted by a lay community at the time of an individual's death. As historians consider the extent to which the practices of the general, lay population resembled the practices of the religious elite, the manuscript from Orsières offers a specific point of investigation.[2]

This particular lay community was small. In the first half of the fourteenth century (when the deathbed ritual in GSB 3 was recorded), census records show the population of Orsières growing from 304 to 402 taxable inhabitants.[3] Yet the village was accustomed to visiting travelers: Orsières is located along a pilgrimage and trade route, the Via Francigena, that extended from Canterbury to Rome. The bridge across the Danse River funneled

---

[2] John Van Engen provides a summary of the scholarly line of inquiry in "The Christian Middle Ages as an Historiographical Problem," *The American Historical Review* 91, no. 3 (1986): 519–552. Other historians have similarly critiqued scholarship that assumes large differences between "elite" and "popular" religious practices. To name a few: Carl Watkins, "'Folklore' and 'Popular Religion' in Britain during the Middle Ages," *Folklore* 115, no. 2 (Aug. 2004): 140–150; Peter Brown, *The Cult of the Saints: Its Rise and Function in Latin Christianity* (Chicago: University of Chicago Press, 1981). A more recent and ongoing line of scholarly inquiry considers the possibility of meaningful religious participation among the general population and in rural areas. Both Van Rhijn and Keefe investigate the religious practices and understandings of the laity in the Carolingian era. Van Rhijn describes the importance placed on the proper religious conduct and the mechanisms for communicating religious ideals to the laity. Her scholarship examines the manuscript evidence of the "local level," including handbooks for priests in rural areas: Carine Van Rhijn, "Charlemagne and the government of the Frankish Countryside," in *Law and Empire: Ideas, Practices, Actors,* edited by Jeroen Duindam, Jozef Frans, Jill Harries, Caroline Humfress, and Nimrod Hurvitz (Leiden: Brill 2013), 157–176. See also Van Rhijn, "The local church, priests' handbooks and pastoral care in the Carolingian period," in *Chiese locali e chiese regionali nell'alto Medioevo; Spoleto, 4-9 Aprile 2013* (Spoleto: Fondazione centro Italiano di studi sull'alto medioevo, 2014), 2: 689–710; Susan A. Keefe, *Water and the Word: Baptism and the Education of the Clergy in the Carolingian Empire* (Notre Dame, Indiana: University of Notre Dame, 2002); and Keefe, *A catalogue of works pertaining to the explanation of the creed in Carolingian manuscripts* (Turnhout: Brepols, 2012). Hen challenges "the image of the ignorant barbarian priest" by examining two liturgical and canonical manuscripts created during the Carolingian period: Yitzhak Hen, "Knowledge of canon law among rural priests: The evidence of two Carolingian manuscripts from around 800," *Journal of Theological Studies* 50, no. 1 (1999): 117–134 (here, 120). Bullough examines the documentary evidence of the laity's "experiences" of liturgy during the Carolingian era: Donald Bullough, "The Carolingian Liturgical Experience," in *Continuity and Change in Christian Worship: Papers read at the 1997 Summer Meeting and the 1998 Winter Meeting of the Ecclesiastical History Society,* edited by R.N. Swanson (Woodbridge, Suffolk, UK: Published for the Ecclesiastical History Society by the Boydell Press, 1999), 29–64. See also John Blair and Richard Sharpe, eds., *Pastoral Care before the Parish* (Leicester: Leicester University Press, 1992). Kurt considers the relationship between the religious practices of "clerical and monastic elites" and those of the laity in the Iberian Visigothic realm: Andrew Kurt, "Lay piety in Visigothic Iberia: Liturgical and Paraliturgical Forms," *Journal of Medieval Iberian Studies* 8, no. 1 (2016): 1–37.

[3] The town's population of taxable inhabitants was 304 in 1313; 402 in 1339; and 259 in 1356, following Albano Hugon, "Orsières," in *Historische Lexikon der Schweiz*, 3 Nov 2009, accessed 14 October 2020 at https://hls-dhs-dss.ch/de/. A history of the community of Grand Saint Bernard is given by Lucien Quaglia, "Les origines de l'hospice du Grand-Saint-Bernard," *Publication du Centre européen d'études bourguignonnes (XIVe-XVIe s)* 15 (1973): 31–36. An overview of life outside of urban communities in the fourteenth century in Western Europe is provided by Paul Freedman, "Rural Society," in *The New Cambridge Medieval History 6. c.1300-c.1415,* edited by Michael Jones (Cambridge: Cambridge University Press, 2000), 82–101.

travelers through the town.[4] The manuscript associated with Orsières, GSB 3, was intended for the use of a priest, in ceremonies that occurred away from the altar (such as blessings of salt and water, rites of baptism, and rites for the sick and dying). The priests administering these rites likely came from the Augustinian community located approximately fifteen miles to the south, at the pass of Grand Saint Bernard (formerly Mont-Joux). The church of Orsières, and presumably also the pastoral care of the town's inhabitants, had been entrusted to this community in the twelfth century.[5] The priests of Saint Bernard were well known for ministering to the area's laity—both travelers and inhabitants—and laity were almost certainly the recipients of the deathbed ritual in GSB 3: its first rubric reads, not COMMENDATIO ANIMAE (COMMENDATION OF THE SOUL), as in the manuscripts from Rome and Sens, but instead, COMMENDATIO ANIMAE COMMUNIS (THE PUBLIC'S COMMENDATION OF THE SOUL).

Few manuscripts containing such rituals are known to survive from lay communities, although historic evidence leads us to search for them. Documentation from the fourth century on reveals clear intentions on the part of religious and political authorities: each person was to be given the opportunity to receive the church's ritual benefits at the time of death. In these earlier centuries, receiving the Eucharist (*viaticum*) was considered to be the essential Christian ritual for the end of life. The Council of Nicea (in 325) declared that *viaticum* should be offered to all, including those who were not in good standing with the church; this decision was confirmed by Innocent I (in 416), Celestine I (in 428), and by the Council of Agde (in 506).[6] Authorities of the Carolingian era reaffirmed this ideal. Paxton has documented the capitularies and statements of church councils concerning deathbed practices; they include: a council statement from 740 urging that no person die without *viaticum* and confession; a council statement from 755 allowing priests to perform baptism if death was imminent; and an additional statement from the following decade allowing a *presbiter degradatus* to perform a baptismal ceremony if death threatened an unbaptized person.[7]

---

[4] One of these travelers, Abbot Maiolus (Mayeul) of Cluny, was purportedly captured near Orsières while traveling in 972 (Hugon, "Orsières").

[5] Hugon, "Orsières." The manuscript shows signs of monastic influence, particularly in the saints listed in the litanies (Leisibach, *Die liturgischen Handschriften*, 87).

[6] The declaration of the Council of Nicea was made amid varying views on the matter. Documentation is summarized by Paxton in *Christianizing Death*, 32–37; Donohue's discussion appears in "The Rite," 158–159; Effros's in *Caring for Body and Soul*, 176–177.

[7] Paxton, *Christianizing Death*, 94–96. The councils cited are: Bavaria, 740 (Albert Werminghoff, ed., *Concilia Aevi Karolini*, Monumenta Germaniae Historica, Concilia 2, 1 [Hannoverae: Impensis

Also from the eighth century, we have evidence that more elaborate rituals for the end of life—rituals that extended beyond the reception of the Eucharist—were being developed. The late eighth-century sacramentary from Autun includes a ritual prescribing not only *viaticum* and confession, but also prayers, psalms, and chants.[8] However, it is not until the ninth century that we have indications of these more extensive deathbed rituals being used outside of monastic or ecclesiastical communities.[9] A manuscript from the second half of the ninth century, Vatican 550, is considered to be a training manual for priests from the Abbey of Lorsch, possibly reflecting use outside the abbey.[10] In the ritual for death and burial, a rubric directs "all brothers or people ... to gather together" (OMNES FRATRES UEL POPULUS AD DOMUM FUNERIS IN SIMUL CONUENIANT).[11] Similarly, a contemporary manuscript created for the Abbey of St-Denis contains a reference to both monks and laity gathering at the deathbed,[12] and the Ivrean Sacramentary—from around 1000—contains miniatures depicting the death of a lay person, attended by his family and a priest.[13]

In sum, documents from the fourth through the sixth as well as the eighth through the tenth centuries show an ideal of giving each person the opportunity to die in good standing with the church, with all the rituals that entailed. These documents reveal an understanding that the essentials of a good,

---

Bibliopolii Hahniani, 1906], cap. 2, p. 52); Verberie, 755 (A. Boretius, ed., *Capitularia Regum Francorum*, vol. 1. Monumenta Germaniae Historica, Legum Sectio II [Hannoverae: Impensis Bibliopolii Hahn, 1883], capit. 1, p. 34); and Verberie, beginning 758 (Boretius, *Capitularia Regum Francorum*, vol. 1, capit. 1, p. 41). For a related discussion (focusing primarily on the twelfth to thirteenth centuries in northern France and present-day Belgium), see Joseph Avril, "La pastorale des malades et des mourants aux XIIe et XIIIe siècles," in *Death in the Middle Ages*, ed. Herman Braet and Werner Verbeke (Leuven: Leuven University Press, 1983), 88–106.

[8] Berlin 1667. The manuscript's ritual for the time of death is included in Sicard's edition (*Liturgie*) as *Ph* and is analyzed in Paxton, *Christianizing Death*, 119–122.

[9] Paxton, *Christianizing Death*, 127. See also Sicard, "La mort," 59–64.

[10] Vatican, Biblioteca Apostolica Vaticana, Pal. lat. 550; discussed in Paxton, *Christianizing Death*, 198–199, and Hieronymus Frank, "Der älteste erhaltene Ordo defunctorum," 360–415. Avril examines the renewed interest in and production of these books in northern France and present-day Belgium during the twelfth through fourteenth centuries: "La pastorale des malades et des mourants."

[11] f. 19.

[12] Paris 2290, discussed in Chapter 2 and edited by Sicard in *Liturgie* as *Den*. Paxton considers its reference to the laity in *Christianizing Death*, 197. See also Sicard, "La mort."

[13] Ivrea, Biblioteca Capitolare d'Ivrea MS 31 (LXXXVI), discussed in Patrick J. Geary, *Phantoms of Remembrance: Memory and Oblivion at the End of the First Millennium* (Princeton, NJ: Princeton University Press, 1994), 51–59; Michael Driscoll, "Per Sora Nostra Morte Corporale: The Role of Medieval Women in Death and Burial Practices," *Liturgical Ministry* 10 (Winter 2001): 14–22; and Michael Driscoll, "Reconstructing Liturgical History before the libri ordinarii: The Role of Medieval Women in Death and Burial Practices," in *Unitas in pluralitate: Libri ordinarii als Quelle für die Liturgiegeschichte*, ed. Charles Caspers and Louis van Tongeren (Münster: Aschendorff Verlag, 2015), 299–326.

Christian death included *viaticum*, prefaced by rites for baptism and reconciliation, if necessary. Manuscripts from ecclesiastical and monastic centers, from the eighth century and later, contain elaborations in the portion of the ritual performed immediately prior to death, and manuscripts from the ninth century and later suggest that these extended rituals could include some sort of lay participation—at least, for laity in proximity to those religious institutions.

The manuscript from Orsières moves the discussion beyond this indirect evidence—the declarations of political and religious authorities and the rubrics in manuscripts from religious institutions—to a specific ritual intended for the laity. The following close examination of the deathbed ritual in GSB 3 indicates that the practices of Orsières shared profound similarities with those of religious institutions. In addition to individual prayers and chants, the essential religious understandings, the essential religious tasks for the gathered community, and the essential religious responses to death appear to have been held in common. Yet although the ritual for Orsières appears to be the same in kind as those of religious institutions, it mirrors none exactly. As will be discussed below, some differences might be accommodations for a lay community, particularly one that was rural and isolated. Other variations, however, appear to have no connection with the community's religious status; instead, they suggest that even into the fourteenth century, rituals for the dying remained unstandardized, and the community of Orsières maintained a version that circulated locally.

The Opening Rubric: Indications for the Ritual's Performance

Incipit commendacio anime communis	The public's commendation of the soul begins
Prius faciat aquam beneditam[14]	First he ought to prepare the blessed water
et aspergat super astamtes[15]	and sprinkle on those gathered
et per domum	and throughout the home
deinde super corpus	then over the body
et dicat respunsum[16]	and recite the responsory

---

[14] beneditam] read as benedictam.
[15] astamtes] read as astantes.
[16] respunsum] read as responsum.

The first rubric expands the customary designation COMMENDATIO ANIMAE to COMMENDACIO ANIME COMMUNIS, indicating that the ritual was intended for the laity. The rubric further indicates that the dying individual was not expected to be alone; a gathering of people is assumed to be present. The rubric directs the celebrant to bless water and sprinkle it *super astantes*—on those standing near. Only after recognizing the gathered community with this blessing was the celebrant to turn his attention to the dying person. Whether this gathering would have included a few family members or a larger circle of acquaintances is not clear, and probably varied in individual instances. Yet regardless of its size, the first rubric clearly indicates that the ritual involved a gathering, as did the deathbed rituals of religious institutions.

In using the term *corpus* to refer to the dying person, the rubric suggests a certain flexibility in the ritual's timing—possibly as an accommodation to a lay community that was rural and isolated. Since the word *corpus* could refer to either a living or a deceased person, the ritual could have been performed appropriately whether the celebrant arrived during the final agony or after death had occurred.[17] This rubric suggests that the inhabitants of Orsières depended upon the presence of a cleric to begin the ritual. Given the lack of a religious community within the town itself, and given the difficulty of traveling through the mountainous terrain, a priest could not always be certain to be present for the moment of death. In allowing for the possibility of beginning either before or after the final breath, the ritual acknowledges the realities of this particular community.

Although the celebrant's role, and the ritual, could begin after the moment of death, we should not assume that the dying person was unattended during the agony. In referring to people already gathered, the ritual's opening suggests a practice of being present with a dying person, even if these practices were not formalized into a ritual. The specific actions and customs of the caregivers and community went unrecorded, but certainly not unperformed.[18]

---

[17] On the ambiguity of the word *corpus* and its use in reference to a living person, see Romedio Schmitz-Esser, *The Corpse in the Middle Ages: Embalming, Cremating, and the Cultural Construction of the Dead Body* (Turnhout: Harvey Miller, 2020), 24.

[18] Geary and Driscoll consider the roles of family members—particularly women—at the deathbed: Geary, *Phantoms of Remembrance*, 51–59; Driscoll, "Per Sora Nostra," and "Reconstructing Liturgical History." See also Sicard, "La mort."

Finally, this first rubric indicates that, although others were assumed to be present, the celebrant carried the primary responsibility for the performance of the first chant. The rubric uses singular, third-person conjugations for the verbs, including DICAT. The singular form DICAT suggests that only one person—the celebrant, or perhaps an accompanying cantor—was required to have full knowledge of the chant. A community gathered, but one person sang. In contrast to the rubrics in rituals from religious communities, then, the first rubric in the ritual of Orsières suggests a separation of roles between the celebrant and other participants.

Responsory and Verse: *Subuenite–Suscipiat*

Subuenite sancti dei	Advance, saints of God
occurrite angeli domini	run, angels of the Lord
suscipientes animam eius	taking his soul
offerentes eam in conspectu altissimi	offering it in the sight of the most high
Suscipiat te Christus	May Christ receive you
qui vo<ca>uit te	who called you
et in sinu Abrahe	and to the bosom of Abraham
angeli deducant te	may angels lead you cf. Luke 16: 22
Offerentes . . .	Offering . . .

As in the manuscripts from Rome and Sens, the prescribed ritual response to death is song. Immediately following the celebrant's blessing of the community and the dying (or recently deceased) person, the rubric in GSB 3 prescribes a performance of the responsory *Subuenite*, along with the verse *Suscipiat*.[19] These are the precise chant texts that open the ritual from Sens. It appears that these elements of the *Ordo XLIX* tradition experienced an

---

[19] The text of the chant complex appears in Sicard, *Liturgie*, 66–68; Paxton, *Christianizing Death*, 39–40; Donohue, "The Rite," 124–125; Hesbert, *CAO*, 7716 and 7716v. Donohue's discussion of the chants' texts as a response to death occurs in "The Rite," 164–169. Ottosen edits the responsory as number 90 and the verse as number 221 (*Responsories*, 228, 401, and 418). Paxton's edition and translation appear in *The Death Ritual at Cluny*, 114–115; see also 211.

extended transmission that encompassed both a cathedral community and an Alpine village.[20]

In the rituals from both Sens and Orsières, the responsory and verse were intended to be sung, not spoken. The scribe of GSB 3 planned to provide music notation for these chants but left the task incomplete. As seen in Figure 3.1, the chant texts appear below empty staff lines. The way in which the chants' texts are written indicates that the scribe considered the melody as he worked. In certain positions, the spacing of the syllables below the staff lines allows room for the notation of extended musical gestures. For example, extra space was left after the word *dei* on Line 1, suggesting that the melody conveyed the final syllable of the word with a melismatic gesture of four or more pitches. Similar instances appear on Line 2 (after the second syllable of *domini*) and Line 3 (after the first syllable of *altissimi*). Additionally, at the end of the verse (not pictured in the image), the scribe included a cue (the single word *offerentes*) directing the singer to repeat a portion of the responsory. Although the melody was not recorded, it determined the manner in which the scribe wrote the chants' texts (whether he worked from his own memory or copied from an exemplar with notation). The manuscript does not reveal why he left the notation unfinished, but it does indicate that the responsory and verse were intended to be sung with melody, not simply spoken or recited with a formulaic tone.

The manner in which the chant texts are written—coordinated to an unnotated melody—provides enough evidence to compare some aspects of the melodic content with versions in other manuscripts. The spacing of the text's syllables in GSB 3 suggests that the responsory's melody resembled, but was not identical to, the melodic versions of Sens (Paris 934, in Chapter 2 as Music Transcription 2.1) and the Abbey of Saint Mary the Virgin and Saint Francis without Aldgate (Cranston 2322, in Chapter 4 as Music Transcription 4.1). In some positions, the additional space left for melismatic, multi-note gestures corresponds to the position of such gestures in these other manuscripts. (Positions of correspondence include Line 1, the final syllable of *dei*; Line 2, the final syllable of *angeli*; and Line 3, the first syllable of *altissimi*.) It appears that in all three versions of the chant, melismas occur with these syllables, even though we cannot know if the specific number and sequence of pitches—and indeed, the pitch content—were

---

[20] The tradition is documented from the eighth century and associated with Rome; see Chapters 2 and 5.

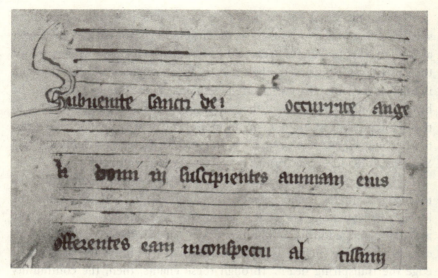

Figure 3.1 *Subuenite* with incomplete music notation (GSB 3, f. 30v). Image © Archives du Gd-St-Bernard. Reproduced by permission of the Archives du Gd-St-Bernard.

identical. In some positions, however, the version of GSB 3 appears to differ from the others. The scribe did not allow additional space for melismas where they occur in other versions. (One such instance appears with the second syllable of *occurrite*: a melisma conveys this syllable in the version from Cranston 2322, but not in the version from Paris 934; neither does space for a melisma appear in GSB 3.) In sum, although we have no notation of the responsory's melody in GSB 3, its text underlay (the number of pitches accorded to individual syllables) probably resembled other versions of the melody, without being identical. The ritual from Orsières shares chant texts with others, but an identical melody does not seem to have been transmitted among them.

Even without music notation, the scribal work reveals much of what the responsory and verse contributed to the ritual from Orsières. The text of *Subuenite* functions as a concise litany, calling upon members of the heavenly community—saints and angels—to aid the dying person's soul. In this way, the responsory expands the community of participants beyond those gathered in the room. The text entreats these heavenly protectors and entrusts them with the task of bringing the dying person's soul into the presence of God.

Whether the ritual began prior to or soon after death, this first chant speaks to the moment of transition, the "migration of the soul."[21] The angels are told to "run" or "hurry," because the movement is happening; the time for their assistance has arrived. The words of the responsory transfer the soul, in the listeners' imaginations, from its residence in the human body into the heavenly realm. The words of the responsory's verse, addressed directly to the dying person, speak to a soul in motion: "Christ has called you" (past tense); "may Christ receive you" (in the future). The chants *Subuenite* and *Suscipiat* thus address and bridge the moment of transition.

The chants also articulate acceptance. In calling upon heavenly protectors to engage with the soul's journey, the sung text acknowledges that the journey is happening. The soul is leaving the body; death is occurring. By articulating hope for the soul's future ("May Christ, who has called you, receive you"), those singing or otherwise participating in the chant acknowledge the transpiring death. Through these chants, then, the community conceded the end of life and directly addressed the dying person with prayers and blessings—just as in the rituals from Rome and Sens.

With their vivid images, the chants offer the ritual's participants and listeners a coherent narrative of death and the afterlife: the soul travels, accompanied by angels and saints, to the presence of the "most high." The request to the angels—to carry the soul to the bosom of Abraham—echoes the parable of poor Lazarus and the wealthy man in the gospel of Luke. Following the verse, a cue prescribes the repetition of the final line of the responsory: "offering [the soul] in the sight of the most high." This repetition conflates two images in performance: while in the bosom of Abraham, the soul is also in the "sight of the most high." With these specific metaphors, the chants describe the movement of the unseen soul, and the lay community partook of the same images as the communities of elite religious institutions.

Kyrie and *Pater noster*

Following these chants, the manuscript's scribe wrote cues for the *Kyrie* and the *Pater noster*, which are also incorporated into the ritual from Rome. As discussed in Chapter 1, these items were typically recited or sung

---

[21] On the pre-Carolingian use of this metaphor, see Paxton, *Christianizing Death*, 54.

collaboratively, although GSB 3 gives no specific indication of their manner of performance in Orsières. Yet regardless of the performance practice, the text of the *Pater noster* asserted an intimate, familial connection between the dying person and God, and also among those gathered. The text defines a community of those who say or hear it. Since these two items were part of the Mass (a liturgy open to the laity), it is not unreasonable to assume that those attending a ritual for the dying in Orsières would have been familiar with them and able to participate to some extent—either by actively reciting or listening with familiarity.

Prayers: *Pie recordacionis* and *Deus cui omnia viuunt*

The two prayers that follow the *Pater noster* are not unique to the ritual from Orsières; they appear in some of the earliest sources containing deathbed liturgies, as well as later sources from prominent religious institutions, such as the canonry of Klosterneuburg and the abbey of Cluny.[22] In these sources, the prayers (standardized as *Pio recordationis* and *Deus cui omnia vivunt*) are often prescribed for the moments immediately following an individual's death. One of the oldest manuscripts preserving *Pio recordationis* places the prayer after the rubric: "When the sister leaves her body."[23] Likewise, in manuscripts preserving the Cluniac rite for the time of death, the prayer follows the rubric: "When . . . they do not doubt that he is dead."[24] The prayer's text also indicates that it was intended for the moments immediately following the last breath: it refers to the deceased person in the past

---

[22] Sicard documents the early sources containing the prayers in *Liturgie*: *Pio recordationis*, 262–264; *Deus cui omnia vivunt*, 90–92. Cluniac sources are documented by Paxton, *The Death Ritual at Cluny*, with the prayers edited and translated on 106–109. Deshusses edits *Pio recordationis* in *Le sacramentaire grégorien* as numbers 1398 and 4047 and *Deus cui omnia vivunt* as number 1399; the prayers also appear in Klosterneuburg 1022A, f. 30. The specific versions of the prayers preserved in GSB 3 contain the textual revisions made by Benedict of Aniane in the early ninth century—revisions that highlighted the individual's responsibility for sin. On these revisions, see particularly Paxton, *Christianizing Death*, 140–143; *The Death Ritual at Cluny*, 206; and Sicard, *Liturgie*, 90–95 and 262–264.

[23] ". . . QUANDO MIGRAT SOROR DE CORPORE" (Caesarius, *Sancti Caesarii Episcopi Arelatensis opera omnia* [N.p.: Marietoli, 1942], 2:127); see also Sicard, *Liturgie*, viii and 260–264; and Paxton, *Christianizing Death*, 52–53. Rosamond McKitterick's research provides further insights into the roles the women in this community played in creating liturgical books and administering their own affairs: "Nuns' Scriptoria in England and Francia in the Eighth Century," *Francia* 19, no. 1 (1992): 1–35.

[24] CUM AUTEM IAM EUM NON DUBITAVERINT OB[I]ISSE (edited and translated in Paxton, *The Death Ritual at Cluny*, 104–105).

tense (as she or he "whom the Lord has called from the temptations of this world") but uses the future tense to refer to God's upcoming care of the soul ("that he may deign to grant him a quiet and pleasant dwelling").[25] *Pio recordationis* was said on behalf of a person who had already died but was still journeying to a destination in the afterlife. The inclusion of *Pio recordationis* and *Deus cui omnia vivunt* indicates that the ritual from Orsières—although it was intended for the laity—contains some of the same items found in the rituals from religious institutions and places them in similar liturgical positions.

Whether for the laity of Orsières or the members of elite religious institutions, the prayers consider those gathered at the deathbed to be a community; they address the people's shared actions and responsibilities. From *Pio recordationis*: "In the pious activity of remembrance, most dear brethren, let us commemorate."[26] Regardless of whether the people around the bedside recited the prayer collectively, the text addresses them as having specific, shared obligations. Their task, at this point, is to remember and pray. Likewise, the prayer *Deus cui omnia vivunt* articulates a common action for those gathered: of entreating God to provide safe passage and refuge for the soul.

These two prayers offer specific conceptualizations of death: life ends when God "calls" a person; the deceased goes to a safer place, away from the temptations of the world; God grants a dwelling in the afterlife. *Deus cui omnia vivunt* offers a vision of life for the moment of death: "God in whom all things live, and through whom our bodies do not perish by dying but are changed into something better."[27] Images from the parable of Luke appear again: the prayer asks that the soul be "gathered up" by angels and "let down in the bosom of your friend Abraham the patriarch." In these ways, the prayers offered specific understandings concerning the gathered community, its role during the death of one of its members, and the transformative processes that the dying person underwent. The presence of these prayers in the deathbed ritual of GSB 3 indicates that such understandings were not unique to practitioners at ecclesiastical centers.

---

[25] Unless otherwise noted, translations in the following discussion are from Paxton, *The Death Ritual at Cluny*, 106–109.
[26] Translation from Paxton, *Christianizing Death*, 53.
[27] *Deus cui omnia viuunt et cui corpora nostra moriendo non pereunt sed mutamtur in melius* (as it appears in GSB 3, f. 31). Translations here and following are from Paxton, *The Death Ritual of Cluny*, 106–109.

Antiphon and Psalm: *Suscipiat te Christus–In exitu Israhel*

Versus	Verse	
Suscipiat te Christus qui vocauit te	May Christ receive you who called you	cf. Luke 16:22

Spalmus Dauid	Psalm of David	
I\<n\> exitu Israhel	When Israel came out ...	Psalm 113[28]

The chant *Suscipiat te Christus* and Psalm 113 (the items following these prayers) are held in common with the ritual from Sens and others that partake of the *Ordo XLIX* tradition; the ritual of Orsières thus shares with many others the image of death as a release from captivity.[29] This common understanding of death is not affected by the small variants seen between the versions of Sens and Orsières: the scribe of Orsières used a neutral term, Versus, to introduce the chant, while the scribe of Sens used no designation at all; in GSB 3, the verb "called" (*vocauit*) replaces "created" (*creauit*) found in Paris 934;[30] the scribe of GSB 3 included a shortened version of the text, either as an extended incipit, or as a reflection of the fact that the text was actually reduced to the first blessing for the dying person (omitting the second clause, which depicts angels leading him to the bosom of Abraham). These variants do not negate the overriding commonality: the portrayal of death as a return to Christ and as an escape from captivity was broadly transmitted, reaching even lay communities.

With Psalm 113, the scribal work in GSB 3 offers additional indications that the ritual was intended for a lay community: the psalm is written in its entirety. In the manuscripts of religious institutions, psalms are customarily indicated with only an incipit showing the first words—a reflection of the fact that psalms were typically memorized, and also readily available in other manuscripts. This position in GSB 3 also reveals that the ritual of Orsières underwent a process of review and correction. The primary scribe omitted two verses of Psalm 113 (vv. 6 and 18), which were later written in the margins, with points of insertion added to the main text. These corrections show that the ritual was read and improved in a secondary scribal effort. Rather than

---

[28] Translation from Alter, *The Hebrew Bible*, 3:270 (as Psalm 114).
[29] See Sicard, *Liturgie*, 66–69, and Paxton, *The Death Ritual of Cluny*, 114–115 and 130–131. *Suscipiat te Christus* is edited in Hesbert, *CAO*, as number 5092.
[30] Sicard's edition notes the frequency of this variant: *Liturgie*, 66–68.

being unused, the document seems to have served as an aid to facilitating correct performances.

Oratio: *Suscipe domine animam famuli tui ... quam de ergasculo*

The prayer following Psalm 113 occurs not only in the ritual from Orsières, but also in the deathbed rituals from Cluny and Klosterneuburg.[31] Its text continues the themes of Psalm 113 by articulating an understanding that death frees a person from bondage. In the prayer's metaphors, the world is a prison, and by dying, the inmate is released from "places of pains ... the bond of ... sins." Death is caused by God's call, and it offers an entry into a "blessedness of quiet and eternal light." Although some specific images differ, the prayer continues the understandings put forth in the ritual's previous items: the final agony is the gateway to a better existence.

Antiphon and Psalms: *Chorus angelorum—Dilexi quoniam—Credidi propter*

Versus	Verse	
Chorus angelorum te suscipiat	May the choir of angels take you up	cf. Luke 16:22
ut cum Lazaro quondam paupere	so that with Lazarus, once poor,	
eterna\<m\> habeas requiem	you may have eternal rest	
Spalmus[32] Dauid	Psalm of David	
Dilexi quoniam exaudiet dominus	I love the Lord, for He has heard ...	Psalm 114[33]
Requiem eternam	Rest eternal ...	

---

[31] Klosterneuburg 1022A, f. 30; the text is edited in Deshusses, *Le sacramentaire grégorien*, as number 1400; Cluniac sources are edited and translated in Paxton, *The Death Ritual at Cluny*, 108–109 (from which the translations in the following discussion are drawn).

[32] Spalmus] read as Psalmus.

[33] Translations (also in the following discussion) are from Alter, *The Hebrew Bible*, 3:273 (as Psalm 116).

Spalmus[34]	Psalm	
Credidi propter	I trusted, though I did speak—	Psalm 115[35]

Once more, with the chant *Chorus angelorum* and its accompanying psalms, the ritual from Orsières incorporates items from the *Ordo XLIX* tradition, as does the ritual from Sens.[36] *Chorus angelorum* reiterates metaphors of the afterlife: angels take the soul to a place of rest, where it joins Lazarus. Following this chant, however, GSB 3 prescribes fewer psalms than does the ritual from Sens. Rather than indicating Psalms 114–119, the manuscript from Orsières prescribes only two (Psalms 114 and 115). Omitting Psalms 116–119 appreciably reduces the amount of recited text and shortens the ritual's performance time. Also, since the scribe of GSB 3 wrote the entirety of the ritual's psalms, excluding four reduced the amount of labor and manuscript space required. The shortened version perhaps reflects the understanding that the ritual might be sung after death had occurred, rather than as an accompaniment to a potentially extended final agony. The ritual from Orsières partakes of much of the same sung material as the ritual from Sens, but in a shortened form.

Although fewer psalms are prescribed, they convey the same message of hope. "I love the Lord, for He has heard my voice, my supplications.... The cords of death encircled me.... I plunged down, but me He did rescue." The psalmist soothes himself: "Return, my being, to your calm, for the Lord has requited you." In reciting this psalm next to the deathbed, the community associated the faith and redemptive experiences of the psalmist with the dying person. God's successful rescue of the psalm's narrator offered hope to those experiencing the ritual. Psalm 115 conveys reassurance specific to the end of life: "Precious in the eyes of the Lord is the death of His faithful ones." The scribe included a cue (*Requiem eternam*) between the two psalms, likely indicating a versicle and response.[37] In this way, the psalms of rescue and reassurance are surrounded by the chant's specific images of the soul being brought into a place of peace. The ritual of Orsières fully conveys the poetic

---

[34] Spalmus] read as Psalmus.

[35] Translations (also in the following discussion) are from Alter, *The Hebrew Bible*, 3:274 (as Psalm 116:10).

[36] The chant's text is edited by Hesbert, *CAO*, as number 1783; Ottosen, *Responsories*, as number 405; Sicard, *Liturgie*, 69–71. On the use of Psalm 114 in rituals for the time of death, see Sicard, *Liturgie*, 74–75.

[37] Edited by Hesbert, *CAO*, as number 8183.

images and comforting messages found in the *Ordo XLIX* tradition, even with a reduced number of psalms.

Annotated Psalm Incipit: *De profundis*

| De profundis | From the depths... | Psalm 129 |

A later addition to the ritual from Orsières—and another indication of a secondary scribal effort to review and revise the ritual—is found in the margins of folio 33v. This later annotation consists of the incipit *De profundis* (Psalm 129), a psalm that belongs to the "penitential" grouping found in the ritual from Rome (SP F 11).[38] The psalms appearing earlier in the ritual from Orsières contain expressions of confidence and victory; in contrast, the narrative voice of Psalm 129 waits for divine mercy to compensate for his own wrongdoings and inadequacies. The scribe who added this psalm to GSB 3 introduced an element of repentance into a ritual that had been largely free from it. His editorial work indicates not only that the ritual was revised, but also that the revisions altered the depictions of the relationship between the dying person and God.

Kyrie, *Pater noster*, and Versicles with Responses

Kyrieleyson   Lord, have mercy...

Pater noster   Our father...   Matthew 6
Et ne nos   and lead us not...

VERSUS
In memoria eterna   An eternal remembrance the just   Psalm 111:7[39]
  erunt justi   shall be...
Ab audi<ti>one   From evil rumor...

---

[38] On the psalm's inclusion in the Cluniac rites for the time of death, see Paxton, *The Death Ritual of Cluny*, 76–77.

[39] Translations here and in the following discussion are based on Alter, *The Hebrew Bible*, 3:268 (as Psalm 112:6–7).

Anima eius in bonis demorabitur	His life will repose in bounty	Psalm 24:13[40]
Et semen	And his seed …	
Non intres in iudicium	Do not come into judgment …	Psalm 142:2[41]
Quia non iustificabitur	For no living thing is acquitted …	
Ne tradas bestiis	Do not deliver to the beasts …	Psalm 73:19
Et animas pauperem	And the souls of the poor …	
In finem	In the end	

The ritual next prescribes a series of items that were customarily performed collaboratively. The inclusion of these items suggests that during the deathbed ritual, the lay community of Orsières assumed tasks similar to the communities of religious institutions. Following a repetition of the *Kyrie* and the *Pater noster*, a series of short statements appear, written in a manner that suggests they were intended to be recited in alternation.[42] The first four statements refer to the just, generally, and the deceased person, specifically: "An eternal remembrance the just shall be. From evil rumor <they shall not fear>"; "His life will repose in bounty, and his seed <will inherit the earth>." The second set of statements are prayers to God on behalf of the deceased person: "Do not come into judgment <with Your servant>, for no living thing is acquitted <before You>"; "Do not deliver to the beasts <the souls that acknowledge you>; and the souls of the poor do not forget in the end." The first statements extend the confident vision of the afterlife heard earlier in the ritual, while the last statements extend the plea for mercy evident in the preceding *Kyrie*. Although some of these individual verses appear in other rituals for the dying, I have not yet found a concordance for this entire series of versicles and responses. The lack of an obvious concordance suggests a lack of widespread standardization in rituals for the dying, even into the fourteenth century: local versions seem to have persisted.

---

[40] Translations here and in the following discussion are from Alter, *The Hebrew Bible*, 3:74 (as Psalm 25:13).
[41] Translations here and in the following discussion are from Alter, *The Hebrew Bible*, 3:324 (as Psalm 143).
[42] The first versicle and response are edited by Hesbert, *CAO*, as number 8096; the second as number 7947.

While this exact series of versicles and responses does not appear in other manuscripts (to my knowledge), the genre, along with its implied performance practice, does. These versicles and responses are recorded in GSB 3 as if the lay community, along with the celebrant, could successfully complete their collective recitation. As seen in SP F 11 (Chapter 1), the scribal work in GSB 3 divides the statements with colored initials, suggesting that the performance alternated between two groups, or between the celebrant and other participants. I see no indications in the manuscript from Orsières that the responsibility for the performance of these items lay with a single individual. The ritual for the laity in GSB 3 contains the same types of items as rituals from religious institutions, even when the customary performance practices of those items assumed collective participation.

PSALMUS	PSALM	
Miserere mei deus	Be merciful to me, O God...	Psalm 50[43]
Requiem eternam dona	Rest eternal give...	cf. IV Esdras 2:34–35
Domine exaudi orationem	LORD, O hear my prayer...	Psalm 101:2[44]
Dominus vobiscum	The Lord be with you...	
Non intres \<in iudicium\> cum seruo tuo	Do not come into judgment with Your servant...	cf. Psalm 142:2[45]

ALIA ORATIO	ANOTHER PRAYER
D\<e\>us vite dator et humanorum corporum reparator	O God, giver of life...[46]

The penitential tone and commonalities with the ritual from Rome, seen with *De profundis* (Psalm 129), appear again in the next items. As discussed in Chapter 1, Psalm 50 was traditionally understood to give voice to the

---

[43] Translation from Paxton, *The Death Ritual at Cluny*, 68–69.
[44] Translation from Alter, *The Hebrew Bible*, 3:236 (as Psalm 102).
[45] Translations based on Alter, *The Hebrew Bible*, 3:324.
[46] Translations here and in the following discussion are from Paxton, *The Death Ritual at Cluny*, 112–115.

remorse of David, when confronted with his transgressions. The psalm's inclusion in the deathbed ritual of Orsières reveals an understanding that repentance on the part of the dying person was necessary, but that reconciliation with God was likely. "A pure heart create for me, God, and a firm spirit renew within me. . . . A broken, crushed heart God spurns not."[47]

After *Requiem eternam* and a versicle and response (which are also part of the ritual from Sens), the prayer *Non intres <in iudicium> cum seruo tuo* introduces the ritual's most judicial language.[48] In its two sentences, the text refers multiple times to God's retribution; it assumes that the dying person will be confronted with a demanding judge. The prayer presents arguments in favor of the deceased person's soul: "the true supplication of Christian faith commends [him] to you"; "he ... was marked with the sign of the trinity while alive." With this prayer, the ritual from Orsières participates in a long and broad transmission pattern: Benedict of Aniane included this text in his early ninth-century liturgy; it also appears in later sources from Cluny.[49]

The final prayer of the deathbed ritual is also found in Benedict of Aniane's liturgy and the ritual from Cluny; the text of *Deus vite dator* appeals to God as the "giver of life and restorer of human bodies" and entreats, "May you see fit to free [the soul] from the torments of hell."[50] Immediately following this dire image, the prayer depicts a more positive image of the afterlife: "Gather [the soul] up among the company of your saints . . . order that it be clothed in celestial and immortal garments and cared for in the pleasantness of paradise." The God to whom this prayer is addressed can make good what is not. Although these texts—with their legalistic, judgmental tenor—differ from many other aspects of the ritual in GSB 3, they provide further evidence that the lay community of Orsières shared material with the rituals of religious institutions, and that the lay community engaged in one of the primary tasks given to the communities of ecclesiastical and monastic centers: supplicating God on the dying person's behalf.

---

[47] Translation from Alter, *The Hebrew Bible*, 3:134, as Psalm 51:12 and 19. On the psalm's inclusion in other rituals for the time of death, see Sicard, *Liturgie*, 137–139; Paxton, *Christianizing Death*, 123–124; and Paxton, *The Death Ritual at Cluny*, 68–69.

[48] Edited by Deshusses, *Le sacramentaire grégorien*, as number 1401; edited and translated in Paxton, *The Death Ritual at Cluny*, 126–127 (from which the translations in the following discussion are taken).

[49] On the prayer's inclusion in the liturgy of Benedict, see especially Paxton, *Christianizing Death*, 141 and 143–144.

[50] *infernorum cruciatibus*. The prayer is edited in Deshusses, *Le sacramentaire grégorien*, as number 1407; edited and translated in Paxton, *The Death Ritual at Cluny*, 112–115 (from which the translations are quoted); see also Paxton, *Christianizing Death*, 141 and 146.

All Gather: Moving the Body from the Home

POSTEA CONUENIANT OMNES	AFTERWARDS LET ALL GATHER
UT DEFERANT CORPUS AD ECLESIAM[51]	IN ORDER TO CARRY TO BODY TO THE CHURCH
ET ANTEQUAM ABTRAHATUR[52] DE DOMO	AND BEFORE IT IS REMOVED FROM THE HOME
DICAT RESPONSUM	THE RESPONSORY SHOULD BE RECITED
Subuenite sancti	Advance, saints...
Kyrieleyson	Lord, have mercy
Pater noster	Our father... Matthew 6
ORACIO	PRAYER
Deus vite dator	O God, giver of life...[53]
ALIA ORACIO	ANOTHER PRAYER
Deus qui humanarum animarum	O God who is the eternal lover of human souls...[54]
TUNC LEUETUR CORPUS	THEN LET THE BODY BE LIFTED
ET PORTETUR AD ECCLESIAM	AND CARRIED TO THE CHURCH
DICENDO ANTIPHANA	SINGING THE ANTIPHON
In paradisum deducant te angeli	May angels lead you into paradise....[55]

The final portion of the ritual in the home reveals further activities of the lay community. The rubric in this position indicates that the gathering grows larger—"all should assemble" (CONUENIANT OMNES)—to carry the body from the home to the church. The rubric's wording suggests that some people

---

[51] ECLESIAM] read as ECCLESIAM.
[52] ABTRAHATUR] read as ABSTRAHATUR.
[53] Translations here and in the following discussion are from Paxton, *The Death Ritual at Cluny*, 112–115.
[54] Translations here and in the following discussion are from Paxton, *The Death Ritual at Cluny*, 114–115.
[55] Translations here and in the following discussion are from Paxton, *The Death Ritual at Cluny*, 130–131. The additional chants prescribed in GSB 3 for the procession with the body to the church are listed in the Appendix.

who had not been present during the final agony now arrive, or that some who had dispersed while the body was washed and prepared now return. The physical labor of moving the body necessitated such a gathering, yet the rubric indicates that even these necessary activities were subsumed into a ritual. As people gathered to work, they joined an ongoing liturgy.

All should gather, but they are instructed not to move the body immediately; the ritual first prescribes chants and prayers. The same responsory heard at the beginning of the ritual, *Subuenite*, is repeated (with responsibility for the performance again assigned to a single person with the verb DICAT), along with other items recited immediately after death: *Kyrie* and the *Pater noster*. With the repetition of these items, even those who were not present at the ritual's beginning had the opportunity to hear depictions of the soul's first movements in the afterlife and to participate in the plea for mercy and the Lord's prayer. According to the ritual, the journey continued for the soul, and the shared responsibilities continued for the community. (These items are followed by the prayer *Deus vite dator*—also repeated from earlier in the ritual—and another prayer concordant in the ritual of Cluny, *Deus qui humanarum animarum*.[56]) Even for laity, then, the ritual for the dying encompassed an entire community; death was not an event for the individual alone or even for the immediate family alone. Others of the community participated in the ritualized transition as the body was moved from the home to the church.

Summary: Evidence for Deathbed Rituals, as Practiced among the Laity

The vast majority of deathbed rituals that survive from the Middle Ages appear in the manuscripts of prominent cathedrals, monasteries, and religious orders, prompting the question of whether these liturgies were practiced with the laity, or if they remained solely within the domain of religious and political elites. Indirect evidence from the late Antiquity through the early Middle Ages suggests that rituals for the time of death were—at the very least—intended to be practiced with the laity. From the fourth century on, documents from political authorities, church leaders, and councils assert that rituals considered to be beneficial at the time of death should be offered

---

[56] Edited by Deshusses, *Le sacramentaire grégorien*, as number 1408; edited and translated by Paxton, *The Death Ritual of Cluny*, 114–115.

to all people. In addition to these statements, some deathbed rituals from prominent religious institutions—beginning in the ninth century—refer to laity in their rubrics, suggesting that they might have gathered at the bedside.

The fourteenth-century manuscript from Orsières offers evidence of a different type—an actual ritual, recorded in a liturgical manuscript and directed toward a lay community. I tend toward caution when assessing the relationship between the contents of a manuscript and the liturgical practices of a community—after all, books are not always used—yet in this instance, editorial emendations and discoloration on the outer edges of the folios offer concrete indications that the ritual of GSB 3 was reviewed and revised, and that the manuscript was open to these pages many times. The scribe of GSB 3 does not dazzle with beautiful handwriting, elegant use of the page, or erudite Latin; rather, we see idiomatic spellings, dropped words, and little attempt at aesthetic ornamentation. This manuscript was not created to impress, but to be used. The modest book provides a rare opportunity for historians: a chance to view a reflection of the practices of a rural, lay community at the time of an individual's death.

Commonalities with the Rituals of Religious Institutions

The ritual from Orsières has much in common with those of ecclesiastical and monastic centers. It contains the same genres, including those that were customarily performed collaboratively: psalms, responsories, the *Kyrie*, the *Pater noster*, and versicles with responses. Even more strikingly, the ritual from Orsières shares specific prayers and chants with the deathbed rituals from monasteries and cathedral communities. Indeed, each item in the ritual from Orsières (with the exception of a few versicles and responses) has concordances with the known rituals of religious institutions. These include (with standardized spellings) the prayers *Pio recordationis*, *Deus cui omnia vivunt*, and *Deus vitae dator*, which are present in the Cluniac customaries; the chants *Subvenite–Suscipiat*, *Suscipiat te Christus*, and *Chorus angelorum*, which appear in Paris 934 (from the cathedral community of Sens) and the broader transmission of the *Ordo XLIX* tradition; and Psalms 50 and 129 (*Miserere mei* and *De profundis* from the penitential psalms), which are held in common with SP F 11 (from Rome).

With these shared items come shared understandings of death and shared images of the afterlife. In the chants and psalms of the *Ordo XLIX* tradition, the ritual of Orsières uses metaphors that depict the soul resting in the bosom of Abraham; angels and saints protecting the soul in its journey away from the body; and death offering an escape from slavery. In the understanding of the penitential psalms and the prayers *Non intres <in iudicium>* and *Deus vitae dator*, human contrition and divine mercy counteract the deceased person's wrongdoings in a post-mortem judgment.

The ritual of GSB 3 prescribes similar roles for the lay community as Paris 934 and SP F 11 prescribe for their respective communities. All these manuscripts assume that the dying individual is surrounded by people who conduct a liturgy on his or her behalf, including praying for the soul, singing chants, and reciting psalms. Whether in Orsières, Sens, or Rome, the community was entrusted with the essential tasks of the ritual: witnessing, acknowledging, and accepting the death; calling on members of the heavenly community to assist the departing soul; supplicating God on its behalf. The deathbed ritual offered a framework for the lay community of Orsières to experience and respond to the death together, just as the deathbed rituals of religious institutions did. The death of an individual was understood to be an occurrence for the community, and the community's first response to death was song.

The ritual from Orsières shows another commonality with the rituals from Sens and Rome; these three liturgies provide the same moments with ritual structure. I have focused on the portion of the rituals encompassing the moment of death, but GSB 3, like the manuscripts of religious communities, also provides liturgical material for the time prior to the death agony—the anointing of the sick—and also for the post-mortem period, including transporting the body to the church and later to the burial grounds. These manuscripts record the rite at the deathbed as part of a larger ritual expanse, one that offers material for the entirety of a life's ending. When viewing this larger expanse, GSB 3 holds even more in common with other manuscripts. For example, the seven penitential psalms that begin the ritual for the dying in the manuscript from Rome are found in the ritual for the sick in the manuscript from Orsières. The chant sung closest to the moment of death in Orsières, the responsory *Subuenite*, appears in the manuscript from Rome, but during the vigil with the body in the night before burial. In short, the ritual from Orsières, like those of religious communities, reveals the intention to sacralize the experiences of sickness, suffering, and death, and it contains similar acknowledgments of suffering and assertions of an intimate relationship between the sufferer and creator. In rituals from both religious and lay communities, we hear appeals to heavenly protectors and see the bosom of Abraham as a depiction of the afterlife. In terms of ritual process, we see the involvement of the gathered community and a flexibility that allows the ritual to be applied to the unpredictable timing of an individual's death.

Differences between the Ritual for the Laity and the Rituals of Religious Institutions

Even with these commonalities, the ritual from Orsières does not appear to duplicate any specific liturgy from a religious community; it is not a copy or a shortened version of a Cluniac model, for example. These differences suggest that rituals for the deathbed had not been standardized in the fourteenth century; local versions were still in use. Although the ritual for the lay community of Orsières appears to be the same in kind as those of religious institutions and orders, it reveals its own specificities in its liturgical accompaniment for a dying individual.

Some differences between the ritual of Orsières and the rituals of Sens and Rome might be accommodations to a lay community. For instance, the manuscript of Orsières provides no material specific to the agony. While its ritual could appropriately begin prior to death, the first rubric also indicates that it could begin after death had occurred. In the community of Orsières, the final agony might have been attended by family and caregivers in ways that went undocumented in written form. Unlike the ritual from Rome, which begins with the penitential psalms—songs that articulate suffering—the first psalm of the ritual from Orsières is Psalm 113, the song of release. GSB 3 also contains a shorter, more efficient deathbed ritual, when compared with the rituals from Rome and Sens. As one example, the ritual from Orsières retains only two psalms in a position where six are listed in Paris 934. That these psalms are written out in full in GSB 3, and that only one person (likely the celebrant) is directed to sing the chant *Subuenite*, also points to the use of the manuscript within a lay community.

Conclusion: Considering Understanding

The comparison of the ritual for the dying in GSB 3 with the rituals found in manuscripts of religious institutions reveals an agreement in the fundamentals and variation in their expression. In its overall resemblance to the rituals of religious elites, the deathbed rite from Orsières supports Van Engen's caution against "treating medieval religious life as comprised of two cultures." The manuscript from Orsières suggests that the deathbed rituals were one of the "many elements . . . that were shared" between the general population and the well-educated religious.[57]

Van Rhijn's characterization of pastoral care in the Carolingian era seems apt, even for this later time period. She states, "Good practices were considered to be of the highest importance, but 'good' could take many different forms."[58] The "good practices" of the rituals for the dying—the community's presence and involvement at the departure of an individual, their pleas for intercession, their affirmation of beliefs concerning the afterlife—these practices are evident in manuscripts from elite, urban religious communities as well as a manuscript from a small, remote, lay community. Even with a variety of "good forms," the religious understandings, the religious tasks, and the religious responses to death appear to have been held in common.

When considering the performance of these rituals, beyond the evidence provided by the manuscripts themselves, questions of language and comprehension arise—particularly concerning the laity. To what extent can we imagine a ritual conveying meaning, if we are not sure of the Latin literacy of the participants? The vibrant metaphors of the afterlife, the exhortations to the community: How much would the people of Orsières have understood? Before we assume that ignorance created a barrier between the people of Orsières and the ritual's intellectual substance, it is worth considering some factors that might have offered lay individuals familiarity and insight into the ritual's content.

Priest as Teacher and Pastoral Care Giver

The laity of Orsières could have gained knowledge of the deathbed ritual through the priests who conducted it. Van Rhijn's work documenting the roles and responsibilities of priests during the Carolingian era suggests this

---

[57] Van Engen, "The Christian Middle Ages as an Historiographical Problem," 552.
[58] Carine Van Rhijn, "The Local Church, Priests' Handbooks and Pastoral Care in the Carolingian Period," in *Chiese locali e chiese regionali nell'alto medioevo; Spoleto, 4–9 Aprile 2013* (Spoleto: Fondazione centro Italiano di studi sull'alto medioevo, 2014), 689–710; here, 705.

possibility, also for the fourteenth century. In a direct chain of command—and education—that extended from the emperor and his advisors to the laity, "Carolingian bishops monitored the quality of local churches via their priests, and attempted to make sure these men knew what they were doing."[59] The hierarchical structures of the church were used to offer pastoral care, sacraments, and instruction to the general population. The evidence of the Carolingian era lies at great distance from the manuscript of Orsières, yet it reveals a functional hierarchy—and expectations of each level of the hierarchy—that still existed in the fourteenth century. It opens the possibility that the laity of Orsières understood the ritual for the dying and could participate in it meaningfully, through the instruction and explanations given by the clergy.

Evidence from the Carolingian era also suggests the possibility that the laity might have known and been able to recite the *Pater noster*, which occurs three times within the portion of the ritual conducted in the home of the dying person in the manuscript from Orsières. Although written at a distance of 150 miles and five centuries, a statute by Bishop Haito of Basle gives insight into the mechanisms established for pastoral care and religious education. As described by Van Rhijn: "One important tool for such education in the basics of the Christian religion was teaching the people the Lord's Prayer and the Creed, both in Latin and in the local language, and explaining to them what the prayers meant and how they should be understood."[60] The possibility exists that the *Pater noster* could have been comprehended and recited collectively by those gathered around a dying individual at Orsières. The ritual's limited repertory—in particular the repetitions of the chant complex *Subuenite–Suscipiat*, as well as the *Pater noster*—reveals a ritual of manageable scope.[61]

---

[59] Van Rhijn, "The Local Church," 700.

[60] Van Rhijn, "Charlemagne and the Government," 172–173. The statute is edited by Peter Brommer, *Capitula episcoporum I* (Hannover: Hahnsche Buchhandlung, 1984), 210–219: "§II Secundo iubendum, ut oratio dominica . . . et symbolum apostolorum . . . ab omnibus discatur tam latine quam barbarice, ut, quod ore profitentur, corde credatur et intellegatur." McKitterick analyzes the evidence indicating "didactic intentions" on the part of clergy and ecclesiastical authorities, including an early ninth-century ordinance indicating that laity should learn the Creed and the Lord's Prayer (*Capitulare missorum*, 802): Rosamond McKitterick, *The Frankish Church and the Carolingian Reforms, 789–895* (London: Royal Historical Society, 1977), 115–154.

[61] Cannon considers similar questions in his study of whether the Latin elements of English sermons in the Middle Ages might have led laity to become more familiar with the Latin language: Christopher Cannon, "What Did the Medieval Laity Hear When They Heard Latin?" Paper presented at the national conference of the Medieval Academy of America, Virtual Version, March 27–29, 2020, accessed October 15, 2020, at https://www.medievalacademy.org/page/MAA2020VirtualMeeting.

Scribal Work

As the ritual is written in GSB 3, the participation of the lay community seems to be assumed, at the very least in the versicles and responses. The scribal work includes capitalized and colored initial letters normally associated with changes of speakers, suggesting that the statements were expected to be recited in alternation between the celebrant and participants.

Additional scribal work suggests that importance was attached to providing an error-free ritual. Not only was the effort of creating the manuscript and writing the ritual undertaken, but scribal annotations also indicate that the ritual was edited and improved. The prayers *Pie recordacionis, Deus cui omnia viuunt, Non intres <in iudicium>, Deus vite dator,* and *Deus qui humanarum animarum* show corrections, as does the text of Psalm 113 in two positions; *De profundis* (Psalm 129) was added in the margins of folio 33v. This ritual was not written once and then set aside; the hands of multiple editors worked to provide the lay community of Orsières with high-quality material.

Participation does not have to be literate to be meaningful. Even without being able to understand or recite the texts, those gathered might have felt that they were fully participating in the rites for the dying person. The ritual, as it is documented in GSB 3, allows for the community to experience and respond to the death together, with or without knowledge of the texts and chants.

What were the actual, literate levels of participation? What was the quality of the Latin pronunciation, the expertise in singing? What percentage of those gathered participated vocally in the chants, psalms, and prayers? How much of the ritual's words, images, and metaphors did they understand? The answers to these questions must have varied with each occurrence of the ritual, and with each individual celebrant and participant. Such queries lie largely beyond any possible scholarly inquiry.

Yet rather than assuming general ignorance on the part of the laity, historical considerations and manuscript evidence allow us to keep such questions open, awaiting further insights from subsequent research, and—if none arise—accepting the limitations inherent in scholarly investigations. It is possible that the people of Orsières stood passively and inattentively while the celebrant conducted the liturgy; it is also possible that they participated wholeheartedly, understood well, and found great meaning in the ritual at the deathbed.

4

Among Women

Abbey of Saint Mary the Virgin and Saint Francis without Aldgate (England)

Manuscript Source: Reigate (Surrey), Parish Church of St Mary Magdalene, Cranston Library, Ms. 2322
(Cranston 2322)

Just outside the medieval walls of London, half a mile north of where the Tower fronts on the Thames River, a community of women lived enclosed in the "Abbey without Aldgate."[1] The liturgical care that these women provided one another at the time of death is reflected in a manuscript that survives from the second half of the fifteenth century (Reigate, Surrey, Parish Church of St Mary Magdalene, Cranston Library, Ms. 2322; hereafter referred to as Cranston 2322).[2] This small book—measuring approximately 8 by 5½

---

[1] The abbey without Aldgate was founded in the late thirteenth century and disbanded in 1539 by Henry VIII. Recent scholarship on the community's history includes Anna Campbell, "Franciscan Nuns in England, the Minoress Foundations and Their Patrons, 1281–1367," in *The English Province of the Franciscans (1224–c. 1350)*, ed. Michael Robson (Leiden: Koninklijke Brill, 2017), 426–447; Elizabeth M. Makowski, *English Nuns and the Law in the Middle Ages: Cloistered Nuns and Their Lawyers, 1293–1540* (Woodbridge: Boydell Press, 2011); Jennifer Ward, *English Noblewomen in the Later Middle Ages* (London: Longman, 1992; repr. London: Routledge, 2014). Earlier studies include Anne F. C. Bourdillon, *The Order of Minoresses in England* (Manchester: The University Press, 1926); Eileen Power, *English Medieval Nunneries, c. 1275–1525* (Cambridge: Cambridge University Press, 1922); Walter W. Seton, ed., "The Rewle of Sustris Menouresses Enclosid," in *A Fifteenth-century Courtesy Book and Two Franciscan Rules*, ed. R. W. Chambers and Walter W. Seton (London: Published for the Early English Text Society by Kegan Paul, Trench, Trübner and Humphrey Milford, Oxford University Press, 1914), 63–125; William Page, ed., "Friaries: The Minoresses without Aldgate," in *A History of the County of London*: Vol. 1, *London within the Bars, Westminster and Southwark* (London: Victoria County History, 1909), 516–519, accessed November 5, 2020, through *British History Online*, http://www.british-history.ac.uk/vch/london/vol1/pp516-519; Edward Murray Tomlinson, *A History of the Minories: London* (London: Smith, Elder, & Co., 1907). The community's manuscript holdings are documented in David Bell, *What Nuns Read: Books and Libraries in Medieval English Libraries* (Kalamazoo, MI: Cistercian Publications, 1995), 149–152. Historical maps that include the location of the abbey are provided online by the University of London School of Advanced Study, Institute for Historical Research, "Layers of London," https://www.layersoflondon.org/map (accessed November 5, 2020).

[2] I am indebted to Anne Bagnall Yardley for informing me of this manuscript and helping me to view images. Manuscript descriptions are found in Yardley, "Clares in Procession: The Processional

inches—was likely made for the use of a cantrix, to facilitate the performance of music that occurred outside of the Office and Mass liturgies. The women who used this manuscript would have borne the responsibility for leading processions and the music of other community functions, such as grace at mealtimes, the professions of new sisters, and the ritual for the dying.[3]

The abbey of Aldgate was founded as part of the Franciscan's "Second Order" of Saint Clare, and so it is not particularly surprising that the deathbed liturgy contained in manuscript Cranston 2322 conforms closely to the Ritual of Last Sacraments of 1260, prescribed and promulgated by the Franciscan Order.[4] Yet in some ways, the inclusion of the Franciscan ritual in Cranston

and Hours of the Franciscan Minoresses at Aldgate," *Women & Music: A Journal of Gender and Culture* 13 (2009): 1–23; Yardley, *Performing Piety: Musical Culture in Medieval English Nunneries* (New York: Palgrave Macmillan, 2006), 102–111; N. R. Ker and A. J. Piper, *Medieval Manuscripts in British Libraries* (Oxford: Clarendon Press, 1992), 4:201–203. Clear evidence reveals the manuscript's provenance: The liturgies included within the manuscript indicate a Franciscan community; the saints included in the calendar indicate a Franciscan community in England; the adaptations seen in the ritual for the dying (discussed below) further associate the manuscript with a community of women; an inscription on folio 190 connects the manuscript specifically with Aldgate. As translated by Yardley ("Clares in Procession," 4) the inscription reads: "Note that Dame Agnes Porter gave this book to Dame Anne Frenell, minoress of Aldgate (London) to bequeath it after her death, with the permission of her sovereign, to whomever she will." For a comprehensive summary of extant liturgical manuscripts from English Franciscan communities, see Nigel J. Morgan, "The Liturgical Manuscripts of the English Franciscans c. 1250–c. 1350," in *The English Province of the Franciscans (1224–c. 1350)*, ed. Michael J. P. Robson (Leiden: Brill, 2017), 214–245. (Cranston 2322 is mentioned on 214, note 1.)

[3] As a book type, Cranston 2322 seems to have functioned as a processional and a ritual for a women's community; in addition to material for processions, it contains liturgies that could be performed without a priest. Yardley provides a complete inventory of the manuscript's contents ("Clares in Procession," 4) and a summary of evidence that the manuscript was created for the use of a cantrix (*Performing Piety*, 103, and "Clares in Procession," 23). Boynton provides a context for the liturgy celebrated at Aldgate: Susan Boynton, "Monastic Liturgy, 1100–1500: Continuity and Performance," in *The Cambridge History of Medieval Monasticism in the Latin West*, ed. Alison I. Beach and Isabelle Cochelin (Cambridge: Cambridge University Press, 2020), 958–974. The role of the cantor (cantrix) in female monastic communities is explored by: Katie Ann-Marie Bugyis, "Female Monastic Cantors and Sacristans in Central Medieval England: Four Sketches," in *Medieval Cantors and Their Craft: Music, Liturgy and the Shaping of History, 800–1500*, ed. Katie Ann-Marie Bugyis, A. B. Kraebel, and Margot E. Fassler (Woodbridge: York Medieval Press, 2017), 151–169; Alison Altstatt, "Re-membering the Wilton Processional," *Notes: The Quarterly Journal of the Music Library Association* 72, no. 4 (2016): 690–732; Alison Altstatt, *Wilton Abbey in Procession: Religious Women's Music and Ritual in the Thirteenth-century Wilton Processional* (forthcoming, University of Liverpool Press); and Yardley, *Performing Piety*.

[4] The Franciscan ritual gained broad transmission in the thirteenth century as friars established communities throughout Europe. Following Van Dijk and Walker, the Franciscan rites for the sick and dying were revised after Haymo's death in 1243 and issued as part of the breviary of 1260 (Van Dijk, *Origins*, 280–291). A critical edition of the ritual is provided by Van Dijk, *Sources*, 2:390–392; his discussion appears at 1:135. All references to the 1260 version in the following discussion are taken from his edition. Donohue considered several medieval rites—including that of the thirteenth-century Franciscans—as forerunners of the now-current version published by the Roman Catholic Church in the early 1980s. His translation and discussion of the Franciscan rite of 1260 occurs in Donohue, "The Rite," 217–231. Van Dijk, "Some Manuscripts of the Earliest Franciscan Liturgy," *Franciscan Studies* 16, no. 1 (1956): 60–101; Andrew W. Mitchell, "The Chant of the Earliest Franciscan Office" (PhD diss., University of Western Ontario, 2003); Anna Welch, *Liturgy, Books and Franciscan Identity in*

2322 is remarkable: it indicates that the women of Aldgate (referred to as the "Minoresses" or "Minories") had a level of education and liturgical sophistication beyond what was required of them. Following the rule that governed their abbey, sisters were permitted to substitute liturgies with repetitions of simple prayers, such as the *Pater noster*.[5] Cranston 2322 indicates that the women of Aldgate surpassed this lower standard: at the time of an individual's death, the manuscript prescribes—and facilitates the performance of—the extensive liturgy of the Franciscan Order. The contents of Cranston 2322 (as well as an appendix to a manuscript copy of the abbey's rule, discussed below) reveal a competent community dedicated to a robust and thorough practice of the Franciscan liturgies, including the rites for the dying.[6]

Medieval Umbria (Leiden: Brill, 2015); and Patrick J. Whittle, "Franciscan Liturgical Practice and the Liturgy of Rome from Francis of Assisi to Haymo of Faversham: Reassessing Current Assumptions" (PhD diss., The Catholic University of America, 2022) investigate the relationships among the earliest Franciscan liturgies, the papal liturgies, and the later, revised Franciscan liturgies. See also Donohue, "The Rite," 200–205, where he discusses the "unsolved problems of origin and composition" of the Franciscan Commendation of the Soul.

[5] The women of Aldgate followed the "Isabelline Rule," with the revisions of Pope Boniface VIII. This rule states: "The sisters who can read and sing shall do the office reverently and moderately, following the customs and order of the friar minors, and the other [sisters] shall say 20 *Pater noster* for matins, 5 for lauds, 7 each for prime, terce, sext, none and compline, and 12 for evensong. And in this same manner all things of the office of our Blessed Lady shall be kept, with devout prayers for the dead. And if there are any sisters who are suitable and knowledgeable, the abbess, if she thinks them good, should order and appoint one of them as a mistress, suitable and honest, to teach the nuns song so that they may perform the offices and service of God steadfastly" (as translated from Aldgate's Middle English version by Yardley, *Performing Piety*, 40; the passage is edited in the original language by Seton, "The Rewle of Sustris Menouresses," 85). The Isabelline Rule was originally approved for the community of Longchamp (France) in the mid-thirteenth century (after the death of Clare). On the rule and the relationship of women's liturgical practices to those of the Franciscan Order, see Yardley, "Clares in Procession," 2–4; Mary Natvig, "Rich Clares, Poor Clares," *Women & Music: A Journal of Gender and Culture* 4 (2000): 59–70; and Seton, "The Rewle of Sustris Menouresses," especially 63–71. Andrews provides the most recent contribution to the history of the early Franciscan Order, including the women involved and the rule(s) of Isabelle: Frances Andrews, "The Early Mendicants," in *The Oxford Handbook of Christian Monasticism*, ed. Bernice M. Kaczynski (Oxford: Oxford University Press, 2020), 264–284. Hirbodian provides a valuable case study of women religious (including those associated with the Franciscan order) in Strasbourg in a contemporaneous time period: Sigrid Hirbodian, "Religious Women: Secular Canonesses and Beguines," in *The Oxford Handbook of Christian Monasticism*, ed. Bernice M. Kaczynski (Oxford: Oxford University Press, 2020), 285–299.

[6] The abbey's English translation of the Isabelline Rule, as well as an appendix with a more detailed prescription of the abbey's liturgical practices, are preserved in Oxford, Bodleian Library, MS 585, Part 2 (Summary Catalogue no. 2357). Manuscript descriptions are provided by the University of Oxford, "Medieval Libraries of Great Britain (MLGB3) 2015," accessed November 5, 2020, at http://mlgb3.bodleian.ox.ac.uk/mlgb/book/3809/?search_term=585&field_to_search=shelfmark&page_size=500. See also "Medieval Manuscripts in Oxford Libraries: MS. Bodl. 585–Part 2 (2019)," accessed November 5, 2020, at https://medieval.bodleian.ox.ac.uk/catalog/manuscript_1603; and Seton's introduction to "The Rewle of Sustris Menouresses," particularly 72–73. Both the English translation of the rule and the appendix are edited by Seton, "The Rewle of Sustris Menouresses," 77 and 98–116; see also Yardley, *Performing Piety*, 41–42.

The following examination of the deathbed ritual in Cranston 2322 gives further evidence of the community's competence. Small but significant changes to the standardized Franciscan version appear: the ritual was modified to make it more appropriate for the women's community. Not only were the Minoresses confident and skilled enough to attempt performances of the complex Franciscan liturgy, they also tailored it for their own use. Even more strikingly, the manuscript indicates that the women of Aldgate were able to perform the ritual without the assistance of a friar or priest. As detailed in the analysis below, the abbey's surviving documentation leaves behind an impression of a self-sufficient, capable community, dedicated to providing dying sisters with the liturgical care prescribed by the Franciscan Order, tailored specifically for a woman, and conducted entirely by the women of Aldgate themselves.

For these reasons, the following analysis contributes to the growing body of scholarship that investigates and articulates areas of autonomy practiced by medieval female religious. The rite for the dying in the manuscript from Aldgate offers an indisputable and fascinating example of two related phenomena that scholars have observed in other women's communities of the time period: liturgical material being adapted specifically for the use of a women's community, and women exerting a degree of independence in their liturgical practices.[7]

---

[7] Bugyis examines the types of pastoral care women provided to one another in Benedictine communities in the tenth through thirteenth centuries: Katie Ann-Marie Bugyis, *The Care of Nuns: The Ministries of Benedictine Women in England during the Central Middle Ages* (New York: Oxford University Press, 2019); Yardley examines the same issue in women's communities of multiple orders from the thirteenth century on: Yardley, *Performing Piety* and *Clares in Procession*. Nardini's work demonstrates the compositional activities of women in religious communities in Benevento: Luisa Nardini, *Chants, Hypertext & Prosulas: Re-texting the Proper of the Mass in Beneventan Manuscripts* (Oxford: Oxford University Press, 2021). Other notable examples of scholarship on women's communities and women's areas of agency include: McKitterick, "Nuns' Scriptoria"; Alison I. Beach, *Women as Scribes: Book Production and Monastic Reform in Twelfth-Century Bavaria* (Cambridge: Cambridge University Press, 2004); Lester, *Creating Cistercian Nuns*; Claire Taylor Jones, *Ruling the Spirit: Women, Liturgy, and Dominican Reform in Late Medieval Germany* (Philadelphia: University of Pennsylvania Press, 2018) and *Fixing the Liturgy: Friars, Sisters, and the Dominican Rite, 1256–1516* (Philadelphia: University of Pennsylvania Press, 2024); Margot E. Fassler, "Women and Their Sequences: An Overview and a Case Study," *Speculum* 94, no. 3 (2019): 625–673; Gisela Muschiol, "Gender and Monastic Liturgy in the Latin West (High and Late Middle Ages)," in *The Cambridge History of Medieval Monasticism in the Latin West*, ed. Alison I. Beach and Isabelle Cochelin (Cambridge: Cambridge University Press, 2020), 803–815; Diane Watt, *Women, Writing and Religion in England and Beyond, 650–1100* (London: Bloomsbury Academic, 2020); and Lucy Barnhouse, "Disordered Women? The Hospital Sisters of Mainz and Their Late Medieval Identities," *Medieval Feminist Forum* 55, no. 2 (2020): 60–97. In a related area of scholarship, Michael Driscoll and Patrick Geary examine the roles women played in caring for the dying and deceased: Driscoll, "Per Sora Nostra" and "Reconstructing Liturgical History"; Geary, *Phantoms of Remembrance*.

Additionally, examinations of the chants within the deathbed ritual reveal the functions of music: emphasizing and drawing connections among the vivid images of the sung words, embellishing textual depictions of the afterlife with distinctive soundscapes, and guiding the community through the process of taking leave of a sister.

The Ritual's Beginning: Litany for a Dying Woman

ORDO COMMENDACIONIS ANIME	ORDER OF THE COMMENDATION OF THE SOUL
PRIMO DICANTUR LETANIE	FIRST ARE SUNG THE LITANIES
Kyrieleyson	Lord, have mercy
Christeleyson	Christ, have mercy
Kyrieleyson	Lord, have mercy
Sancta Maria ora pro ea	Holy Mary, pray for her...

The beginning of the deathbed ritual in Cranston 2322 shows both fidelity to the Franciscan version of 1260 and also a willingness to make it more appropriate for the women of Aldgate. The opening rubric gives the same directions as the 1260 version, but with fewer words: PRIMO DICANTUR LETANIE in Cranston 2322 replaces PRIMUM FIANT LITANIE BREVES IN HUNC MODUM.[8] The litany that follows this rubric in Cranston 2322 is identical to the 1260 version—Francis occupies a prominent position as the first among monks and hermits—but the version of Aldgate changes the references to the dying person. *Ora pro eo* ("Pray for him") appears as *Ora pro ea* ("Pray for her"). Thus, the litany faithfully follows the version of the Franciscan Order but adapts it in ways that make it appropriate for a dying woman. References to the dying person using the feminine forms of pronouns appear consistently throughout the litany. While other manuscripts, such as Paris 934 (Chapter 2), have the feminine forms written as alternatives (above the primary text with masculine forms), such is not the case in Cranston 2322. The feminine forms of pronouns were part of the initial scribe's work; the understanding that the litany would be sung for the benefit of women guided the creation of the manuscript. In singing the litany, then, the women of Aldgate referred specifically to their dying sister while calling upon the heavenly community for assistance.

---

[8] Van Dijk, *Sources*, 2:390.

During the Soul's Exit: Prayers

In exitum anime	During the exit of the soul
Oracio	Prayer
Proficiscere anima Christiana	Go forth, Christian soul...
Responsio	Response
Amen	Amen
Deus misericors deus clemens	Merciful God, gentle God...
Commendo te omnipotenti deo soror mea karissima	I commend you to omnipotent God, my dear sister...
Responsio	Response
Amen	Amen
Oracio	Prayer
Suscipe domine ancillam tuam	Receive, Lord, your handmaid...
Responsio	Response
Amen	Amen
Oracio	Prayer
Commendamus tibi domine animam famule tue	We commend to you, Lord, the soul of your servant...
Responsio	Response
Amen	Amen
Oracio	Prayer
Delicta iuuentutis et ignorancias eius	The transgressions of youth and her ignorance...
Responsio	Response
Amen	Amen

Similarly, the next portion of the ritual, intended for the final moments of life ("DURING THE EXIT OF THE SOUL"), shows both a conformity to the 1260 version as well as adaptations making it appropriate for the community of Aldgate. The rubric of the 1260 version (DEINDE PRO VICINO MORTI, CUM IN

AGONE SUI EXITUS ANIMA VISA FUERIT ANXIARI, FIANT HEE ORATIONES[9]) is changed in Cranston 2322 to three efficient words: IN EXITUM ANIME. This shorter rubric gives only the briefest indication of how to coordinate the following prayers to the physical events of a life's ending; it reads as a succinct reminder to a person who already knows when and how the material should be performed. In contrast, the rubric of the 1260 version contains a more complete, detailed description that could be useful to people less familiar either with the dying process or with the coordination of liturgical material to that process. With the brief rubric in Cranston 2322, the manuscript's scribe seems to have assumed a certain amount of knowledge on the part of the manuscript's user. The rubric provides further evidence that the manuscript was created for the use of a knowledgeable and liturgically skilled community (or perhaps even a specific individual).

The prayers prescribed to accompany the soul's exit in Cranston 2322 are those of the 1260 version;[10] as with the litany, the collection of prayers demonstrates fidelity to the earlier ritual of the Franciscan Order. These prayers offer detailed, vibrant images of the soul's successful passage away from the body, in which dangers are conquered through the help of the saints and the mercy of God, and the soul is finally received into the heavenly community. The prayers populate the experience of dying with heavenly companions and advocates.

Yet the Franciscan prayers are modified in Cranston 2322 to make the texts appropriate for a woman. For example: *Commendo te omnipotenti deo frater karissime* ("I commend you, dear brother, to omnipotent God") appears in Cranston 2322 as *Commendo te omnipotenti deo soror mea karissima* ("I commend you, my dear sister, to omnipotent God"); *Suscipe domine servum tuum* ("Receive, Lord, your servant") is altered to *Suscipe domine ancillam tuam* ("Receive, Lord, your handmaid"). As the prayers appear in Cranston 2322, the dying person is consistently addressed and referred to as a woman. In the prayers, as in the preceding litany, these changes to the 1260 version appear as part of the initial scribe's work; the possibility of performing the prayers for a man is not given.

---

[9] Van Dijk, *Sources*, 2:392 ("THEN, FOR THE NEARNESS TO DEATH, WHEN, IN THE STRUGGLE OF ITS EXIT, THE SOUL IS SEEN TO BE ANXIOUS, LET THESE BE THE PRAYERS").
[10] Editions and discussions of the prayers occur in Donohue, "The Rite," 71–101 and 223–228; Sicard, *Liturgie*, 275–279 and 361–372; Dumas, *Liber sacramentorum Gellonensis*, numbers 2888 and 2892; Deshusses, *Le sacramentaire grégorien*, number 1396; and Paxton, *Christianizing Death*, 77 and 117–119.

In Case of Anxiety: Psalms

SI ANXIATUR ADHUC ANIMA	IF THE SOUL IS STILL UNEASY	
DICANTUR HII PSALMI	THESE PSALMS OUGHT TO BE PERFORMED	
Confitemini domino quoniam	Acclaim the LORD, for ...	Psalm 117
Beati immaculati	Happy whose way is blameless ...	Psalm 118
VSQUE AD PSALMUM	UNTIL THE PSALM	
Ad dominum cum tribularer	To the LORD when I was in straits ...	Psalm 119[11]

The subsequent rubric and psalm assignments duplicate the 1260 version of the ritual: Psalms 117–119 were to be sung in cases of anxiety. The performance practices of the women of Aldgate probably also followed that of the friars: the psalms were most likely sung.[12] An appendix to a manuscript copy of the rule that governed life at Aldgate includes a description of the community singing psalms in a procession from the refectory to the church.[13] "The lead singer [*chaunterere*] shall begin to go to the monastery with *Miserere mei deus* [Psalm 50], and all the convent and then the choir on that one side shall take its verse and the choir on the other side shall take another verse. And as soon as they have bowed to the image reverently, they shall go into the church singing the same melody."[14] This description, along with others in the text, depicts a community with robust practices of singing: practices that included a skilled cantrix and a choir that could perform psalms in alternation. A community with such practices was capable of singing the psalms in the liturgy for the dying, as well. The women of Aldgate not only made use of the same liturgical items as the Franciscan friars, they likely also made use of the customary performance practices. The reassurance offered by these psalms (they depict God as a source of rest and comfort for a suffering person) might well have been delivered with the sisters gathered around the bed, singing the psalms' verses in alternation.

---

[11] Translations of the psalms follow Alter, *The Hebrew Bible*, 3:276–291.
[12] On the use of the psalms in other rituals for the dying, see Sicard, *Liturgie*, 74–75, 227, and 229; also Paxton, *The Death Ritual at Cluny*, 134–139. Donohue's discussion of their use in the 1260 version occurs in "The Rite," 228–229.
[13] The rule and appendix are contained in Bodleian 585, a manuscript contemporaneous with Cranston 2322; see above, note 6.
[14] Translated from Seton's edition in "The Rewle of Sustris Menouresses," 103.

At the Soul's Departure: *Subuenite–Suscipiat–Requiem eternam*

EGRESSA ANIMA DE CORPORE	AT THE DEPARTURE OF THE SOUL FROM THE BODY
DICATUR HOC RESPONSORIUM	THIS RESPONSORY OUGHT TO BE PERFORMED
Subuenite	Advance...
Versus	VERSE
Sus<ci>piat te Christus	May Christ receive you... cf. Luke 16:22

For the moment of death, Cranston 2322 prescribes the same liturgical response—the chant *Subuenite* with its verse *Suscipiat*—as the 1260 version.[15] The scribe of Cranston 2322 also followed the scribal practices seen in manuscripts containing the earlier version of the ritual: the chants first appear in abbreviated form (when they are prescribed at the moment of death) and later appear in their entirety, with music notation (when prescribed following the funeral Mass). Although they appear without music notation in the material sung at the deathbed, the chants were likely intended to be sung. The scribal practice of notating a chant fully only in one position, while using cues to refer to it in other positions, was typical during the Middle Ages and made efficient use of a manuscript's space. In Cranston 2322, the prominent discoloration on the outer edge of folio 124, where the chants are notated in full, suggests that the music notation was referred to frequently, perhaps even when the cantrix performed it at the moment of death. (The following transcription and analysis use the complete, notated version of the chants from folio 124.)

One small difference between the 1260 version and the version in Cranston 2322 is evident. When the chant complex appears in the material

---

[15] The text of the responsory appears in Sicard, *Liturgie*, 66–68; Paxton, *Christianizing Death*, 39–40; Donohue, "The Rite," 124–125; Hesbert, *CAO*, numbers 7716 and 7716v. Donohue's discussion of the text as a response to death occurs in "The Rite," 164–169. Ottosen edits the responsory as number 90 and the verses as numbers 198 and 221 (*Responsories*, 228, 401, 417, and 418). Paxton's edition and translation appear in *The Death Ritual at Cluny*, 114–115; see also 211. A transcription of the chants from a thirteenth-century manuscript containing the 1260 version of the ritual appears in Elaine Stratton Hild, "The Role of Music in a Franciscan Liturgy for the End of Life as Evidenced in Manuscript Newberry 24," in *Death and Disease in the Medieval and Early Modern World: Perspectives from Across the Mediterranean and Beyond*, ed. Lori Jones and Nükhet Varlık (Woodbridge, Great Britain: York Medieval Press and Boydell & Brewer Ltd., 2022), 151–175. The manuscript investigated is Chicago, Newberry Library, Vault Manuscript 24 (Newberry 24).

for the moment of death, the cue for a second verse, *Requiem eternam*, is missing. Yet this verse does appear with the complete, notated version of the chant complex found later in the ritual (f. 124, Music Transcription 4.1). The omission of the cue in the material for the moment of death is ambiguous: either it reflects the intended performance practice (at the moment of death, the responsory *Subuenite* should be sung only with the verse *Suscipiat*, not with the second verse *Requiem eternam*), or it reflects the abbreviated nature of the scribal work at this position in the manuscript (the responsory *Subuenite* should be sung with two verses—*Suscipiat* and *Requiem eternam*—yet the scribe chose to indicate these chants with only the first words of the responsory and the first verse). In either case, the deviation from the 1260 version is minor. Melodic variations are minor, as well. With a few exceptions (noted below, where pertinent), the scribe of Cranston 2322 recorded the same melody and text underlay as the scribe of the manuscript Newberry 24, which contains a version of the ritual from around 1240.

Responsorium	**Responsory**	
Subuenite sancti dei	Advance, saints of God	
occurrite angeli domini	run, angels of the Lord	
suscipientes animam eius	taking her soul	
offerentes eam in conspectu altissimi	offering it in the sight of the most high	
Versus	**Verse**	
Suscipiat te Christus	May Christ receive you	
qui uocauit te	who called you	
et in sinu Abrahe	and to the bosom of Abraham	cf. Luke 16:22
angeli deducant te	may angels lead you	
Susci\<pientes\>	Taking \<her soul offering it in the sight of the most high\>	
Versus	**Verse**	
Requiem eternam dona eis domine	Rest eternal give them, Lord	cf. IV Esdras 2:34–35
et lux perpetua luceat eis	and may light perpetual shine on them	

Music Transcription 4.1 *Subuenite–Suscipiat–Requiem eternam* (Cranston 2322, f. 124)

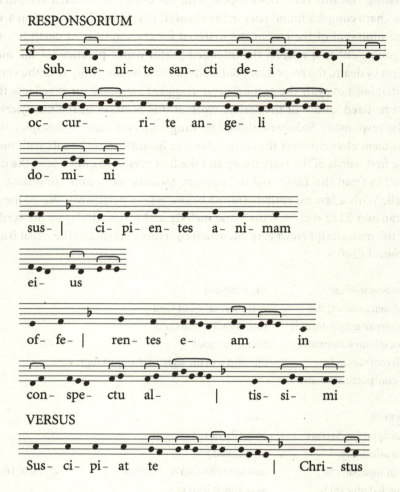

The responsory *Subuenite*, along with its verses *Suscipiat* and *Requiem eternam*, offers a ritualized structure for experiencing the transition of death. As recorded and notated on folio 124 of the manuscript, the chants guide the gathered community through the process of taking leave of a sister. The responsory begins by entreating the heavenly community for help; through its performance, the community at the bedside requests specific assistance for the dying sister. The first two lines of text address saints and angels, asking them to "advance" (*subuenite*) and "run" (*occurrite*) to her. The following lines explain specifically what these members of the heavenly community are

Music Transcription 4.1 (cont.)

expected to do: their role is to bridge the human and the heavenly realms by taking the soul of the dying sister to God—"offering it in the sight of the most high." With this text, the chant offers the community a way to petition on behalf of the suffering person in their midst.

The chant's music contributes to the textual images as it conveys them. Two participle phrases describe the activities of the heavenly community: *suscipientes animam eius* and *offerentes eam*. The musical setting draws connections between these actions and emphasizes them in performance. These two textual phrases are conveyed with the same melodic material (adapted to accommodate their differing numbers of syllables); in a performance of the chant, the melodic repetition associates the multiple actions the heavenly community accomplishes for the dying person's soul. Similarly, melodic repetition makes explicit the connection between the angels and the "most high." The final syllable of *angeli* and the word *domini* are conveyed with the same melodic material as the word *altissimi*. With this repetition, the melody draws associations among the different members of the heavenly community. The angels are portrayed as "angels of the Lord" not only in the text, but also in the melody. (This particular melodic repetition is not seen in the 1260 version. In the earlier version of the melody, the melodic gestures are similar, but not exact repetitions.) In these ways, the music animates the textual images for the ritual's listeners and participants as the responsory sounds in performance.

The musical aspects of the chant also elaborate on the textual image of the afterlife. After the text calls upon the saints and angels, it references the soul in the presence of the most high (*in conspectu altissimi*); the melody embellishes this image by creating a distinctive expanse of sound. The chant's lowest pitch conveys the word *in*; the melody then ascends from this low point while conveying the word *conspectu* and reaches the chant's highest pitch ("b-flat") with the word *altissimi*. The broad, sweeping melodic ascension occurs only in this one position in the chant. According to the melody, then, when the soul has ascended into the sight of the "most high," it inhabits a spacious and expansive place. The melody adds to the textual depiction of the soul's destination.

The process of leave-taking continues with the verse *Suscipiat*. This verse directly addresses a final blessing to the dying woman. In contrast to the preceding responsory, the verse's text refers to the dying person with a second-person pronoun. Rather than speaking *about* the dying person (as the narrative voice of the responsory does), the narrative voice of the verse speaks *to* her. The melody emphasizes this direct address by conveying the word *te* ("you") with an extended melisma—with eleven pitches, the longest heard in the chant until this point. Such emphasis of the word *te* shows an unusual use of this particular melody, which conveys other responsory verse texts as a standard, repeated melody (or *tone*) for Mode 4. Placing the melisma with the final syllable of the first word is a typical text underlay for this particular responsory verse melody.[16] In the verse *Suscipiat*, one would expect the melisma to convey the final syllable of the first word, *suscipiat*.

---

[16] As documented in the CANTUS database: University of Waterloo, "CANTUS: A Database for Latin Ecclesiastical Chant," https://cantus.uwaterloo.ca/melody (accessed July 6, 2022). The second verse of Music Transcription 4.1, *Requiem eternam*, offers a convenient example. It is conveyed with the same melody as *Suscipiat*, but the final syllable of the word *requiem* is conveyed with the melisma.

Conveying instead the word *te* (the second word of the verse's text) with the melisma alters the normal pattern of applying the melody to a text and offers the word extraordinary articulation in performance. With this elaborate ornamentation and emphasis of the word "you," the melody of *Suscipiat* brings attention to the act of directly addressing and blessing the dying person.

As the performance continues, the chant shifts from directly addressing the dying person to recalling the actions of the heavenly community. With a cue (*Susci<pientes>*), the scribal work indicates that a repetition of the final lines of the responsory follows the verse *Suscipiat*. The soul's sweeping ascent into "the sight of the most high" is heard again. In this way, the performance repeats the description of the dying person's soul leaving the human community. The increasing distance between the dying person and those surrounding the bedside is again articulated.

The performance of the second verse, *Requiem eternam*, completes the process of leave-taking. While the first verse emphasized a direct address to the dying person, this second verse emphasizes the soul's separation from human activity. An extended melisma of eleven pitches creates a single, melodic focal point of the word *requiem* ("rest"). This second verse also broadens the perspective beyond the individual in the deathbed. Rather than addressing "you" (as the narrative voice of the first verse does), the narrative voice of the second verse refers to "them" (*eis*). With the shift to plural, third-person pronouns, the performance no longer limits itself to the concern of a single soul. Instead, it prays to God on behalf of many: those who have died at different times. This final verse integrates the individual who has just died into the community of the deceased.

The performance ends with this broadened perspective. Customarily, each verse is followed by a cue, indicating a repetition of the responsory's ending. (This typical performance practice is seen after the first verse in Cranston 2322; it also appears after both verses in the 1260 version, as recorded in Newberry 24.[17]) Yet in the case of Cranston 2322, the scribe did not provide a cue after the second verse; a second return to the responsory is not prescribed. The lack of cue leaves some ambiguity regarding the intended performance practice. It is possible that the scribe omitted the cue, assuming that the users of the manuscript would follow the convention of repeating the end of the responsory. Yet it also seems possible that the lack of a written cue indicates an unusual performance practice—that of ending with the second

---

[17] Hild, "The Role of Music," 163.

responsory verse, without a second return to the responsory. One piece of evidence supporting this hypothesis comes from a careful comparison with the earlier, notated version of the chant complex in Newberry 24. The cues in this earlier manuscript indicate a return to the responsory after each of the two verses, but each cue directs singers to a *different* portion of the responsory. (The first cue directs singers to repeat the ending of the responsory from the word *suscipientes*, the second from the word *offerentes*.) Although the practice of repeating the ending of a responsory after a verse was customary, the nuanced technique of repeating from a *different* point after each verse was not. The scribe of Cranston 2322 probably would not have left such intricate details without a notated reference. Instead, it seems more likely that the scribal omission of the second cue in Cranston 2322 indicates that a second return to the responsory was not prescribed. The lack of cue likely indicates a lack of return.

Given the liturgical context, the extraordinary performance practice of ending the chant complex with the second verse would have carried special poignance. The community underwent a decisive change at the final breath of a sister. With the death, those gathered at the bedside did not experience a return to the situation that prompted an urgent cry for help to the heavenly community (heard in the responsory); they also did not experience a return to the situation in which they could directly address the dying person (as in the first verse). Repeating the end of the responsory or the first verse was perhaps understood to be neither necessary nor appropriate. From the perspective of those surrounding the bedside, the dying person had moved beyond the human community into the care of the heavenly. The chants both reflect and accompany the change. The prayer for peace for the deceased heard in the second verse, *Requiem eternam*, acknowledged the new reality and established the new relationship between the sister who had died and her sisters who were still living: they would pray on her behalf. In a performance of *Subuenite* and its verses, the community was guided through the transition that occurred with a sister's death.

Collective Responses to Death: *Kyrie* and Prayers

Kyrieleyson	Lord, have mercy
Christeleyson	Christ, have mercy
Kyrieleyson	Lord, have mercy

Pater noster	Our father...	Matthew 6
Et ne nos	And lead us not...	
RESPONSIO	RESPONSE	
Sed libera	But deliver...	
VERSUS	VERSE	cf. IV Esdras 2:34–35
Requiem eternam dona eis domine	Rest eternal give them, Lord	
RESPONSIO	RESPONSE	
Et lux perpetua	And light perpetual...	
VERSUS	VERSE	
A porta inferi	From the gate of hell...[18]	
RESPONSIO	RESPONSE	
Erue domine animam eius	Save, Lord, her soul...	
VERSUS	VERSE	
Requiescant in pace	May they rest in peace...	cf. Psalm 4:9
RESPONSIO	RESPONSE	
Amen	Amen	
VERSUS	VERSE	Psalm 101:2
Domine exaudi	Lord, hear...	
RESPONSIO	RESPONSE	
Et clamor	And let my outcry...	
ORACIO	PRAYER	
Tibi domine commendamus animam	To you, Lord, we commend the soul...	
RESPONSIO	RESPONSE	
Amen	Amen	

In contrast to the 1260 version, which includes the rubric "AFTERWARDS" (POSTEA),[19] the version of Cranston 2322 contains no rubric designating material specifically for the time after death. While the same items are

---

[18] Translation from Paxton, *The Death Ritual at Cluny*, 107.
[19] Van Dijk, *Sources*, 2:392.

prescribed in both versions, Cranston 2322 groups more items under the earlier rubric EGRESSA ANIMA DE CORPORE. Fewer rubrics probably gave the community—led by the cantrix—more flexibility to sing the material as it seemed appropriate for each individual's circumstances.

The material immediately following the chant complex *Subuenite* allowed the community to respond to the death collectively, since each item was customarily performed in alternation between a leader (in the case of the community of Aldgate, a cantrix) and others present.[20] The prayer *Kyrieleyson* continues the broadened perspective achieved in the performance of the previous chants. Rather than referring to a specific individual, the *Kyrie* offers a universal plea for mercy. As part of the daily liturgy of the Mass, this text would have been familiar. Yet the performance of the text varied, even in the daily liturgies; at times it was spoken, rather than sung, and sung performances made use of different melodies. In the ritual for the dying, the notation in Cranston 2322 (recorded on folio 124v) reveals a melody strikingly beautiful in its simplicity, symmetry, and balance (Music Transcription 4.2).

Kyrieleyson	Lord, have mercy
Christeleyson	Christ, have mercy
Kyrieleyson	Lord, have mercy

Music Transcription 4.2 *Kyrie* (Cranston 2322, f. 124v)

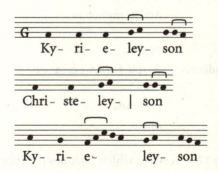

[20] Paxton's discussions and translations of these items occur in *The Death Ritual of Cluny*, 106–107, 112–113, and 166–167; and in *Christianizing Death*, 146 (especially note 66). The prayer *Tibi domine commendamus animam* appears in Sicard, *Liturgie*, 355–358; Paxton, *Christianizing Death*, 147 (especially note 71); Deshusses, *Le sacramentaire grégorien*, as number 1415; and Paxton, *The Death Ritual at Cluny*, 158–159.

The musical setting prioritizes a clear articulation of the text. The melody closely adheres to the text's three syntactic units, using three melodic gestures to convey them. The same arch-shaped gesture (beginning with the pitch "f," rising to "a," and descending again to "f") conveys the prayer's first two statements. The rising and falling gestures mimic a gentle breathing pattern as they define the boundaries of the first two syntactic units.

The musical setting of the third line creates an expansion and intensification of this restrained melodic material. With the first two lines of text, the melody moves only by step and conveys each syllable with only one, two, or three pitches. With the third line, however, a melisma conveys the third syllable with five pitches tracing leaps of thirds. The melodic ambitus, which in the first two lines had encompassed only a third (from "f" to "a"), extends upward in the third line, spanning a fifth (from "f" to "c"). Together, the greater ambitus, the inclusion of leaps, and the melisma create a sense of expansion. If the melody with the first two lines of text mimics gentle breathing, the melody with the third line breathes more deeply. The chant ends by settling to "f," the pitch that began the setting and ended each of the first two gestures. In doing so, the melody conveys the three textual statements as a symmetrical whole.

As the community's collective responses to death continue with subsequent items, the ritual blurs the distinction between the individual woman who has just died, those who have died before, and those who are still living. The *Kyrie* is a general plea for mercy, which might encompass the deceased woman and her community, as well as those previously deceased. The *Pater noster*, as well, can be understood to draw into one community all who were present, as well as those who were not. The versicle *Requiem eternam* asks peace for "them"—in the context of the deathbed liturgy, a reference to the one who had just died as well as those who had died previously. The response *Erue domine* again asks for God's assistance for a single soul, "my soul"—a petition for (and in the voice of) the person who had just died, or for each individual present—while the following versicle, *Requiescant in pace*, asks for peace for multiple people. The prayer that concludes this section of the ritual, *Tibi domine commendamus animam*, returns to the singular, feminine forms referring to the deceased person. So after praying for a broad community of those who were present at the deathbed and those who had died before, the ritual returns its focus to the single woman whose death was most recent. With these varied references, the ritual draws connections between the living and the dead. Death is defined as an experience common to all, and the community performing the ritual is reminded of their shared mortality.

The most notable aspect of this portion of the ritual is what it lacks. The Franciscan version from 1260 includes the versicle customarily performed by a priest and responded to by the gathered community: *Dominus vobiscum / Et cum spiritu tuo*. In fact, every ritual examined in this book—with the exception of the ritual of Aldgate—includes this versicle and response. That the ritual from Aldgate omits them, while otherwise duplicating the 1260 version, gives very strong indications that the scribe who created Cranston 2322 expected that the women would conduct this liturgy with no priest present.

The Liturgy Continues: Preparing and Surrounding the Body

TUNC SORORES QUE PRESENS FUERINT[21] LAUENT CORPUS ET POSTEA PONANT IN FERETRO ET SORORES STENT ORDINATIM IN CIRCUITU FERETRI IUXTA DISPOSICIONEM MAIORIS INCIPIENTE ABBATISSA	THEN THE SISTERS WHO WERE PRESENT SHOULD WASH THE BODY AND AFTERWARDS LAY IT UPON THE BIER AND THE SISTERS SHOULD STAND IN A CIRCLE NEXT TO THE BIER IN ORDER OF RANK BEGINNING WITH THE ABBESS	
Kyrieleyson Christeleyson Kyrieleyson	Lord, have mercy Christ, have mercy Lord, have mercy	
Pater noster RESPONSIO Sed libera	Our father... RESPONSE But deliver...	Matthew 6
VERSUS In memoria eterna erit iusta RESPONSIO Ab auditione mala non timebit	VERSE The just woman will be in eternal remembrance RESPONSE On hearing evil she will not be afraid	Psalm 111:7

---

[21] QUE PRESENS FUERINT] more plausible would be QUE PRESENTES FUERINT.

AMONG WOMEN 129

VERSUS	VERSE	
Ne tradas domine bestiis animam confitentem tibi	Do not deliver to the beasts the soul that confesses you	Psalm 73:19
RESPONSIO	RESPONSE	
Et animas pauperum tuorum ne obliuiscaris in finem	And the souls of your poor do not forget in the end	
VERSUS	VERSE	
Non intres in iudicium cum ancilla tua domine	Do not come into judgment with your handmaid, Lord	cf. Psalm 142: 2[22]
RESPONSIO	RESPONSE	
Quia non iustificabitur	For no living thing is acquitted ...	
VERSUS	VERSE	
A porta inferi	From the gate of hell[23]	
RESPONSIO	RESPONSE	
Erue domine animam meam	Save, Lord, my soul	
VERSUS	VERSE	
Requiescant in pace	Let them rest in peace	cf. Psalm 4:9
RESPONSIO	RESPONSE	
Amen	Amen	
VERSUS	VERSE	
Domine exaudi oracionem	Lord, O hear my prayer ...	Psalm 101:2
RESPONSIO	RESPONSE	
Et clamor	And let my outcry ...[24]	
ORACIO	PRAYER	
Suscipe domine animam famule tue sororis nostre quam de ergastulo	Receive, Lord, the soul of your servant, our sister, which you ... from the prison of this world ...[25]	
RESPONSIO	RESPONSE	
Amen	Amen	

---

[22] Translations based on Alter, *The Hebrew Bible*, 3:324.
[23] Translation from Paxton, *The Death Ritual at Cluny*, 107.
[24] Translation from Alter, *The Hebrew Bible*, 3:236 (as Psalm 102).
[25] Translation based on Paxton, *The Death Ritual at Cluny*, 108–109.

The following rubric adds to the image of the self-sufficient women of Aldgate: the sisters are directed to wash the body, move it to a bier, and then order themselves, by rank, around the corpse. The abbess is named as the summit of this hierarchy. Were a priest expected to be present, his role would likely have been mentioned and his place in the group specified (as it is in the 1260 version of the ritual). This rubric in Cranston 2322 depicts a group of women who, having been present at the deathbed, now prepare the body and continue the liturgy with the corpse at the center.

This all-female image is again confirmed by the second omission of the versicle and response *Dominus vobiscum / Et cum spiritu tuo*. Although it is present at this point in the version of 1260, it is again absent in the version of Cranston 2322. The scribal work in the manuscript from Aldgate repeatedly indicates that a priest was not expected to be present; the ritual is written in a way that allows the women of Aldgate to perform it independently.

This portion of the ritual in Cranston 2322 shows other adaptations for the community of women. Washing and moving the body was a task assigned to the sisters who had been present at the death. The rubric indicates that the attending sisters share the responsibility, while in the Franciscan version of 1260, these tasks are assigned to the brothers who had been directed to complete them (FRATRES QUIBUS PRECEPTUM).[26] The rubric has been altered for the community of Aldgate.

In Cranston 2322, even the texts of the versicles are modified to make them appropriate for women: *In memoria eterna erit iustus* is changed to reference a single female as *In memoria eterna erit iusta*; the versicle *Non intres in iudicium cum servo tuo* reads in Cranston 2322 as *Non intres in iudicium cum ancilla tua*. The manuscript contains a ritual version that was thoroughly adapted for the use of women, without exempting the minor texts of versicles.

With this portion of the ritual (as seen with the earlier versicles and responses), the distinction between the living and the dead blurs. The community performing the versicle and response *A porta inferi / Erue domine animam meam* could be understood to be taking on the voice of the deceased individual or praying for themselves ("From the gate of hell / Save, Lord, my soul"), while the following versicle and response entreats on behalf of multiple deceased individuals: *Requiescant in pace / Amen* ("May they rest in peace"). Other items specifically refer to the recently deceased woman, like the prayer *Suscipe domine animam famule tue sororis nostre* ("Receive,

---

[26] Van Dijk, *Sources*, 2:393.

Lord, the soul of your servant, our sister") and the versicle and response *In memoria eterna erit iusta / Ab auditione mala non timebit* ("The just woman will be in eternal remembrance / On hearing evil she will not be afraid"). The liturgy conducted at the death of an individual sister functioned—in these moments—as a commemorative service for those previously deceased, and as a petition for those who were still alive. From the ritual's perspective, the living and the deceased have the same needs of God.

Moving the Body to the Church

Deinde sorores portent corpus ad ecclesiam decantando	Then the sisters carry the body to the church singing	
Responsorium	Responsory	
Subuenite	Advance...	
Versus	Verse	
Suscipiat	May Christ receive...	cf. Luke 16:22

The final rubric for this portion of the ritual again indicates the competence and self-sufficiency attributed to the women of Aldgate. The wording directs the sisters to carry the body to the church themselves, accompanied by the responsory *Subuenite* and its verse *Suscipiat*. The rubric and the chant assignments speak to a community that was able to accomplish the physical task of moving a corpse even while performing a complex and intricate liturgy. The ritual for the death of a community member, as recorded in Cranston 2322, could have been conducted without involving anyone outside of the community. In their deathbed ritual, the women of Aldgate are the liturgical equals of their male counterparts in the Franciscan Order.

Conclusion: Conducting the Deathbed Ritual within the Boundaries of the Rule

Cranston 2322 provides a version of the Franciscan deathbed ritual that the women of Aldgate could have performed with no outside involvement. But did they? An examination of Bodleian 585—the manuscript contemporaneous with Cranston 2322 containing a copy of the community's rule—offers another way to consider how self-sufficient the women of Aldgate might have been at the time of a sister's death.[27] The rule prescribes guidelines concerning visiting friars and priests. Male religious authorities were allowed to engage with sisters only in limited and carefully controlled situations:

> When any of the sisters being grievously sick—that she is not able to come to the parlor to be confessed or to receive God's body or other sacraments of the holy church—then her confessor arrayed in vestments belonging to a priest except the chasuble shall enter within, and his fellow vested all in white, that then the sick sister confess here in such manner that three other sisters be so near that they may see the same confessor and also she who is confessed. And when the confession shall be heard or any other sacrament ministered, just as they come in vested, so go they out, nor dwell they therein, nor with any other sister speak, but in foresaid manner. And also when any commendation shall be done for souls of sisters, or obsequies for any of them dead, two friar minors or priests priors or three, when the body is brought to internment, shall enter vested with ornaments belonging to a priest, and they for to do all that belongs to a priest in such case. And be they always together all the time that they shall be occupied about the execution of the same office, and that fulfilled, to depart then without tarrying.[28]

This passage of the rule lays out strict guidelines for the presence of men within the community's living quarters. When a sister was too sick to come to a common area, her confessor could go to her, appropriately vested and accompanied by a companion, with three other sisters standing near enough to see both the confessor and the sick sister. At the end of the confession (or other sacrament), the confessor and his companion are instructed to depart without speaking to any other sisters. In this position, the rule provides for a friar or priest to administer the sacraments to a sister who is seriously ill, but it describes them as being administered apart from the ritual at the deathbed.

Regarding the ritual at the deathbed itself, the rule is ambiguous. It states that friars and priests may be present "whan any comendacioun schal be done for sowlis of Sustris" and for funeral services. This phrase "when any

---

[27] See above, note 6.
[28] Edited in the original language by Seton, "The Rewle of Sustris Menouresses," 90–91. My thanks to Anne Bagnall Yardley for her thoughts on the translation of this passage.

commendation shall be done for souls of sisters" is unclear. It could refer to the ritual conducted at the deathbed, but the phrase was also used to refer to the end of the burial ritual or, more generally, to commemorative services for those who were already deceased.[29] Yardley notes that rituals for the dying also came to be used as commemorative services,[30] and the above examination documents how the deathbed ritual in Cranston 2322 blurs the distinctions between the dying individual and others previously deceased. The liturgy might have been appropriately performed at times other than an individual's death. In short, the community's rule states that friars and priests are allowed to be present to commend the souls of sisters, but it does not clarify precisely which liturgy is being referred to.

Even if the rule is interpreted as allowing the presence of friars and priests at the deathbed ritual, it does not indicate their participation for a correct performance. The sentence mentioning the "commendation of souls" is included in a section whose purpose is to severely restrict the presence of men in the women's areas, not to regulate the women's performance of the liturgy. In other words, the rule governing Aldgate might be interpreted as permitting the community to admit friars or priests for the deathbed ritual, but it does not prescribe their presence.

Combine this with the evidence of Cranston 2322: as it is recorded in the manuscript, no part of the ritual requires the presence of a friar or priest. Neither confession nor *viaticum* is included. The 1260 version separates both of these sacraments from the liturgy for the final moments of life, and the ritual in Cranston 2322 follows suit.[31] Furthermore, the rubrics in Cranston 2322 specifically indicate that several aspects of the ritual—including the manual labor of moving the body—should be completed by the sisters. As it appears in Cranston 2322, the ritual does not once mention a priest or friar, or any responsibility—liturgical or otherwise—that would necessitate the presence of an outsider to the community. So although the rule could be interpreted as allowing the presence of a friar or priest at the deathbed, the ritual—as it is recorded in Cranston 2322—does not necessitate it. The manuscript presents a ritual that could be conducted entirely by the women themselves.

---

[29] For the historic uses of the term *Commendatio animae*, see Paxton, *Christianizing Death*, especially 116 and 130–131.
[30] Yardley, "Clares in Procession," 14, note 60.
[31] See Donohue on the change from a *ritus continuus* to three separate rites, with *viaticum* included in the rite for the communion of the sick, rather than in the rite for the moment of death: "The Rite," esp. 207–213.

While evidence does not exist to prove conclusively that the sisters conducted the deathbed ritual by themselves, the abbey's surviving documents suggest that they were capable of doing so. Both the rule and its appendix in Bodleian 585 depict a community with educated and skilled cantrices—sisters who could lead the community's liturgical music, making use of books such as Cranston 2322. The rule recommends that the community sing the Franciscan liturgies and train incoming sisters in singing;[32] the appendix outlines practices like singing psalms in alternation, under the leadership of a cantrix. Cranston 2322 is the type of document that such a capable cantrix—and a self-sufficient community—would have relied upon.

If the women of Aldgate conducted the ritual without a priest, as a close reading of their manuscripts suggests, they were participating in a change that was also occurring throughout the English lay population. In her study on the development of vernacular deathbed rites in England from 1380 to 1540, Appleford shows the ways in which these rites increased lay participation at the deathbed, and even allowed for their performance without a priest.[33] The dating of Cranston 2322 to the second half of the fifteenth century suggests that its deathbed rite, even while maintaining the Latin text, was modified with similar intentions: "in order to allow a lay reader to conduct a version of the ritual in his or her own right, imitating the role of the officiating priest."[34]

Not only did the manuscript Cranston 2322 provide the women of Aldgate a resource for the performance of the deathbed ritual, it also seems to have served its purpose. Discoloration on the lower, outer corners of the folios containing the material for the time of death suggest that the manuscript was used either as an aid in preparation or during the ritual itself. Indeed, the book is small enough to have been easily held while the ritual was occurring. Discoloration is especially prevalent on the pages containing the litany at the ritual's beginning and the notated version of *Subuenite*. As noted in the above discussion, the chant complex *Subuenite–Suscipiat* was prescribed multiple times in the ritual but notated only once (with the material designated for the time period after the funeral Mass). The prominent discoloration on the outer edge of the folio containing the chant notation suggests that it offered useful information to those using the manuscript. The cantrix might have held her hand in that position in order to easily reference the music notation

---

[32] See above, note 5.
[33] Amy Appleford, *Learning to Die in London, 1380–1540* (Philadelphia: University of Pennsylvania Press, 2015).
[34] Ibid., 14.

during earlier stages of the ritual, where the scribe provided only abbreviated, non-notated versions.

Thus, the contents of Cranston 2322 likely offer insights into the community's liturgical practices with the dying; they also speak to an ongoing area of scholarship that considers women's religious communities in the Middle Ages. The deathbed ritual of Cranston 2322 indicates that the practice of the liturgy provided some areas of autonomy for the women of Aldgate. While the rite for the dying contained in Cranston 2322 is largely based on the earlier, widely transmitted version from 1260, it reveals details of implementation that are specific to the women's community. As it is recorded in the manuscript, the liturgy has been carefully thought through and adapted for the sole use of women.

Furthermore, Cranston 2322 indicates that members of the community performed the deathbed rite for one another, rather than relying on the leadership of a male cleric or friar. This finding echoes the scholarship of Bugyis, which examines the types of pastoral care women provided to one another in Benedictine communities in the tenth through thirteenth centuries. In her work, Bugyis examines religious women "not as the passive recipients of sacerdotal ministrations, but as the primary agents of their spiritual and material care."[35] The women of Aldgate, performing the rite for the dying without the presence of a male cleric, provide an additional example of the phenomenon documented in Bugyis's research: "nuns' performances of ministries that have traditionally retained more discernibly sacerdotal or sacramental casts."[36] Where historians might assume or expect the involvement of a priest or friar, we instead find women acting independently as they minister to one another. Cranston 2322 provides further evidence of the phenomenon Bugyis researches, and it also suggests that women's care for one another in liturgical and ministerial roles reached beyond the boundaries of specific religious rules and orders. Cranston 2322 demonstrates for a Franciscan community what Bugyis has documented in communities following the Benedictine Rule.[37]

---

[35] Bugyis, *The Care of Nuns*, 10.
[36] Ibid., 291.
[37] Bugyis herself expected more instances of the phenomenon to surface. The author closes her large-scale investigation of Benedictine communities by stating: "Close studies of the extant documents of practice and other material remains from other women's communities in England during the late Middle Ages may yet unveil more ministers of Christ, charged with the *cura* of fellow sisters and others who sought their hospitality, counsel, instruction, healing, absolution, and intercession. We need only to keep searching for them" (*Care of Nuns*, 296).

136 MUSIC IN MEDIEVAL RITUALS FOR THE END OF LIFE

In sum, a close examination of Cranston 2322 and its ritual for the dying provides clear impressions of the women of Aldgate: ministering to one another at the time of death, rather than waiting for outside assistance; performing the liturgy prescribed by their Order, rather than resorting to simpler alternatives; and tailoring the liturgy specifically for women, making use of thoughtfully created documents to do so.

5
Analysis
Variation and Continuity within the Liturgical Tradition

Each of the previous chapters examines a single ritual as an entity that provides insight into the liturgical ideals (and perhaps the liturgical practices) of a specific community at the time of an individual's death. Comparing these rituals—considering them in the light of one another—helps to respond to the queries of historians who have previously engaged with the material. Such a comparison also reveals how the deathbed rituals engage questions of current interest in the broader scholarly community. These questions now provide a framework for analytical reflection:

1. Were the chants prescribed in the rituals for the dying borrowed from other liturgies, or were they created specifically for the time of an individual's death?
2. Is there a particular ritual (and accompanying chant repertory) that seems to have originated in Rome? To what extent is it possible to determine the practice (or practices) of the medieval Roman church?
3. To what extent did specific geographical areas and institutions maintain their own versions of the deathbed rituals? Conversely, to what extent did standardization across geographical areas occur?
4. Individual rituals show great variation in the items they prescribe and the order in which these items appear. But even with these variations, what commonalities exist among rituals?
5. What do the deathbed rituals tell us about images and conceptions of the afterlife during the Middle Ages?
6. In what ways do the chants of the deathbed rituals inform our understanding of the possible relationships between music and text in plainchant repertories?

Distinctive Chant Repertories?

Evidence suggests that distinctive chant repertories were developed for the deathbed rites. Rather than being borrowed from other liturgies, such as the Office of the Dead, many of the chants sung at the deathbed seem to have been created specifically for the end of life. An examination of the earliest extant sources for both the deathbed rites (liturgies performed on behalf of an individual person during the final agony) and the Office of the Dead (liturgies commemorating the deceased as part of regularly occurring services) helps to understand the development of these chant repertories. The earliest extant sources containing rites for a sick, dying, or recently deceased individual date from the end of the eighth century; the earliest liturgical sources for the Office of the Dead date to around fifty years later, in the mid-ninth century. Because these sources do not contain legible music notation, they appear only peripherally in previous chapters. But in order to determine the extent to which the chant repertories in the deathbed liturgies were distinct and unique, it is worth considering the relationship between these two types of liturgies and the chants they incorporate.

A close investigation of these sources indicates the following: first, the earliest manuscripts containing rites for a sick, dying, or recently deceased individual reveal four *different* repertories; the developments and changes that Paxton traces in the rituals throughout the early Middle Ages are evident in their chants. Changing centers of influence, as well as changing theological understandings, resulted in differing musical content. Second, the Office of the Dead seems to have had multiple beginnings. The desire to commemorate and offer spiritual assistance to the souls of the deceased took different forms, and made use of different chants, in different institutions. Third, the time period between the death of an individual and his or her burial began to be liturgically structured and prescribed with numerous chants around the mid-ninth century. These are the sources—those with extensive prescriptions for the vigil with the body, during the night before burial—that reveal commonalities, and shared chant repertories, with the earliest sources of the Office of the Dead. (Table 5.1 lists, chronologically, the manuscript sources under consideration. Table 5.2 shows the same sources, categorized according to the four different repertories they contain.)

Table 5.1 The earliest sources containing chant repertories in rites for a sick, dying, or recently deceased individual and commemorative liturgies[a]

	sickness	agony	death	death – burial	burial	after burial	commemorative liturgies
775							St Gall 349
		Berlin 1667 ------>					letter: Monte Cassino[b]
800			Hadrianum supplement *Hucusque*[c]	Rheinau 30 ------>			letter: Fulda[d] Aachen reforms[e] letter: Reichenau[f]
825	Paris 12050						
850	Dublin 60 Le Mans 77 New York G 57 Vatican 485 ------> Leningrad Q.v.I.41 Reims 213		München 29164 ------>		------> ------>	------>	Trier 1245/597

(continued)

Table 5.1 Continued

	sickness	agony	death	death – burial	burial	after burial	commemorative liturgies
875		Paris 2290 --------->	--------->	--------->	--------->		
	Paris 2291 Stockholm A 136 --------->	--------->	--------->	--------->	--------->	--------->	
			Vatican 550 --------->	--------->	--------->	--------->	
				Paris 2984 --------->	--------->	--------->	Albi 44
900							

[a] Each manuscript's complete shelf mark can be found in the Index: Manuscripts Cited (with Abbreviations).
[b] Hallinger, *Initia*, 136.
[c] Deshusses, *Le sacramentaire grégorien*, 1:459.
[d] Hallinger, *Initia*, 321.
[e] Ibid., 460.
[f] Ibid., 336.

Table 5.2 Chant repertories in eighth- and ninth-century sources[a]

	1	2	3	4
	sources from 750–810: Frankish use of purportedly Roman material[b]	sources from 800–850: Benedict of Aniane	sources from 800–850: commemorative services	sources from 850–900
manuscript sources	Berlin 1667 Rheinau 30 St Gall 349	Hadrianum supplement *Hucusque* Paris 12050	Monte Cassino letter Fulda letter Aachen reforms Reichenau letter	Dublin 60 München 29164 Trier 1245/597 Le Mans 77 New York G 57 Vatican 485 Leningrad Q.v.I.41 Reims 213 Paris 2290 Paris 2291 Stockholm A 136 Vatican 550 Paris 2984 Albi 44
total chants	12 antiphons 10 psalms	3 specified antiphons 1 versus 1 hymn	1 specified antiphon 2 specified psalms	71 specified antiphons 44 psalms 34 responsories 38 responsory verses 1 hymn 5 versus

[a] Each manuscript's complete shelf mark can be found in the Index: Manuscripts Cited (with Abbreviations).
[b] From Andrieu's *Ordo XLIX* and *XV*: Andrieu, *Les ordines*, 3:121–122 and 4:523–530.

Repertory 1: Franks Develop Rituals for the Final Agony, Incorporating Roman Elements

The first repertory is found in the earliest sources containing developed rites for a sick or dying individual; these rites reveal an intertwining of Frankish and Roman elements.[1] Scholars agree that the late eighth- and early ninth-century sacramentaries Berlin 1667 and Zürich, Zentralbibliothek, Ms Rh 30 (Rheinau 30), were created and used in Frankish territory: in Autun, France, and St Gall or Reichenau, respectively. The acute concern for the dying person that prompted the creation of such rituals seems to have been Frankish. In particular, the understanding that the community of the living, by performing religious and liturgical acts, could assist the soul during and after death, became pronounced in Frankish territories in the late eighth century.[2]

Yet Roman elements are also evident. The sung material in these early rituals asserts a theological confidence and trust that scholars associate more with the Roman church of the late Antiquity and less with the Frankish territories of the eighth and ninth centuries. As Paxton puts it, the chants and selected psalms are "infused with a spirit of optimism concerning the salvation of Christians and the resurrection of the dead."[3] The chants in these rituals include the antiphons *Aperite mihi portas* ("Open the gates of justice to me. I will enter them."[4]) and *Tu iussisti nasci me* ("You ordered me to be born, Lord. You promised that I would rise again"). The psalms of these rituals include number 117: "Confess to the Lord, for he is good, for his mercy is forever."[5]

Additional evidence of this particularly confident attitude in the face of death, associated with Rome, occurs in an eighth-century manuscript held in St Gall (Sankt Gallen, Stiftsbibliothek, Cod. Sang. 349, hereafter St Gall 349). After the rubric "Ad agendas uero mortuorum," an antiphon and psalm verse are listed, first for the introit of a Mass, and then for the communion.[6] The

---

[1] The sources and rites containing this early repertory are described in Paxton, *Christianizing Death*, 92–127.
[2] Ibid., 120 and 126.
[3] Ibid., 38.
[4] The antiphon's text is edited from Cluniac documents and translated by Paxton, *The Death Ritual at Cluny*, 134–135.
[5] Translation from ibid.
[6] St Gall 349, p. 93. Images of the manuscript are available online through University of Fribourg, "E-codices," accessed February 22, 2021, at e-codices.unifr.ch/en/list/one/csg/0349. See also Sicard, *Liturgie*, 78; and Andrieu, *Les ordines*, 3:121–122.

chants are not the same as those contained in the two sources mentioned in the previous paragraphs, but they bear strong similarities. In St Gall 349, *De terra formasti nos* ("From the earth you formed us") strongly echoes the antiphon text *De terra formasti me* ("From the earth you formed me") in the two sources previously examined. The psalm assignment in St Gall 349 differs from those in the other sources but maintains the same intimacy and confidence toward God: Psalm 64 reads, "to you all flesh comes."

Repertory 2: Benedict of Aniane

The second chant repertory evident in these early sources reflects Carolingian reform impulses from the first half of the ninth century, as well as the influence of one particular person, Benedict of Aniane.[7] Scholars have identified Benedict of Aniane as the compiler of the rites for the sick and dying that are most closely associated with the reform attempts of the Carolingian empire. (These are the rite for the time of death within the *Hucusque* supplement to the Hadrianum and the rite for anointing the sick within the Sacramentary of Rodradus.[8]) These rites differ dramatically from those of the eighth-century sources examined in the previous paragraphs. Gone are the assured requests of God and the optimistic confidence; newly apparent is a legal language that emphasizes "personal guilt and responsibility."[9] Benedict included only a bare minimum of sung material in these rites, and this material contains none of the chants seen in earlier sources. For a dying individual, Benedict prescribes only a series of prayers and indicates that psalms should be sung at the moment of death; the psalms are not specified. Benedict's rite for a sick individual contains slightly more melodic material: three antiphons

---

[7] The sources and rituals containing this chant repertory are described in Paxton, *Christianizing Death*, 128–161.

[8] The rite for the time of death is discussed in ibid., 138–148, and edited by Deshusses, *Le sacramentaire grégorien*, 1:457–461. Benedict of Aniane's role in compiling and editing the rite for the dying in the *Hucusque* supplement was established by Deshusses: "Le 'supplement'"; see also *Le sacramentaire grégorien*, 1:66–70 and 3:66–75. The rite for the sick is edited by Deshusses, *Le sacramentaire grégorien*, 3:145–146. Paxton attributes the compilation of the rite for the sick to Benedict of Aniane on the basis of the following evidence: the inclusion of Visigothic material, Benedict's close association with the reforms under Louis the Pious, and the formulations of the texts, which resemble those of the rite for the dying in the *Hucusque* supplement (*Christianizing Death*, 148–154).

[9] "By introducing terms with legal connotations ... Benedict brought a new element of personal guilt and responsibility into the penitential quality of the prayers for the dead" (Paxton, *Christianizing Death*, 140).

and a versicle. The limited transmissions of these chants lend support for two scholarly understandings: first, that Benedict of Aniane was responsible for its compilation (two of the chants he included are seen otherwise only in manuscripts from his home Visigothic region); and second, that the rite remained narrowly disseminated and fairly un-influential, in spite of its association with the most powerful circles of Carolingian leadership.[10]

In summary, the rituals for the sick and dying associated with the Carolingian reforms of the first half of the ninth century tend in a different direction than do earlier versions. A much more limited repertory of chants, possibly of Visigothic origin, and a new emphasis on individual repentance and personal guilt are hallmarks of Benedict of Aniane's work.

Repertory 3: Early Commemorative Liturgies for the Dead

During the same time period that Benedict of Aniane was compiling new versions of the bedside rituals, a related liturgy was taking shape in Frankish territories. From the end of the eighth century and the beginning of the ninth century, we have indications, primarily in letters, that religious communities were beginning to develop liturgies on behalf of the deceased.[11] These liturgies differed from the deathbed rites because they were celebrated in the course of regular monastic services, apart from the death of any specific individual. Scholars consider these commemorative activities to be forerunners of the fully developed Office of the Dead.

The sources reveal great variation in these early commemorations of the dead. A letter from the monks of Monte Cassino indicates that they included Psalm 50, the quintessential psalm of penitence, at each Office service on behalf of the deceased.[12] Psalm 50 is designated as the song of David, when the prophet Nathan confronts him with his offenses; the psalm begins with

---

[10] Each of the three antiphon incipits indicated in the rite has an extremely limited number of concordances in the Cantus Index database. The manuscripts the antiphons appear in are associated with the Old Hispanic tradition or with the region of southwestern France. That the ritual's versicle text (*Deus deorum dominus locutus est*) would have a wider transmission is not surprising, based as it is on the opening verses of Psalm 49. The widespread use of this biblical text likely has little to do with its inclusion in Benedict's ritual. University of Waterloo, "Cantus Index: Online Catalogue for Mass and Office Chants" (Debra Lacoste, project manager), accessed March 10, 2022, at http://cantusindex.org/home.

[11] These forms of commemoration are discussed in Paxton, *Christianizing Death*, 134–138.

[12] The letter is edited by Kassius Hallinger, *Initia consuetudinis Benedictinae: Consuetudines saeculi octavi et noni* (Siegburg: F. Schmitt, 1963), 136, and discussed in Paxton, *Christianizing Death*, 134.

a plea: "Have mercy on me, God." With this psalm, the monks of Monte Cassino rearticulated the voice of a soul in extreme need, a soul that feels itself deserving of condemnation in the face of judgment. The choice echoes the work of Benedict of Aniane with its emphasis on personal guilt, particular judgment, and the soul's need for generosity and leniency. In contrast, a letter from the monks of Fulda indicates that they chose more positive, confident sung material in their liturgies for the deceased. Psalm 64 begins, "A hymn is appropriate for you, O God . . . all flesh comes to you." Their antiphon text was *Requiem aeternam* ("Give them eternal rest, Lord"). These texts recall the simple confidence of the earliest chants examined above as Repertory 1.

The contrast between Fulda's sung material and that of Monte Cassino indicates that the earliest, sung liturgies commemorating the deceased did not stem from a single understanding or model; rather, the liturgies of different institutions diverged in their sung material and, it would appear, in their level of confidence concerning the salvation of the souls of the deceased.

Repertory 4: Further Development of the Deathbed Rites and Commemorations of the Dead

The fourth repertory—greatly expanded from those just discussed—appears in sources from the second half of the ninth century. From this time period, a proliferation of extant manuscripts containing liturgies for the sickness, death, and burial of an individual appear; furthermore, these liturgies contain a proliferation of sung material. As one example, the manuscript Vatican 550 prescribes over 150 chants for the rituals accompanying the agony, death, post-mortem cleansing of the body, transportation of the corpse, and the services of Matins and Lauds between death and burial. From the second half of the ninth century we also have the earliest liturgical manuscripts containing Offices of the Dead: the manuscripts Trier 1245/597 and Albi 44 include Matins responsories and Lauds antiphons for liturgical commemorations of the deceased, unconnected to the death or burial rites of individuals.[13]

---

[13] Trier, Wissenschaftliche Bibliothek der Stadt Trier, Hs. 1245/597 8', and Albi, Bibliothèque municipale Rochegude 44.

These mid- to late-ninth-century sources reveal that liturgies were further developed by monastic communities outside of Rome. The greatly expanded repertories contained in these sources—together over 200 chants—bring us into more familiar scholarly territory. The responsories in these sources form about a third of those found in Ottosen's monumental study, *The Responsories and Versicles of the Latin Office of the Dead*.[14] Scholars have used these responsories, and the order in which they were written, to help determine where manuscripts were created and used. These are the sources in which one can see a shared repertory: chants used both in the rites for specific individuals (at the end of life) and for commemorations of the deceased (celebrated as regularly occurring services).

In summary, an investigation of early sources allows us to securely assert the following: first, the rites for a dying individual and the Office of the Dead developed in the same environments (the monastic institutions of Frankish territories) and from the same understandings (that the community of the living could assist the souls of the deceased with liturgical acts). Second, these liturgies developed around the same time period, with the rites for dying individuals evident in slightly earlier manuscript sources (from the late eighth century). Beginning in the mid-ninth century, the rites for dying and recently deceased individuals began to prescribe more extensive numbers of chants and psalms for the vigil with the body in the night before burial; the earliest extant liturgical sources containing the Office of the Dead also date from the mid-ninth century. Third, some chants appear both in rites for dying individuals and in early versions of the Office of the Dead. For instance, *Subvenite* is prescribed for the moment of death in an eighth-century witness to the *Ordo XLIX* tradition (Berlin 1667), but it also appears in Vatican 550 (from the second half of the ninth century), prescribed for the time before burial, when the body laid in the church. The chant also appears in numerous later sources as part of the Office of the Dead. The exchange of chants between these two types of liturgies might have gone in the other direction, as well. Seven chants in the Old Roman ritual for the dying (SP F 11) appear in earlier, ninth-century sources, assigned to different liturgical positions, such as the Office service of Lauds (Table 5.3). The Office of the

---

[14] Ottosen, *Responsories*, is also available online as an interactive databank: Universität Regensburg, "Cantus planus: Responsories of the Latin Office of the Dead," accessed February 22, 2021, at https://www-app.uni-regensburg.de/Fakultaeten/PKGG/Musikwissenschaft/Cantus/Ottosen/index.html.

Table 5.3 Transmission of chants prescribed in the deathbed ritual of SP F 11[a]

	Textual transmission		Melodic transmission	
	Non-Roman ninth-century sources[b]	CAO[c]	Concordant melodies[d]	Old Roman melodic types[e]
Dirige domine	München 29164 Paris 2984 Vatican 550 Albi 44	CAO 2244	–	–
Secundum magnam ... et exultabunt	–	–	–	opening gesture: G 14
Domine deus in multitudine	Vatican 550	–	–	–
Conuertere domine	München 29164 Paris 2984 Vatican 550 Albi 44	CAO 1921	–	opening gesture: G 14 short melisma: G 10
Nequando rapiat	München 29164 Paris 2984 Vatican 550 Albi 44	CAO 3875	–	opening gesture: G 14
Dextera tua ... anima mea	–	–	–	–
Dominus suscepit me	–	–	–	–
Redemisti me	München 29164 Vatican 550	CAO 4585	–	entire melody: D 2 series i
Animam eius	–	–	–	–
Leto animo ... iussio tua	–	CAO 3573 (M)	–	–
Qui cognoscis	–	CAO 4461 (E)	SP B 79 (also Old Roman)	–
Svscipiat te Christus	Vatican 550	CAO 5092 (M, H)	–	opening gesture: D 2 series ii
Induc eum domine	Vatican 550	–	SP B 79 (also Old Roman)	opening gesture: D 2 series ii

[a] Each manuscript's complete shelf mark can be found in the Index: Manuscripts Cited (with Abbreviations).
[b] In these sources, the chant is not necessarily assigned to the same liturgical position as in SP F 11.
[c] Hesbert, *CAO*.
[d] As documented in the CANTUS database: University of Waterloo, "CANTUS."
[e] Melodic types evident in Old Roman Office antiphons, as documented in Nowacki, "Studies on the Office Antiphons."

Dead and the rites for the dying developed from common roots in common environments, and they share some melodic material.[15]

Yet some chants in the rites for the dying stand out from this common repertory. The eighth-century dating for the earliest sources of deathbed rituals suggests strongly that the chants they contain were created specifically for the time of an individual's death. Because these manuscripts predate the first sources of the Office of the Dead, their chants likely were not borrowed from such commemorative liturgies. The chants that appear in the deathbed rite in Berlin 1667, including *Tu iussisti nasci me*, *Subvenite*, *Suscipiat te Christus*, and *Chorus angelorum*, seem to have been developed expressly for the liturgies conducted at the bedside of a dying individual.

It is also important to note that the rites for the dying and the Office of the Dead have chants they do *not* hold in common. As seen in the previous chapters, the chant repertories prescribed for the deathbed liturgies remained limited to the older, optimistic chants from the *Ordo XLIX* tradition and, in the Old Roman ritual of SP F 11, other chants that most often convey the same spirit of confidence and trust. While the repertories sung at the bedsides of dying individuals did not remain completely distinct from the repertories of the Office of the Dead, they did remain distinctively optimistic concerning the salvation of the soul.

Determining the Practice(s) of Rome

One question arises immediately when comparing the rituals of the previous chapters: what was the practice of Rome? Can any one of these rituals, or any chant repertory contained within them, be identified as an authoritative prescription, or even as a product, of the Roman church? Two different deathbed rituals, containing two distinct chant repertories, have been understood to reflect Roman practice: Manuscript Paris 934 (Chapter 2) transmits the psalms and chants of the *Ordo XLIX* tradition, a widely transmitted repertory that scholars—primarily through the work of Andrieu and Sicard—consider to have originated in Rome. The ritual found in SP F 11 (Chapter 1) is also associated with Rome: scholarly consensus firmly places the origins

---

[15] Ottosen is willing to assert a stronger connection. He argues that the Office of the Dead developed from the liturgies sung between the death and burial of an individual, which were repeated on anniversaries of the individual's death (*Responsories*, 42–44).

and provenance of the manuscript within an elite institution of that city. Thus, SP F 11 and Paris 934 are both understood to contain Roman material: the ritual of SP F 11 because of its manuscript source, the ritual of Paris 934 because of its liturgical contents. Yet the chant repertories and melodies in these two deathbed liturgies differ markedly.[16] How can both of these rituals be Roman, given their stark differences?

The *Ordo XLIX* Tradition as Roman?

Historians have long associated the *Ordo XLIX* tradition—the material edited by Andrieu from a deathbed rite in an eleventh-century manuscript and documented by Sicard in the deathbed rites of over 100 additional medieval sources—with Rome.[17] A scholarly consensus finds that its attitude toward death and the afterlife—a confident reliance on God's love and mercy—has strong resonances with the Roman church of late Antiquity.[18] Andrieu placed the origins of *Ordo XLIX* in Rome based on two additional factors:

1. its inclusion (in the eleventh-century manuscript Vatican 312) alongside a compilation of rituals intended to disperse Roman practices in Frankish territories. (This compilation is referred to in scholarship as Collection A.)
2. its presence in a twelfth-century century Pontifical created at the Lateran. (The scribe of this pontifical presumably would have drawn

---

[16] Of the thirteen chants prescribed in the end-of-life liturgy of SP F 11, Sicard considers only two (*Laeto animo* and *Suscipiat te Christus*) to be a part of the wider *Ordo XLIX* tradition: *Liturgie*, 71–72, 75–76.

[17] Andrieu, *Les ordines*, 523–530. See also Cyrille Vogel, *Medieval Liturgy: An Introduction to the Sources* (Washington, DC: Pastoral Press, 1986), 187. Sicard's more extensive study of the *Ordo XLIX* tradition greatly expanded the manuscript basis used by Andrieu and provided a broader understanding of the transmission patterns of individual items (Sicard, *Liturgie*).

[18] This point is articulated succinctly by Paxton in *Christianizing Death*, 37–46, and more recently in "The Early Growth of the Medieval Economy of Salvation in Latin Christianity," in *Death in Jewish Life: Burial and Mourning Customs among the Jews of Europe and Nearby Communities*, ed. Stefan Reif and Andreas Lehnardt (Berlin: De Gruyter, 2014), 17–41. Donohue's discussion of *Ordo XLIX* occurs in "The Rite," 136–180, where he notes that the *Ordo XLIX* tradition shows an expectation of a Last Judgment rather than a particular judgment (a concept that developed later in the Middle Ages). Brown nuances our understanding by connecting the confident expectation of divine mercy with the political and societal context provided by an absolute ruler. "These liturgies reflect not so much greater confidence in the love of God as a notion of the absolute power of God, rooted in the most formidably autocratic aspects of the late Roman imperial office. Late Roman Christians found it natural to pray to a God for whom the act of mercy was in itself a declaration of almighty power" (Brown, "The Decline," 48).

upon only those materials considered to be authoritative and authentically Roman.[19])

This evidence is suggestive, rather than definitive, as Andrieu himself noted. Adding to the ambiguity around the origins of *Ordo XLIX*, Westwell has recently interrogated and re-evaluated the appropriateness of the label "Roman," as it has traditionally been applied to Collection A (the material that, for Andrieu and others, lent *Ordo XLIX* "Roman-ness" by association).[20] With scholars now suggesting a Frankish influence upon the materials of Collection A, the Roman origins of the material appended to Collection A at later dates—*Ordo XLIX* and its chants—are even more in doubt.

The earliest extant sources of *Ordo XLIX* (dating from the eighth and ninth centuries) are not Roman—they come from Frankish territory. This pattern of source distribution is ambiguous: it certainly does not confirm a Roman origin for the manuscripts' contents, yet it does not necessarily speak against it. McKitterick has noted that many texts originating in Rome have Frankish manuscripts as their earliest extant sources. In her work on the *Liber pontificalis*, McKitterick considers the "remarkable disjuncture between texts emanating from Rome and the origin of the surviving manuscripts thereof. Why so much has disappeared is perplexing." One explanation looks to the material on which Roman documents were written. Based on surviving fragments, papyrus, rather than parchment, might have been the most common.[21]

A Frankish, rather than Roman, origin for the chants of the *Ordo XLIX* tradition is conceivable. Indeed, if it is possible for the chants to have been created in Rome and then transmitted north of the Alps, it is equally possible that the confident understanding of salvation was transmitted north of the Alps and then given concrete manifestation—in the form of chants for the dying—by Frankish composers and liturgists. This second possibility gains credence from Paxton's work, which indicates that much of the development of the liturgies for the dying took place north of the Alps, in Frankish monasteries and institutions.[22]

---

[19] Andrieu, *Les ordines*, 523–530.
[20] Arthur Robert Westwell, "The Dissemination and Reception of the Ordines Romani in the Carolingian Church, c. 750–900" (PhD diss., University of Cambridge, 2018), 13–59.
[21] Rosamond McKitterick, *Rome and the Invention of the Papacy: The Liber Pontificalis* (Cambridge: Cambridge University Press, 2020), 171–223, here, 176.
[22] Paxton, *Christianizing Death*, particularly 126–127.

In sum, we do not have (and most likely will not gain) evidence to show definitively where *Ordo XLIX* and its chants originated. More important, the question seems to be only of recent interest. The concern to show a Roman origin or Roman authority for *Ordo XLIX* is evident in scholarship of the twentieth century, not in the medieval sources themselves. Wherever *Ordo XLIX* and its chants originated, they enjoyed a broad transmission and a sustained period of usage, eventually extending throughout Frankish and Roman territories and throughout the Middle Ages. This popularity might have had more to do with their contents than with their purported origins or attachment to Rome. The chants probably continued to be sung at deathbeds because they seemed fitting and appropriate; they fulfilled meaningful functions for the rituals' compilers, participants, and listeners.

It is possible that precisely the expressions of comforting, confident expectation within these chants made them seem appropriate for the deathbed rites. Paxton notes that the confident tone of *Ordo XLIX* and its chants appears as a "counter-current" in the Carolingian era.[23] Perhaps this explains why they—rather than the items promoted by Benedict of Aniane—experienced a longer and more widespread dispersion. The "counter-current" might have been welcome; the reassuring images of mercy might have seemed important to those who created and sang the rituals for the dying. The attitude toward death revealed within the chants of the *Ordo XLIX* tradition may be associated with the Roman church of late Antiquity, but it continued to find resonance long afterward.

The Deathbed Ritual of SP F 11 as Roman

In his monumental study of the *Ordo XLIX* tradition, Sicard did not consider the possibility that SP F 11 might offer more authoritative testimony to Roman practice, given the manuscript's provenance in Rome. Indeed, it was primarily after the publication of Sicard's work that musicologists engaged in an extended discussion concerning the "Old Roman" tradition—a repertory of liturgical chant preserved primarily in a small group of eleventh- and twelfth-century manuscripts, including SP F 11. Wide-ranging and contentious as this discussion was, musicologists agreed that the Old Roman manuscripts, including SP F 11, provide important witnesses to a Roman

---

[23] Paxton, "The Early Growth," 28–29.

tradition that had previously been transmitted orally, without written notation. In short, it is likely that the ritual for the dying in SP F 11 reflects a Roman practice older than the manuscript itself.[24]

Roman and Non-Roman Elements in the "Roman" Rituals

Two issues prevent us from establishing either the ritual in SP F 11 (as a witness to the Old Roman tradition) or the ritual in Paris 934 (based on the *Ordo XLIX* tradition) as the earlier, more authentic, or more authoritative Roman practice. First, both of the rituals, and their chant repertories, contain Roman and non-Roman elements. Second, it seems likely that the medieval practices of Rome could have encompassed versions of both rituals, with their differing chant repertories. The possibility that multiple versions existed concurrently within the city remains open; indeed, evidence (discussed below) speaks for it.

The deathbed rituals of both Paris 934 and SP F 11 reveal non-Roman elements. As noted above, the chants of Paris 934—part of the *Ordo XLIX* tradition—might be of non-Roman origin, as suggested by the fact that they appear in their earliest extant manifestations in Frankish manuscripts. It is certainly possible that the chants were created in Rome and transmitted to Frankish territory, and that earlier Roman sources have been lost. Yet it seems equally (if not more) likely that the chants were created at institutions in Frankish territories, drawing on the confident attitude known from the earlier Roman church.

In Paris 934, the assignment of multiple chants and psalms to the time period prior to the moment of death shows a deviation from what scholars consider to be Roman practice. As reconstructed by Paxton, and as seen in almost all of its earliest manuscript sources, the *Ordo XLIX* tradition tends to prescribe sung material *after* the moment of death.[25] Sicard deems litanies and psalms assigned to the time period prior to death to be "supplements" to

---

[24] That the Old Roman manuscripts are important witnesses to the historic practices of Rome is not disputed; the most contentious question in the scholarly debate concerns the extent to which the Old Roman tradition—preserved primarily in eleventh- and twelfth-century manuscripts—reflects the chant repertory transmitted to Frankish territories during the eighth and ninth centuries. See particularly Kelly, *Chant and Its Origins*; Nowacki, "Studies on the Office Antiphons"; Pfisterer, *Cantilena Romana* and "Origins and Transmission," 82–88; Maloy, *Inside the Offertory*; and Dyer, "Sources of Romano-Frankish Liturgy and Music."

[25] Paxton, *Christianizing Death*, 39.

the Roman tradition. Paxton notes further that the prescription of extended amounts of liturgical material to accompany the final agony was a Frankish development of the late eighth century.[26] In early sources of the *Ordo XLIX* tradition, the *viaticum* and recitations of the gospel accounts of Jesus' death are the most common liturgical prescriptions for the final moments of life. (One exceptional older source of the *Ordo XLIX* tradition, Berlin 1667, prescribes a single antiphon, psalm, and litany for these final moments.[27]) By shifting the *Ordo XLIX* chants to an earlier position—as an accompaniment to the final agony—the ritual of Paris 934 alters the Roman practice and uses the chant repertory to address what had been originally a Frankish concern—the support of the dying person in the final moments of life.

Non-Roman elements also appear in the deathbed ritual of SP F 11. Seven of the thirteen chant texts have concordances in earlier, ninth-century manuscripts from diverse geographic locations. (Table 5.3 shows the repertory of chant texts prescribed in SP F 11 for the deathbed liturgy [Column 1] and the non-Roman, ninth-century sources that contain concordant versions [Column 2].) Given this pattern of extant sources, it is not possible to determine exactly where each of these chants originated, and which direction the paths of dispersion took. That the chant texts originated in Rome in the eighth or ninth century, were transmitted to these other locations, and were then written down 300 years later in Rome, seems to be the more complex and less likely possibility. Some of the chants assigned to the deathbed liturgy in SP F 11 likely originated outside of Rome; it is only for the six chants without such ninth-century concordances that a Roman origin seems more likely.

The ritual of SP F 11 also shows the Frankish concern of liturgically supporting a dying person in the final moments of life. Although this is done less explicitly than in Paris 934, the ritual of SP F 11 seems to prescribe much sung material for the time period prior to death. The rubrics in SP F 11 do not coordinate individual items to specific stages of the dying process; the first material follows the rubric "Commendation of the Soul" and precedes the rubric "Antiphon for the way. . .". Following these rubrics, the timing of the performance of the ritual's first section of material remains ambiguous: it may have been intended as accompaniment to the final agony, the final breath, or the washing and preparation of the body. Yet the material's

---

[26] Ibid., 114–127, particularly 126–127; see also Sicard, *Liturgie*, 43.
[27] Sicard, *Liturgie*, 6–11 and final table (unnumbered).

content (which takes on the voice of a suffering person and encourages the soul to depart) combined with its quantity (seven psalms, a litany, the *Pater noster*, four versicles and responses, and fourteen prayers) suggests strongly that these items were intended to accompany the potentially long death agony. The rituals of both SP F 11 and Paris 934, then, have a non-Roman, Frankish element to them, in that they provide extended prescriptions of liturgical material (including sung material) for the final agony.

In fact, the ritual of SP F 11 might be understood as a Roman response to an impulse—received from Frankish areas—to liturgically support a dying person in the final moments of life. The ritual's compilers and practitioners might have made use of some existing, widely circulating chant texts (the seven listed in Table 5.3 that have non-Roman, ninth-century sources); six additional chant texts might have been created for this specific liturgy or incorporated from local practices. The ritual's melodies, however, are likely products of Rome: all display the distinctive Old Roman melodic characteristics. The CANTUS database, which contains transcriptions of Office melodies from medieval manuscripts throughout Europe, provides data with which to investigate the transmission patterns of the melodies. In searching this database, I have found no melody in the deathbed ritual of SP F 11 with a concordant version outside of Rome. (Please see Column 4 of Table 5.3.) Three melodies (conveying the chants *Dirige domine*, *Conuertere domine*, and *Nequando rapiat*) share some commonalities with versions in non-Roman manuscripts and might be considered "different realizations of the same underlying musical structure"[28] (meaning that the Roman and non-Roman versions might have originated in a common melody). In fact, only two chants, *Qui cognoscis* and *Induc eum domine*, have any melodic concordances documented in the CANTUS database: very similar melodies appear in SP B 79, another manuscript transmitting the Old Roman tradition.[29] The melody of one additional chant text in SP F 11's deathbed ritual, *Redemisti me*, uses a formulaic melody found with other texts in the Old Roman antiphon repertory, as documented by Nowacki.[30] The melodies of the deathbed liturgy in SP F 11, then, are likely Roman creations.

With six distinctive chant texts and thirteen distinctive melodies, SP F 11 preserves a ritual for the deathbed that is unique among existing sources.

---

[28] Maloy, *Inside the Offertory*, 107.
[29] Vatican, Biblioteca Apostolica Vaticana, Archivio del Capitolo di San Pietro B 79.
[30] Nowacki, "Studies on the Office Antiphons," 1:165–166.

The liturgical assignments of the chants reveal an additional distinctive feature: ninth-century manuscripts that contain concordant versions of the chant texts do not share the liturgical assignments seen in SP F 11; instead, earlier sources prescribe these chants for the vigil with the body, the burial, or a commemoration of the deceased person. Only SP F 11 assigns these chants to the moments immediately following death. The ritual for the dying in SP F 11 is unique among extant sources, even when viewed alongside others thought to document Roman practices—the sources containing the *Ordo XLIX* tradition, and even the later, thirteenth-century sources containing the deathbed ritual attributed to the papal curia, which was dispersed by the Franciscans.[31] The deathbed ritual in SP F 11 did not originate entirely in Rome, nor was it disseminated as an authoritatively Roman product; instead, SP F 11 reveals a ritual that existed in Rome and for which only one written manifestation survives.

Multiple Practices in Rome

From this evidence, there is good reason to doubt that Rome had a single, standardized deathbed ritual in the twelfth century or earlier. A related liturgy—the Office of the Dead—provides further indications that the deathbed liturgy probably did not exist in one, authoritative version, even in Rome. In his study of the Office of the Dead, Ottosen notes that responsories within the Office were usually standardized in local traditions. In other words, observing the responsories and their ordering in a specific version of the Office of the Dead gives good indications of the location in which the liturgy was used. This pattern of local standardization holds true, *except* with the Old Roman tradition. Ottosen considers several explanations for this exceptional variability within Roman practice, including the possibility that the archcantor at Saint Peter's Basilica enjoyed great latitude in assembling liturgies.[32] Regardless of its causes, such variation should guide

---

[31] On the thirteenth-century liturgy of the papal chapel, see particularly Van Dijk, *Sources*, 135-139, and Mitchell, "Chant," 11-15.

[32] "There may be several reasons for this exception to the general rule of stability. . . . It must be assumed that St. Peter's in Rome and other prominent churches in Rome were the scene of a number of fashionable funerals which required Offices of the Dead especially composed for the occasion. The Old Roman liturgy is characterized by the use of a restricted number of sung elements, compared with the Gregorian, which made it necessary to supplement the series by using responsories taken from other parts of the Liturgy of Hours, a procedure which made it easy to rearrange the series.

our expectations: if we do not find liturgical continuity in Rome, even with the Office of the Dead (a liturgy known for stability in other locations), we should not expect to find it with the deathbed liturgy (which is characterized by greater variability).[33]

The Old Roman version of the deathbed ritual found in SP F 11—with its distinctive repertory and melodic characteristics—does not necessarily cast doubt on the "Roman-ness" of the *Ordo XLIX* tradition. Both chant repertories could have been present in the practices of Rome. In fact, in their shared characteristics, the two traditions invite us to define "Roman-ness" (in terms of deathbed liturgies) broadly—not as a fixed sequence of liturgical items, but as shared images of the afterlife, shared understandings of a dying person's relationship to God, and perhaps a broad, shared repertory, from which chants could be drawn and assigned to different liturgical positions. The chants of the Old Roman and *Ordo XLIX* traditions share similar images of the afterlife (the bosom of Abraham serves a metaphor for the repose of the deceased person's soul) and similar portrayals of the relationship between the dying person and God (the relationship of creation to creator). As noted above, scholars associate both of these aspects with the Roman church of late Antiquity. The two traditions also share repertory: *Subvenite*, *Suscipiat te Christus*, *Chorus angelorum*, and *Tu iussisti nasci me* (from the *Ordo XLIX* tradition) appear in SP F 11, assigned in the material for the time after death (entering the church with the body, during the vigil with the corpse, after the funeral Mass, and carrying the body to the grave). This common repertory of chants—with differing liturgical assignments—suggests that the corpus of chants known in Rome was fashioned into multiple ritual versions.

In sum, the existence of the Old Roman deathbed ritual in SP F 11—so different from the *Ordo XLIX* tradition, also associated with Rome—suggests

Finally, it must be assumed that the archchantor at St. Peter's in Rome was allowed more freedom in the arrangement of the liturgy than was enjoyed elsewhere" (Ottosen, *Responsories*, 325–326).

[33] From my perspective, it does not seem fruitful to attempt to associate the *Ordo XLIX* tradition and the Old Roman tradition (with their respective chant repertories for the end of life) with separate institutions in Rome—to argue, for instance, that the ritual of SP F 11 originated in and was practiced by the community of Saint Peter's Basilica, or that the *Ordo XLIX* tradition represents the practice of the papal chapel at the Lateran. Beyond the six chants for which SP F 11 is the earliest known extant source, it seems likely that the chants in these rituals had early and broad transmissions, and that the locations in which they were composed, and extent of the geographic areas in which the rituals were sung, will remain unknown. Musicologists' documentation of the sources of the Old Roman tradition—of which SP F 11 is a part—indicates that it reached beyond the boundaries of Rome (see especially Huglo, "Le chant"); the same can be said for the *Ordo XLIX* tradition, as shown by Sicard's work (*Liturgie*) with over 100 sources from diverse geographic locations.

that a search for a single, authoritative Roman ritual for the dying in the twelfth century and earlier is misguided. These two different traditions instead point to the likelihood of multiple practices existing within the single city. Yet the two traditions' shared, underlying assumptions and vocabulary concerning the afterlife suggest that Roman practices held some foundational understandings in common, even if they did not share common liturgical articulations of those understandings.

Persistence (and Replacement) of Local Traditions

Multiple practices existed outside of Rome, as well. Standardization cannot be found when observing the medieval deathbed rituals of Western Europe as a whole—even during the eighth and ninth centuries, a time period for which scholars have traditionally posited strong efforts toward liturgical conformity. Local versions were maintained throughout the Carolingian era.[34] This volume's index titled "Items from All Rituals" offers an overview of the specific items contained in the four rituals examined in the previous chapters; it reveals the variability among these rituals. Almost two-thirds of the items appear in only one ritual; only three items—the prayers *Pater noster* and *Tibi domine commendamus*, and the versicle and response beginning *Domine exaudi*—appear in all four. This variability offers an indication of the extent to which local traditions were maintained within specific geographic areas and institutions. The ritual of Sens in Paris 934, for example (Chapter 2), reveals the same specific series of liturgical items preserved in manuscripts from the region 300 years earlier. The fifteenth-century manuscript from Aldgate, the Franciscan community in London (Chapter 4),

---

[34] Recent scholarship has re-evaluated the extent to which the liturgy was standardized during the Carolingian era. See, for example, Westwell, "Dissemination," 2: "What occurred under the Carolingians in the liturgy did not involve the imposition of the Roman rite from above. What was 'Roman' and 'correct' was decided by individuals, each in their own case, and they created and edited texts for what they needed." DiCenso pursues a similar investigation using musicological evidence: DiCenso, "Sacramentary-Antiphoners." Hen goes so far as to state: "Charlemagne's attempt to unify the Frankish rite by importing a Roman sacramentary and invoking a Roman precedent did not so much reform the liturgy as sow the seeds for a proliferating confusion" (Hen, "When Liturgy Gets out of Hand," 212). See also Yitzhak Hen, *The Royal Patronage of Liturgy in Frankish Gaul to the Death of Charles the Bald (877)* (London: Boydell Press, 2001), particularly 78–95 (here, 94): "Roman books and liturgical practices were undoubtedly introduced to the Frankish kingdoms, both voluntarily and by legislation, but the traditional non-Roman rites were neither deliberately suppressed nor lost." On the limited transmission and reception of Benedict of Aniane's work, see Paxton, *Christianizing Death*, 154–161.

contains the same series of liturgical items as the version dispersed by the Franciscan Order approximately 200 years earlier, in 1260.

The extant manuscripts, however, suggest an eventual coalescence around a core repertory of chants. Chant assignments for the time period immediately prior to death—in the presence of a dying person—seem to have become more streamlined and standardized throughout the Middle Ages. Apart from the Old Roman tradition in SP F 11—which seems to have had little influence on other deathbed rituals—the manuscripts surveyed here contain only four chant texts (leaving aside the psalms, the Kyrie, and *Requiem aeternam* as a versicle and response). In rituals outside of the Old Roman tradition, then, chant repertories appear to have been limited to a few chants that originated in the *Ordo XLIX* tradition. *Chorus angelorum* appears in two of the four manuscripts examined in this volume; the responsory *Subvenite-Suscipiat* appears in three; *Suscipiat te Christus* appears as an antiphon in three. Rather than a variety of local repertories, manuscripts from the thirteenth century and later show a homogeneity in the chants assigned for the time of death.

Subvenite–Suscipiat

As the chant repertories of the deathbed rituals narrowed and standardized during the Middle Ages, a single chant complex—the responsory *Subvenite* and its verse *Suscipiat*—became prominent. This chant complex, often referred to in manuscripts by only its first word, *Subvenite*, gained a widespread and stable liturgical assignment as the item indicated for the moment of death. For the laity of Orsières, the cathedral community of Sens, the Augustinian canons and canonesses of Klosterneuburg, and Franciscans from Italy to England, singing *Subvenite* was the prescribed response to a person's last breath.[35] Yardley's observation, that the fifteenth-century ordinal of Barking Abbey refers to the deathbed ritual simply as "*Subvenite*," offers another indication of this trend: the chant became so associated with the deathbed ritual that the ritual itself came to be designated by the chant.[36]

---

[35] *Subvenite* is also indicated in some of the earliest sources of deathbed rituals from the eighth and ninth centuries. On its sources and liturgical placements, see particularly Sicard, *Liturgie*, 66–68. On the deathbed rituals of Klosterneuburg, see Hild, "Rites."

[36] Yardley, "Clares in Procession," 14, note 60, and *Performing Piety*, 104 and 276, note 39. As Yardley discusses in "Clares in Procession," this reference to the ritual *Subvenite* suggests that it was sometimes used as a commemorative liturgy.

Subvenite became known as the primary liturgical response to death, such that the entire ritual could be referred to by its first word. The Franciscan ritual for the dying, widely dispersed throughout Europe in the thirteenth century, likely played a role in the prominent position this chant gained.[37]

In this broad transmission, the text of *Subvenite* shows more stability than its melody. Even the two versions of the chant's melody recorded in manuscripts from Franciscan institutions reveal variants.[38] Yet certain aspects of the melody remain consistent. Where manuscripts contain legible, pitch-specific music notation, the melody of *Subvenite* can almost always be categorized as Mode 4.[39] The defining characteristics of Mode 4—the final pitch of "e" and the ambitus that primarily inhabits the octave above this final—remain consistent.[40] Such consistency is noteworthy, given the amount of variability otherwise found in the deathbed rituals.

This stable aspect of transmission in the melody of *Subvenite* provides a connection with the abbey of Cluny, France. Cluny developed an extended and complex liturgy for the dying, preserved in manuscripts of the eleventh century.[41] The ritual clearly included large portions of sung material, including antiphons, psalms, and responsories, but the melodies sung for dying monks at Cluny are lost to us. The scribes who documented the abbey's version of the ritual did not include music notation; chants are indicated in the extant sources only by their first words. (In fact, few Cluniac manuscripts containing music notation survived the French Revolution, and those that have survived contain none of the chants sung for the dying.[42])

Yet references to music survive in the abbey's architecture. In particular, two capitals of the "Cluny III" buildings (consecrated in 1130) contain illustrations of the eight melodic modes; a visual image and a short inscription

---

[37] See Donohue, "The Rite," 197–237, and Hild, "The Role of Music."

[38] These manuscripts are Chicago, Newberry Library, Vault Manuscript 24 (with the chant edited in Hild, "The Role of Music"), and Cranston 2322 (Chapter 4).

[39] In addition to the manuscripts used in this study, the CANTUS database lists fourteen manuscripts containing the chant; thirteen of these melodies are designated as Mode 4. The exception is a manuscript from the Worcester Cathedral, in which *Subvenite*'s melody is designated as Mode 1. University of Waterloo, "CANTUS," accessed November 10, 2020, at http://cantus.uwaterloo.ca/search?op=starts&t=subvenite&genre=All&cid=&mode=&feast=&volpiano=All. See also Huglo, "Remarques."

[40] Hiley provides an introduction to the medieval understandings of modes in *Western Plainchant*, especially 454–455; Atkinson offers the definitive, detailed study of the reception of Greek music theory in the European Middle Ages: Charles M. Atkinson, *The Critical Nexus* (Oxford: Oxford University Press, 2008; repr. 2015).

[41] Paxton's edition primarily relies upon Paris, Bibliothèque nationale de France, lat. 13875. For source documentation of the Cluniac liturgy, see Paxton, *The Death Ritual at Cluny*, 22–27 and 39–41.

[42] Extant music manuscripts from Cluny are listed in Hiley, *Western Plainchant*, 575.

characterize each type of melody.[43] Of particular interest to this investigation is the capital representing the fourth mode. Its inscription reads, *Succedit quartus simulans in carmine planctus* ("Next comes the fourth, simulating lamentation in song").[44] This inscription draws a connection between the fourth melodic mode and active mourning—the word *planctus* connotes an outward expression, even a vocalization, of grief.

Not only in this inscription, but also in many deathbed rituals, the fourth mode is associated with outward expressions of mourning. The connection occurs through the chant *Subvenite*. The chant's melody—in almost every known version—comfortably conforms to the characteristics of Mode 4, and in the rituals that incorporate it, *Subvenite* is consistently placed at moments of decisive leave-taking: at the last breath, to mark the moment when death had occurred; bringing the body into the church, to mark the moment when the person, who was recently a living member of the community, entered a public space as a corpse that would soon be buried.[45] These are moments of separation: the chant's text speaks of the soul going into the "sight of the most high"; yet the body remains below, to be washed, clothed, and buried. These are moments of grief.

The broad and stable transmission of the chant *Subvenite* with a fourth-mode melody associates this mode with vocal expressions of grief; the Cluniac capital makes the same connection. Regardless of whether the previously existing chant *Subvenite* inspired the designer of the Cluniac capital, or whether the capital and the chant were both shaped by a previously existing characterization of the mode, *Subvenite* offered communities a ritualized way to vocalize loss. The capital of Cluny suggests that the chant's Mode 4

---

[43] The extensive literature concerning these capitals includes Sébastien Biay, "Building a Church with Music: The Plainchant Capitals at Cluny, c. 1100," in *Resounding Images: Medieval Intersections of Art, Music, and Sound*, ed. Susan Boynton and Diane J. Reilly (Turnhout: Brepols Publishers, 2015), 221–236; Sébastien Biay, "Les chapiteaux de rond-point de la troisième église abbatiale de Cluny (fin XIe–début XIIe siècle), étude iconographique" (PhD diss., Université de Poitiers, 2011); Isabelle Marchesin, "Les chapiteaux de la musique de Cluny: une figuration du lien musica," in *Les représentations de la musique au Moyen Âge*, ed. Martine Clouzot (Paris: Cité de la Musique Editions, 2005), 84–91; Kirk Ambrose, "Visual Poetics of the Cluny Hemicycle Capital Inscriptions," *Word & Image* 20, no. 2 (2004): 155–164; Charles E. Scillia, "Meaning and the Cluny Capitals; Music as Metaphor," *Gesta* 27 (1988): 133–148; Jacques Chailley, "Les huit tons de la musique et l'éthos des modes aux chapiteaux de Cluny," *Acta musicologica* 57 (1985): 73–94; Kathi Meyer, "The Eight Gregorian Modes on the Cluny Capitals," *The Art Bulletin* 34 (1952): 75–94; Walter Muir Whitehall Jr., "Gregorian Capitals from Cluny," *Speculum* 2 (1927): 385–395.

[44] The transcription and translation are drawn largely from Paxton, *The Death Ritual at Cluny*, 38.

[45] In the Cluniac ritual, the chant is prescribed for the moment when the body was brought into the church (Paxton, *The Death Ritual at Cluny*, 114–115). For the positions of the chant in the liturgy from Farfa, see Boynton, "A Monastic Death Ritual," 63.

melody might have been part of the musical expression of lamentation.[46] The prominence of *Subvenite–Suscipiat* in deathbed rituals from varied locations throughout the Middle Ages suggests that the chant complex—along with its fourth-mode melody—became firmly associated with the moment of death, and by extension, with grief.

Commonalities in Liturgical Practices

For all of their individualities, the rituals investigated in this book appear to be the fragmentary remnants of a liturgical practice that was widespread in Western Europe, and not confined to one region or one portion of the population. These rituals share the assumption that a dying person—and the soul—could benefit from the presence and liturgical efforts of a community. The rituals seem to integrate two aspirations: alleviating the suffering that occurred in the death agony and ensuring a positive afterlife for the soul.[47] Both intentions seem to be involved in these rituals; intercessory prayer intertwines with the beauty of melody. The rituals share the goals of benefiting the soul and comforting the person.

The manuscript sources examined in the previous chapters also reveal an understanding that the same liturgies were appropriate, regardless of the gender or religious vocation of the dying person. Cranston 2322 (Chapter 4) adapts the Franciscan ritual of 1260 for the benefit of women, without changing any items; Paris 934 (Chapter 2) contains alternative, feminine endings for words that refer to the dying person, in order to make the

---

[46] A similar connection might be at play between the Cluniac capital portraying the third mode and another chant in the repertory of deathbed rituals. For the third mode, the capital of Cluny states: *Tertius impingit Christumque resurgere fingit* ("The third rushes forth and represents Christ who has risen" [Translation based on Paxton, *The Death Ritual at Cluny*, 36–37]). The inscription characterizes the third mode as vigorous and joyful, a reflection of resurrection. The chant *Chorus angelorum*, as seen in the ritual of Paris 934, portrays the energetic ascension of a soul that has just left a body—an ascension understood in the Christian tradition to imitate the resurrection of Christ. It is possible that the tradition that produced the chant *Chorus angelorum*, with a melody in the third mode, also produced the Cluniac capital characterizing the third mode as a rising from the dead. Lacking more evidence, however, this remains an intriguing possibility rather than an arguable assertion. Meyer (in "The Eight Gregorian Modes") proposes that Mode 4 was associated with lamentation through the antiphon *Media vita*; while Chailley ("Les huit tons") regards the numbers identifying the modes as symbolic, rather than descriptive of their associations in chant.

[47] As Paxton states: "Not so much a commending of the soul to God as a ritual of aid to the dying.... This Frankish contribution to deathbed rituals completed the change of emphasis from the exclusive concern with the fate of the soul to the needs of the dying person" (*Christianizing Death*, 205–206).

ritual appropriate for a woman; similar alterations are seen in the manuscript GSB 3 (Chapter 3).[48] The ritual for the laity of Orsières (in GSB 3) follows the same structure and contains many of the same items as rituals used by religious institutions; the only major difference is the possibility—not the requirement—of beginning the liturgy after death had occurred.

Conceptions of the Afterlife

The rituals also share depictions of a soul's experiences after death, and these depictions nuance our understanding of how the afterlife was conceptualized during the time period. Scholars trace changes in the images used to portray the afterlife throughout the Middle Ages, and even note variations among geographic locations.[49] Alongside the image prevalent in the Roman church of late Antiquity—of the deceased person (as a soul) resting in the bosom of Abraham until the final judgment—came other, harsher images: the deceased person (as a soul) facing a Particular Judgment at the moment of death and being assigned to heaven, hell, or purgation.

Yet rather than single images, the rituals examined in this book contain multiple portrayals of the afterlife. One hears the reassurance of the chants from the *Ordo XLIX* tradition, addressing God as the creator of each person and describing a place of welcome and rest for the earthly sojourner. Even in the deathbed ritual of SP F 11 (which contains a chant repertory that is largely independent of the *Ordo XLIX* tradition), chant texts make use of these reassuring images. One also hears contrasting images in these rituals—primarily in prayers and versicles introduced during the Carolingian era—of God as a demanding judge who determines the soul's fate at the moment of death. Viewing together all the items of the deathbed rituals—including prayers, versicles, and responses, as well as chants and psalms—multiple and varied depictions of the afterlife appear. An image of judgment can be juxtaposed with an image of a welcoming heavenly community. Visions of hell emerge among depictions of a safe haven. God is often referenced as the creator and welcomer of a dying person's soul, but sometimes as judge. The passage to the afterlife contains threats as well as protecting angels. The deathbed rituals, with their multiplicity of metaphors, offer supporting

---

[48] Leisibach, *Die liturgischen Handschriften*, 84.
[49] Pivotal contributions are noted in Chapter 2, note 43.

evidence for Brown's findings concerning the multiple, changing "imaginative structures" in the late Antiquity and early Middle Ages: "Faced with so many vivid narratives [of the journey of the individual's soul after death], we should be careful not to endow any one of them with universal validity."[50]

The deathbed rites examined in this volume show a lack of interest in conveying a single, consistent depiction of the afterlife. One senses a reluctance to eliminate the older, comforting images. None of the deathbed rituals analyzed in the previous chapters was entirely "updated" with images of God as judge and understandings of purgatory from the twelfth and thirteenth centuries. Ottosen's observation concerning the Office of the Dead also seems applicable to the deathbed liturgies: "The idea of a First Judgment [at the moment of death] did not completely oust the biblical concept of sleep as the best metaphor to illustrate the state of the departed until the Second Coming of Christ."[51] Even when the images of God as judge became prevalent in theological discourse and other liturgical texts, and even after the doctrine of purgatory had been articulated by the Council of Lyons in 1274, deathbed rituals from various institutions and locations continued to include items that portray God as creator, Christ as welcomer, and the bosom of Abraham as the place of repose. Among the multiple, contrasting images of the afterlife seen in each ritual, positive and reassuring images are prominent.

Scholars have noted a similar emphasis in later, related liturgies conducted on behalf of the deceased. As Nardini states: "A common element in the mass formularies for the Dead is that all texts are characterized by generically positive references to the eternal rest and quiet of the soul.... [In contrast to theological writings and visual church depictions], liturgical prayers and chants for the Dead more directly focused on the theme of the mercy of God."[52] Rather than a single, consistent portrayal of what happened to a soul immediately following the death of the body, we find liturgical images contrasting with theological discourses and the visual depictions in church architecture. Within the varied possibilities, positive images of a loving God are given prominence in liturgies conducted in proximity to a dying person and grieving loved ones. The needs of accompanying and supporting a dying

---

[50] Brown, "The Decline," 44.

[51] Ottosen, *Responsories*, 48.

[52] Luisa Nardini, "The Masses for the Dead in Beneventan Manuscripts: Issues of Formulary Organization and Chant Manipulation," in *Proceedings of the 17th Meeting of the International Musicological Society—Cantus Planus Study Group, Venice (Italy), July–August 2014*, ed. James Borders (Venice: Fondazione Levi, 2021), 481–494; here, 490–491. See also Effros's discussion in *Caring for Body and Soul*, 169–170.

person and the surrounding community seem to have taken precedence over doctrinal consistency and correctness.

When viewing the chants of the deathbed rituals alone, much variation in the presentation of the afterlife disappears. The chants prescribed for the dying offer an emotionally consistent portrayal of the soul's future. They serve as the primary vehicles for conveying reassuring images of the afterlife. Within the chants, God is the creator, never the judge; angels and saints serve the soul as able, constant protectors; the bosom of Abraham—the place of rest—serves as the predominant metaphor for the soul's residence after death.

Music-Text Relationships

The chants' melodies underscore these positive images. Musicologists have established that plainchant melodies can be oriented toward different aspects of the texts they convey (with the most commonly articulated aspect being a text's syntactic units).[53] Within the chants of the deathbed rituals, melodies do occasionally articulate the beginnings and endings of syntactic units. For example, cadential gestures create divisions at the endings of clauses and other word groupings in the chant *Leto animo* (SP F 11, Chapter 1). The melody structures the performance of the lengthy text into meaningful units. At other times within the repertory, the syllables accented in spoken performance receive musical emphasis, as in *Nequando rapiat* (also SP F 11, Chapter 1). But most often, the melodies of the deathbed liturgies are oriented toward the texts' semantic contents—the meanings of the sung words. In this, the chants for the dying prove to be an exceptional plainchant repertory.

DiCenso's survey of analytical tendencies notes the reluctance of chant scholars to acknowledge meaningful relationships between melodic material and the semantic content of sung texts.[54] Yet in the chants of the deathbed liturgies, the close orientation of melody to word meaning is difficult to ignore. It forms a prominent and pervasive feature of the repertory.

A few examples drawn from Chapters 1 to 4 illustrate the point:

---

[53] DiCenso provides an important perspective and a literature review in "Moved by Music," especially 42–43.
[54] Ibid.

1. Melismas emphasize significant words in the texts. In the responsory verse *Suscipiat* (Chapter 4), the melisma conveying the word *te* ("you") intensifies the final blessing given directly to the dying person. In *Chorus angelorum* (analyzed in Chapter 2), the melisma with the name *Habrahe* embellishes the depiction of the soul's future place of rest—the bosom of Abraham.
2. At times, the melodic movement imitates a movement depicted in the text (creating a mimetic relationship between music and words). In *Subuenite* (as transcribed and analyzed in Chapter 2), melodic patterns of ascension reflect the textual depiction of the soul rising to God. In *Redemisti me* (Chapter 1), a large, upward melodic leap coincides with the textual depiction of the dying person placing his soul into God's hands.
3. Melodic repetition draws connections between words, with meaningful implications. The "great mercy" of God is joined with the "humbled bones" of the dying person in *Secundum magnam* (Chapter 1), suggesting that the prayer for mercy is—or will soon be—fulfilled. In the ritual from Sens (Chapter 2), melodic repetition brings together the words depicting the dying person (*Suscipiat te Christus*) and the words depicting the rescued Israelites (Psalm 113), suggesting that the relief of the historic community might soon be replicated in the dying person.
4. Cadential gestures create a sense of finality and closure in significant positions. In *Chorus angelorum* (Chapter 2), a cadential gesture brings the melody to a point of rest as the text depicts the soul resting in the bosom of Abraham.
5. Contrasting areas of pitch content create distinct sonic spaces, which are associated with distinct textual images in performance. In *Conuertere domine* (Chapter 1), contrasting areas of pitch content underscore different depictions of the soul's two possible fates. An ascending melodic line and a higher area of pitch content depict the positive fate—God's capture of the soul—while a descending melodic line and a lower area of pitch content depict the danger—the possibility of the soul's death. In *Chorus angelorum* (Chapter 2), differing areas of pitch content musically echo the contrast between Lazarus' earthly poverty and his peaceful afterlife.

These examples, along with the other instances analyzed in Chapters 1 to 4, reveal a repertory of plainchant that is noticeably, consistently oriented toward the semantic contents of the sung texts. The chants' melodies are closely responsive to the meanings and images of the words they convey.

This finding alone makes the repertory intriguing for chant scholars. Yet the text-to-music relationships of the repertory are not only interesting, they are also poignant—because the nuanced articulation of textual images tends in a single, striking direction. The melodies convey their texts in ways that promote reassuring interpretations of the sung words. They articulate empathetic understandings of the dying person and comforting visions of the soul's future. Created for moments of uncontrollable suffering and crisis, these chants use musical means to console. With this repertory, one cannot claim that the melodies are neutral mechanisms for conveying texts. The melodies themselves seem to be shaped by, and offer a vehicle for, compassion.

Final Considerations

Why Sing?

A study of the deathbed rituals' music brings rich academic gains (and this conclusion ties together some of the most important ones from the preceding chapters), but it also moves compellingly beyond academic concerns. Ironically, it seems, such an academic investigation requires an engagement with situations in which intellectual considerations fade to insignificance. To study the music of medieval end-of-life rituals, I am continually contacting historic moments in which people stood at the bedsides of dying loved ones and lay in bed dying while loved ones stood near them. Academic methods do not shield me from identifying with the people who created the music, the liturgies, and the manuscripts; the people who sang the music and the liturgies and held the manuscripts; the people who stood at the bedside and the people who lay in bed. I myself will be at the bedside of a dying loved one; I will lie in bed with my loved ones near. As I engage with the historic material, the knowledge that these situations will be my own maintains a constant presence. Even while I work to apply rigorous academic standards, a very non-intellectual reaction persists—a reaction that, for me, borders on shock and awe. Sing? While I watch my beloved breathe for the last time? The following discussion first summarizes some of the academic insights gained from a study of the medieval deathbed rituals' music before concluding with a question that lingers at the edges of the scholarly investigation: why sing? What could music possibly have brought to the final moments of life and the community who witnessed it?

Academic Gains

Prior scholarship has established that the practice of singing at the bedside of a dying person formed part of a long and broadly transmitted liturgical tradition. Paxton documents the tradition's pivotal developments in Frankish

Music in Medieval Rituals for the End of Life. Elaine Stratton Hild, Oxford University Press.
© Oxford University Press 2024. DOI: 10.1093/oso/9780197685914.003.0007

territories of the eighth century, as well as the tradition's forerunners in earlier, more localized practices.[1] Sicard's monumental work chronicles both the tradition's geographic breadth—in manuscripts from religious institutions and orders throughout Western Europe—and its chronological extent—into the seventeenth century.[2] This book attempts a first investigation of the tradition's melodies: the music sung at the bedside.

The search for sources with legible music notation has brought forth additional manuscript witnesses to supplement those used in earlier studies. These additional sources reveal the liturgical tradition's incorporation into different parts of society. The deathbed liturgies were not only for elite religious practitioners in urban areas, but also for laity living in rural communities. The rites were practiced not only by and for men, but also by and for women. Extant sources containing deathbed rituals appear to be the fragmentary remnants of a widespread and widely practiced liturgical tradition.

The investigation of musical material in the deathbed rites reveals the extent to which these liturgies remained unstandardized for much of the Middle Ages. Rather than a single, shared ritual, we see variations on a shared tradition. Various versions of the rituals contain differing items, and even when chants are shared, melodic variations are evident. Yet the sources also reflect the growing influence of the Franciscan movement from the thirteenth century on, most notably in the increasingly consistent assignment of the chant complex *Subvenite-Suscipiat* for the moment of death.

Visions of the afterlife appear in the rituals. The deathbed liturgies—particularly their chants—served as repositories for older and entirely hopeful understandings of the soul's future after the body's death. The rituals indicate that conceptions of the afterlife in the Middle Ages did not consistently reflect the changes evident in contemporary theological discourses. Images of judgment and an infernalized purgatory are given little room in the deathbed rituals; images of the soul peacefully resting in the bosom of Abraham abound. A multitude of metaphors coexisted, and at the time of death, comforting images gained prominence. The rituals appear to have been a means of providing pastoral care—care of the suffering person, care of the soul, care of those who gathered at the deathbed. The liturgical practices at the bedside were shared, compassionate efforts of the dying person's

---

[1] Paxton, *Christianizing Death*.
[2] Sicard, *Liturgie*.

community, and these compassionate efforts involved depicting the afterlife in heartening ways.

Why Sing?

One question remains—and if it is not fundamental for the academic study, it is fundamental for the person who encounters the historic material. Why sing? The final reception of the Eucharist, *viaticum*, formed the central focus of deathbed rituals prior to the Carolingian era; in the liturgical tradition investigated in this book, however, that privileged position is given to music. Rather than offering the Eucharist as close to the moment of death as possible, the singing of *Subvenite–Suscipiat* most often marked the decisive moment. The medieval liturgies consistently name music as the resource with which to encounter death. But they are silent on the question of why. Direct evidence concerning the motivations for singing at the bedside of a dying person is lacking; however, several hypotheses seem plausible.

Conveying words with melody provided an additional, dynamic element to the texts' performances. The analyses of the previous chapters show that music played an interpretive role in the delivery of texts. The melodies heightened expressions of empathy for the dying person, depictions of the mercy of God, and portrayals of a welcoming afterlife. By controlling the texts' manner of conveyance, the melodies codified interpretive performances that promoted positive theological understandings. Music played a vital role in expressing reassurance. Communities might have sung at the deathbed to offer comfort to a suffering person.

Philosophical and metaphysical understandings with broad currency in the Middle Ages might also have provided reasons to sing at the end of an individual's life. Plato's dialogue *Timaeus* (widely known through the fourth-century translation and commentary by Calcidius) describes the creation of both the universe and the human soul.[3] In this account, the creator uses

---

[3] As Somfai summarizes: "The *Timaeus* is the only one of Plato's dialogues to have been continuously available in Latin translation in the West from the time of classical antiquity." Anna Somfai, "The Eleventh-Century Shift in the Reception of Plato's Timaeus and Caldicius's Commentary," *Journal of the Warburg and Courtauld Institutes* 65, no. 1 (2002): 1–21. Hicks documents the presence and influence of Neoplatonic concepts in the Middle Ages: Andrew J. Hicks, *Composing the World: Harmony in the Medieval Platonic Cosmos* (New York: Oxford University Press, 2017), and "The Regulative Power of the Harmony of the Spheres in Medieval Latin, Arabic, and Persian Sources," in *The Routledge Companion to Music, Mind and Well-Being*, ed. Penelope Gouk, James Gordon Kennaway, Jacomien Prins, and Wiebke Thormählen (New York: Routledge, 2019), 33–45.

mathematical ratios—the same ratios that define musical consonances—to determine the structure of both. Both the world's soul and the human soul are divinely ordered, and they share mathematical and musical underpinnings. These divinely given commonalities have beneficial consequences for the human soul, in that music ("the divine music ... not ... the music that delights the common crowd") can restore order and harmony to a soul that is wayward or "out of tune."[4]

Plato goes so far as to state that music is a divine gift to humans. "All audible musical sound is given us for the sake of harmony, which has motions akin to the orbits in our soul, and which ... is not to be used, as is commonly thought, to give irrational pleasure, but as a heaven-sent ally in reducing to order and harmony any disharmony in the revolutions within us."[5] In commenting on this portion of the dialogue, Calcidius states, "Plato is of the opinion that this music can, at long last, recall souls that are wandering astray from the right path to their former harmony. ... [Music] recalls [the soul] to its pristine nature and renders it such as it was when god the creator had made it in the very beginning."[6] Hicks points out the emphasis Calcidius places on the "therapeutic utility of music—its ability, through a kind of soul therapy, to restore the soul to its former harmony."[7] In Plato's understanding, stated in *Timaeus* and transmitted to the Middle Ages through Calcidius, music offers the human soul restorative properties.

The medieval liturgies for the dying, consisting largely of sung material, might have been understood as a utilization of these restorative properties. As we have seen, the deathbed liturgies depict the soul in a state of transition, vulnerable enough to benefit from the protection of the heavenly community. The therapeutic benefit Plato attributes to music might have been seen as a potent resource for the time of a soul's transition. Perhaps the practitioners of the deathbed rituals employed music as they employed the litany—as part of a mobilization of resources for the benefit of the departing soul.

---

[4] The translation of Calcidius is from Hicks, *Composing the World*, 58. Pieragostini considers how Neoplatonic ideas, particularly "the Boethian synthesis of Pythagorean and Platonic views," motivated the use of music in circumstances apart from the end-of-life rituals ("toward curative ends") during the Middle Ages: Renata Pieragostini, "The Healing Power of Music? Documentary Evidence from Late-Fourteenth-Century Bologna," *Speculum* 96, no. 1 (2021): 156–176 (here, 156).

[5] Translation by Desmond Lee, Plato, *Timaeus and Critias* (London: Penguin Books, 1977), 65. Pentcheva explores how music in the medieval Easter liturgy was used to "attune" human participants to the divine: Pentcheva, "Performative Liturgies and Cosmic Sound."

[6] Hicks's translation of Calcidius, *Composing the World*, 58.

[7] Ibid., 58–59.

The writings of Macrobius (another commentator working with Neoplatonic understandings) directly associate music with the time of death. In his fifth-century commentary on the *Dream of Scipio*, Macrobius states, "The practices of diverse peoples have ordained that it was proper to have musical accompaniment... in funeral processions, too... owing to the belief that souls after death return to the source of sweet music, that is, to the sky."[8] In Neoplatonic understandings, the concordant commonalities between the universe and the human soul made music appropriate for the time of death. The divinely created music of the universe was echoed in the human soul, and the human soul, once released from the body, would be subsumed into the greater harmony. Platonic metaphors associate the human soul, music, and the greater motions of the universe with a divine purity; Macrobius' writings show how these associations could create impulses to sing at the time of death.

To my knowledge, we have no texts linking these philosophical and metaphysical ideas with the medieval, liturgical practices of singing at the bedside of a dying person. (Indeed, Hicks notes that the music theorists working with Neoplatonic ideas in the twelfth century were not inclined to create connections between the theoretical and the practical.[9]) But perhaps the liturgies themselves are evidence of such a connection. The rites for the dying, which grant a privileged position to singing, suggest the formative and pervasive nature of the Neoplatonic understandings.[10] Within the fertile nexus of images and ideas provided by Platonic texts and Neoplatonic discourses, singing at the moment of death took on profound resonances. Liturgies crafted for the dying depict a soul in motion and offer material to console, protect, and guide it. The presence of music within these rituals suggests an understanding that it, too, could provide protection and guidance. Neoplatonic discourses of the time, which imagine sacred music recalling the soul to its divinely given order, offer a plausible explanation of why singing was considered beneficial at the time of death.

The liturgical music, as much as any other ritual element, might have served to sacralize the death chamber. Chanting sacred texts brought the

---

[8] Ambrosius Aurelius Theodosius Macrobius, *Commentary on the Dream of Scipio*, trans. William Harris Stahl (New York: Columbia University Press, 1990), 195 (Book II, Chapter 3, 6). My thanks go to Andrew Hicks for pointing out this passage.

[9] Hicks concurs with Gushee on this point: "These twelfth-century authors have little to say on such matters... the 'practical concerns of standard plain-chant.'" Cited in Hicks, *Composing the World*, 8.

[10] My thanks to Konrad Küster of the Universität Freiburg for the suggestion.

"religious soundscape" to a room where physical processes otherwise took foremost prominence. Haug's description of the "reading singers" of the fourth century pertains also to those who conducted and participated in the later deathbed rituals: "They made the sacred text an object of sensual perception, or, in modern terms, they made it an object of 'aesthetic' experience."[11]

Reassuring images, heightened by their musical conveyance, provided comfort for the suffering; melody became the vehicle for intercessory prayer; gathering and singing were the actions the community undertook to support a dying loved one. A study of the deathbed rituals "puts us in the presence of the paradox of human existence, which is the simultaneity of life and death, loss and survival, endurance and change."[12] A study of the rituals' music puts us in the presence of beauty used for a specific purpose: to assist the dying person and the gathered community as they moved through the suffering and change of death. This was music intended for moments of crisis and transition.

My own sense, from experiences both as a performing musician and as a deathbed witness, is that the choice to sing at the end of life might have had pragmatic aspects. The use of song in the moments surrounding death might have been motivated by music's ability to structure time. Music is the art form that unfolds over time and thus controls it, for both performers and listeners. We have to diligently follow the pacing of music to sing it or attend to it. While we sing or listen, the music guides us through seconds, minutes, and hours. As physicist Tom McLeish puts it, "Music orders time, domesticating without trivializing it. . . . [Music] consists of and conveys pattern and regularity."[13] Music offered—and continues to offer—loved ones a way to sustain a vigil at the bedside, through time when ordinary activities and conversation are not possible. Music can progress through circumstances of uncertainty and time periods of uncertain duration.

Brought to bear at the bedside of a dying person, the music of the medieval rituals provided a counterbalance: situations of unpredictability were countered with structure, suffering was countered with comfort, the horrors of a failing body with sweet sound. Music offered a constructive action for moments otherwise filled with powerlessness. By chanting, the community

---

[11] Andreas Haug, "Singing from the Book: The End of Sacrifice and the Rise of Chant in the Fourth Century," *Musical Quarterly* 104, no. 3–4 (2021): 370–391; here 373.
[12] Bynum, *The Resurrection of the Body*, xxviii, in reference to the study of the Middle Ages, more broadly.
[13] Tom McLeish, *The Poetry and Music of Science* (Oxford: Oxford University Press, 2019), 200.

used the intangible medium of its breath to create a flow of beauty. As one person's breathing became irregular and ceased, the community's breathing continued audibly. The patterns of chant, and the disciplined breathing required to produce them, moved singers and listeners through the time when time itself feels strangely suspended. The community and the dying person passed through pain and profound transition with chant as the guiding thread.

APPENDIX

Contents of Individual Rituals

Spellings reflect those found in each manuscript source.
* indicates that the scribe wrote only an incipit.

The publications referred to in the "text edition" column are:
CAO: Hesbert, *Corpus Antiphonalium Officii*
Deshusses: *Le sacramentaire grégorien*
Paxton (1990): *Christianizing Death*
Paxton (2013): *The Death Ritual at Cluny*
Sicard, *Liturgie*

SP F 11

Biboliteca Apostolica Vaticana, Archivio del Capitolo di San Pietro F 11 A
Rome, Old Roman tradition
early twelfth century

folio	Rubric (ritual)	Rubric (item)	incipit	notation	biblical source	text edition
f. 33	Incipit Commendatio Anime					

(continued)

folio	RUBRIC (RITUAL)	RUBRIC (ITEM)	incipit	notation	biblical source	text edition
	IN PRIMIS DICANTUR	VII PSALMI SPECIALES CUM LETANIA			Psalm 6, 31, 37, 50, 101, 129, 142	Paxton (2013), 60-81
	POST HEC		Kyrie Christe Kyrie*			
			Pater noster*		Matthew 6	Paxton (2013), 112
f. 33v		CAPITULUM RESPONSUM	In memoria eterna erit iustus Ab auditu malo non timebit		Psalm 111:7	CAO 8096
			A porta inferi			CAO 7923
		RESPONSUM	Erue domine animam eius			Paxton (2013), 106
		RESPONSUM	Requiescat in pace Amen		cf. Psalm 4:9	Paxton (2013), 166
		RESPONSUM	Domine exaudi orationem meam Et clamor meus ad te perueniat		Psalm 101:2	CAO 8025
			Dominus uobiscum			
		OREMUS	Omnipotens sempiterne deus conseruator animarum			Deshusses 2794

f. 34	ALIA ORATIO	O anima tibi dico	
f. 34v	ORATIO	Proficiscere anima Christiana	Dumas 2892 Sicard (1978), 362-368 Paxton (1990), 118, n. 77
f. 35v	ALIA ORATIO	Omnipotens sempiterne deus qui humano corpori animam	Deshusses 4077 Sicard (1978), 272-273 Paxton (1990), 178, n. 39
f. 36	ORATIO	Partem beate resurrectionis optineat	Deshusses 4072
f. 36v	ALIA ORATIO	Ascendant ad te domine preces nostre et animam famuli tui gaudia	Deshusses 2850
f. 36v	ORATIO	Commendamus tibi domine animam famuli tui in manibus patriarcharum	
f. 37	ALIA ORATIO	Commendamus tibi domine animam famuli tui et precamur propter quam ad terram	cf. Deshusses 4065 Sicard (1978), 275-279
f. 37v	ALIA ORATIO	Commendamus te omnipotenti deo eique te cuius es creatura	
f. 39	ALIA ORATIO	Svscipe domine seruum tuum in bonum habitaculum libera domine	

(continued)

folio	Rubric (ritual)	Rubric (item)	incipit	notation	biblical source	text edition
f. 40		ALIA ORATIO	Tibi domine commendamus animam famuli tui			Deshusses 1415[a] Paxton (1990), 147, n. 71 Paxton (2013), 158 Sicard (1978), 355–358
		ALIA ORATIO	Deus cui soli competit medicinam prestare post mortem			Deshusses 3019
		ALIA ORATIO	Absolue quesumus domine animam famuli tui ab omni uinculo delictorum			Deshusses 1016 Paxton (2013), 160
f. 40v		ALIA ORATIO	Deus omnipotens qui dedit potestatem beato Petro apostolo et ceteris apostolis			
		ANTIPHONA PER UIAM	Dirige domine	notation	cf. Psalm 5:9	CAO 2244
		ANTIPHONA	Secundum magnam	notation	Psalm 50:3, 10	
		ANTIPHONA	Domine deus in multitudine	notation	cf. Psalm 5:8–9	
f. 41		ANTIPHONA	Conuertere domine	notation	Psalm 6:5–6	CAO 1921
		ANTIPHONA	Nequando rapiat	notation	Psalm 7:3	CAO 3875

APPENDIX 179

	ANTIPHONA	Dextera tua	notation	cf. Psalm 17:36
f. 41v	ANTIPHONA	Dominus suscepit me	notation	cf. Psalm 117:13 cf. Psalm 26:13
	ANTIPHONA	Redemisti me	notation	Psalm 30:6 Luke 23:46	CAO 4585
	ANTIPHONA PSALMUS	Animam eius Ad dominum dum tribularer*	notation notation	Psalm 119
f. 42	ANTIPHONA	Leto animo	notation	cf. Genesis 2:7	CAO 3573 Sicard (1978), 71-72
	PSALMUS	De profundis*	notation	Psalm 129	Paxton (2013), 76
	ANTIPHONA PSALMUS	Qui cognoscis Secundum magnam*	notation notation	cf. Psalm 18:13 Psalm 50	CAO 4461 Paxton (2013), 68-70
f. 42v	ANTIPHONA	Svscipiat te Christus	notation	cf. Luke 16:22	CAO 5092
QUANDO INGREDIUNTUR ECCLESIAM	ANTIPHONA	Induc eum domine	notation	cf. Exodus 15:17

ᵃ Benedict of Aniane uses this prayer in his supplement, but the version found in SP F 11 retains the wording of the earlier Rheinau sacramentary. See Paxton, *Christianizing Death*, 147 and note 71.

Paris 934

Paris, Bibliothèque nationale de France, lat. 934
Cathédrale Saint-Étienne de Sens (Cathedral of Saint Stephen, Sens)
late twelfth–thirteenth centuries

folio	Rubric (ritual)	Rubric (item)	incipit	notation	biblical source	text edition
f. 113v	Incipit					
	Commendatio anime					
	Cum igitur anima in agone					
	sui exitus					
	dissolutione corporis					
	uisa fuerit laborare					
	cum uenire studebunt					
	fratres uel clerici quique					
	fideles					
	et agatur hoc modo					
	commendatio					
		Responsorium	Subuenite sancti dei	notation		CAO 7716 Paxton (2013), 114 Sicard (1978), 66
f. 114		Versus	Suscipiat eam Christus	notation of incipit	cf. Luke 16:22	CAO 7716v Paxton (2013), 114 Sicard (1978), 66-68

	ORATIO	Tibi domine commendamus animam famuli tui		Deshusses 1415 Paxton (1990), 147, n. 71 Paxton (2013), 158 Sicard (1978), 355-358
	ALIA	Misericordiam tuam domine sancte pater omnipotens		Deshusses 4071 Paxton (1990), 178, n. 38 Sicard (1978), 323-325
f. 114v		Suscipiat te Christus In exitu Israhel*	notation notation	cf. Luke 16:22 Psalm 113	CAO 5092 Paxton (2013), 130-132
		Omnipotens sempiternę deus qui humano corpori animam . . . letifica clementissime deus animam serui tui			Deshusses 4077 opening: Paxton (1990), 178, n. 39 Sicard (1978), 272-273
f. 115v	ANTIPHONA	Chorus angelorum te suscipiat	notation	cf. Luke 16:22	CAO 1783 Sicard (1978), 69-71
	PSALMUS VSQUE	Dilexi quoniam* Ad dominum cum tribularer*	notation	Psalm 114 Psalm 119	
	ORATIO	Diri uulneris nouitate			Deshusses 4059 Sicard (1978), 305-308

(continued)

folio	Rubric (ritual)	Rubric (item)	incipit	notation	biblical source	text edition
f. 116	TUNC ROGET SACERDOS PRO EO ORARE		Pater noster* Et ne nos*		Matthew 6	Paxton (2013), 112
			Non intres in iudicium*		Psalm 142:2	
			A porta inferi*			CAO 7923 Paxton (2013), 106
			Requiem eternam*		cf. IV Esdras 2:34–35	CAO 8183 Sicard (1978), 72 Paxton (1990), 146, n. 66 Paxton (2013), 106
			Domine exaudi*		Psalm 101:2	CAO 8025
			Dominus uobiscum Et cum spiritu tuo			
		Oratio	Partem beatę resurrectionis obtineat			Deshusses 4072
	TUNC PONATUR CORPUS IN FERETRO ET PORTETUR IN ECCLESIAM CANENDO	Psalmus	Miserere mei*		Psalm 50	Paxton (2013), 68-70

GSB 3

Bourg-Saint-Pierre, Hospice du Grand-Saint-Bernard, ms. 3 (ancien 10091)
Parish of Orsières, Switzerland (Canton Valais)
early fourteenth century

folio	RUBRIC (RITUAL)	RUBRIC (ITEM)	incipit	biblical source	text edition
f. 30	INCIPIT COMMENDACIO ANIME COMMUNIS				
f. 30v	PRIUS FACIAT AQUAM BENEDITAM[b] ET ASPERGAT SUPER ASTAMTES[c] ET PER DOMUM DEINDE SUPER CORPUS ET DICAT	RESPUNSUM[d]	Subuenite sancti dei		CAO 7716 Paxton (2013), 114 Sicard (1978), 66
			Suscipiat te Christus Offerentes*	cf. Luke 16:22	CAO 7716v Paxton (2013), 114 Sicard (1978), 66-68
			Kyrieleyson		
			Pater <noster>*	Matthew 6	Paxton (2013), 112
f. 31			Pie recordacionis		Deshusses 1398 Paxton (2013), 106 Sicard (1978), 262-264

(continued)

184 APPENDIX

folio	RUBRIC (RITUAL)	RUBRIC (ITEM)	incipit	biblical source	text edition
		ALIA ORATIO	Deus cui omnia viuunt		Deshusses 1399 Paxton (2013), 106-108 Sicard (1978), 90-92 (Forme II)
f. 31v		VERSUS SPALMUS DAUID	Sucipiat te Christus qui vocauit te I\<n\> exitu Israhel	cf. Luke 16:22 Psalm 113	CAO 5092 Paxton (2013), 130-132
f. 32v		ORATIO	Suscipe domine animam famuli tui... quam de ergasculo		Deshusses 1400 Paxton (1990), 143, n. 55 Paxton (2013), 108
		VERSUS	Chorus angelorum te suscipiat	cf. Luke 16:22	CAO 1783 Sicard (1978), 69-71
		SPALMUS DAVID	Dilexi quoniam exaudiet dominus	Psalm 114	
f. 33			Requiem eternam*		CAO 8183
		SPALMUS	Credidi propter	Psalm 115	
f. 33v			De profundis*e Kyrieleyson	Psalm 129	Paxton (2013), 76
			Pater noster* Et ne nos*	Matthew 6	Paxton (2013), 112

VERSUS	In memoria eterna erunt justi Ab audi<ti>one*	Psalm 111:7	CAO 8096
	Anima eius in bonis demorabitur Et semen*	Psalm 24:13	CAO 7947
	Non intres in iudicium* Quia non iustificabitur*	Psalm 142:2	Paxton (2013), 106
	Ne tradas bestiis Et animas pauperem[f] In finem	Psalm 73:19	
PSALMUS	Miserere mei deus*	Psalm 50	Paxton (2013), 68-70
	Requiem eternam dona*	cf. IV Esdras 2:34-35	CAO 8183 Paxton (1990), 146, n. 66 Paxton (2013), 106 Sicard (1978), 72
	Domine exaudi orationem*	Psalm 101:2	CAO 8025
	Dominus vobiscum*		
	Non intres <in iudicium> cum seruo tuo	cf. Psalm 142:2	Deshusses 1401 Paxton (1990), 144, n. 56 Paxton (2013), 126 Sicard (1978), 201

(continued)

folio	RUBRIC (RITUAL)	RUBRIC (ITEM)	incipit	biblical source	text edition
		Alia oratio	D<e>us vite dator et humanorum corporum reparator		Deshusses 1407 Paxton (2013), 112-114
f. 34	Postea conueniant omnes ut deferant corpus ad eclesiam et antequam abtrahatur[g] de domo dicat responsum				
			Subuenite sancti*		CAO 7716 Paxton (2013), 114 Sicard (1978), 66
			Kyrieleyson*		
			Pater noster*	Matthew 6	Paxton (2013), 112
		Oracio	Deus vite dator*		Deshusses 1407 Paxton (2013), 112-114
		Alia oracio	Deus qui humanarum animarum		Deshusses 1408 Paxton (2013), 114
f. 34v	Tunc leuetur corpus et portetur ad ecclesiam dicendo	Antiphana[h]	In paradisum deducant te		CAO 3266 Paxton (2013), 130 Sicard (1978), 135

f. 35v	Spalmus	Ad te leuaui animam meam	Psalm 24	
		Requiem eternam*	cf. IV Esdras 2:34-35	CAO 8183 Paxton (1990), 146, n. 66 Paxton (2013), 106 Sicard (1978), 72
	Antiphona	Tu iussisti nasci		CAO 5213 Sicard (1978), 133
	Spalmus Dauid	Te decet hymnus deus	Psalm 64	
f. 36	Responsorium	Libera me domine		CAO 7091 Paxton (2013), 128 Sicard (1978), 167
	Dum intratur ecclesiam dicatur			

b BENEDITAM] read as BENEDICTAM.
c ASTAMTES] read as ASTANTES.
d RESPUNSUM] read as RESPONSUM.
e marginal annotation.
f pauperem] read as pauperum.
g ABTRAHATUR] read as ABSTRAHATUR.
h ANTIPHANA] read as ANTIPHONA.

Cranston 2322

Reigate (Surrey), Parish Church of St Mary Magdalene, Cranston Library 2322 Abbey of Saint Mary the Virgin and Saint Francis without Aldgate fifteenth century (second half)

folio	Rubric (ritual)	Rubric (item)	incipit	notation	biblical source	text edition
f. 117v	Ordo commendacionis anime					
	Primo dicantur	Letanie	Kyrieleyson Christeleyson Kyrieleyson			
			Sancta Maria ora pro ea			
f. 118v	In exitum anime	Oracio	Proficiscere anima Christiana			Dumas 2892 Paxton (1990), 118, n. 77 Sicard (1978), 362-368
f. 119		Responsio	Amen			
			Deus misericors deus clemens			Deshusses 1396 Dumas 2888 Paxton (1990), 77, n. 115
f. 119v			Commendo te omnipotenti deo soror mea karissima			
f. 120v		Responsio	Amen			

APPENDIX   189

f. 121v	ORACIO	Suscipe domine ancillam tuam in locum Amen	
	RESPONSIO		
	ORACIO	Commendamus tibi domine animam famule tue N.ⁱ precamurque Amen	cf. Deshusses 4065 Sicard (1978), 275-279
f. 122	RESPONSIO		
	ORACIO	Delicta iuuentutis et ignorancias Amen	Sicard (1978), 378-380
f. 122v	RESPONSIO		
SI ANXIATUR ADHUC ANIMA DICANTUR HII	PSALMI	Confitemini domino quoniam bonus*	Psalm 117
	VSQUE AD PSALMUM	Beati immaculati* Ad dominum cum tribularer*	Psalm 118 Psalm 119
EGRESSA ANIMA DE CORPORE DICATUR HOC	RESPONSORIUM	Subuenite*	CAO 7716 Paxton (2013), 114 Sicard (1978), 66
	VERSUS	Sus<ci>piat te Christus*	CAO 7716v Paxton (2013), 114 Sicard (1978), 66-68

(continued)

APPENDIX

folio	Rubric (ritual)	Rubric (item)	incipit	notation	biblical source	text edition
			Kyrieleyson			
			Pater noster*		Matthew 6	Paxton (2013), 112
			Et ne nos*			
		Responsio	Sed libera*			
		Versus	Requiem eternam dona eis domine		cf. IV Esdras 2:34–35	CAO 8183 Paxton (1990), 146, n. 66
		Responsio	Et lux perpetua*			Paxton (2013), 106 Sicard (1978), 72
		Versus	A porta inferi			CAO 7923
		Responsio	Erue domine animam eius			Paxton (2013), 106
		Versus	Requiescant in pace		cf. Psalm 4:9	Paxton (2013), 166
		Responsio	Amen			
		Versus	Domine exaudi*		Psalm 101:2	CAO 8025
		Responsio	Et clamor*			
		Oracio	Tibi domine commendamus animam famule tue sororis nostre			Deshusses 1415 Paxton (1990), 147, n. 71 Paxton (2013), 158 Sicard (1978), 355-358
f. 123		Responsio	Amen			

TUNC SORORES QUE
PRESENS FUERINT[1]
LAUENT CORPUS
ET POSTEA PONANT IN
FERETRO ET SORORES
STENT ORDINATIM IN
CIRCUITU FERETRI IUXTA
DISPOSICIONEM MAIORIS
INCIPIENTE ABBATISSA

	Kyrieleyson		
Responsio	Pater noster* Sed libera*	Matthew 6	Paxton (2013), 112
Versus	In memoria eterna erit iusta	Psalm 111:7	CAO 8096
Responsio	Ab auditione mala non timebit		
Versus	Ne tradas domine bestiis animam confitentem tibi	Psalm 73:19	
Responsio	Et animas pauperum tuorum ne obliuiscaris in finem		
Versus	Non intres in iudicium cum ancilla tua domine	cf. Psalm 142:2	Paxton (2013), 106
Responsio	Quia non iustificabitur		

(continued)

APPENDIX

folio	Rubric (ritual)	Rubric (item)	incipit	notation	biblical source	text edition
		Versus	A porta inferi			CAO 7923
		Responsio	Erue domine animam meam			Paxton (2013), 106
		Versus	Requiescant in pace		cf. Psalm 4:9	Paxton (2013), 166
		Responsio	Amen			
		Versus	Domine exaudi oracionem		Psalm 101:2	CAO 8025
		Responsio	Et clamor*			
f. 123v[k]		Oracio	Suscipe domine animam famule tue sororis nostre quam de ergastulo Amen			Deshusses 1400 Paxton (1990), 143, n. 55 Paxton (2013), 108
		Responsio				
	Deinde sorores portent corpus ad ecclesiam decantando	Responsorium	Subuenite*			CAO 7716 Paxton (2013), 114 Sicard (1978), 66
		Versus	Suscipiat*		cf. Luke 16:22	CAO 7716v Paxton (2013), 114 Sicard (1978), 66-68

[i] N.] read as Nomen, indicating the name of the dying person.
[j] QUE PRESENS FUERINT] more plausible: QUE PRESENTES FUERINT.
[k] The folio change occurs after the rubric ORACIO.

Bibliography

Alter, Robert. *The Hebrew Bible: A Translation with Commentary*. 3 vols. New York: W. W. Norton, 2019.

Altstatt, Alison. "Re-membering the Wilton Processional." *Notes: The Quarterly Journal of the Music Library Association* 72, no. 4 (2016): 690–732.

Altstatt, Alison. *Wilton Abbey in Procession: Religious Women's Music and Ritual in the Thirteenth-century Wilton Processional*. Exeter Studies in Medieval Europe. Liverpool: University of Liverpool Press, forthcoming.

Ambrose, Kirk. "Visual Poetics of the Cluny Hemicycle Capital Inscriptions." *Word & Image* 20, no. 2 (2004): 155–164.

Andrews, Frances. "The Early Mendicants." In *The Oxford Handbook of Christian Monasticism*, edited by Bernice M. Kaczynski, 264–284. Oxford: Oxford University Press, 2020.

Andrieu, Michel. *Les ordines Romani du haut moyen âge: Les Textes; Ordines XXXV–XLIX*. Louvain: Spicilegium Sacrum Lovaniense, 1956.

Appleford, Amy. *Learning to Die in London, 1380–1540*. Philadelphia: University of Pennsylvania Press, 2015.

Ariès, Philippe. *The Hour of Our Death*. Translated by Helen Weaver. New York: Alfred A. Knopf, 1981.

Atkinson, Charles M. *The Critical Nexus*. Oxford: Oxford University Press, 2008; repr. ed. 2015.

Aubrey, Elizabeth. "Vernacular Song I: Lyric." In *The Cambridge History of Music*, edited by Mark Everist and Thomas Forrest Kelly, 382–427. Cambridge: Cambridge University Press, 2018.

Augustine. *Sermons: Vol. III (51–94) on the New Testament*. Translation and notes by Edmund Hill. Edited by John E. Rotelle. Brooklyn, NY: New City Press, 1991.

Avril, Joseph. "La pastorale des malades et des mourants aux XIIe et XIIIe siècles." In *Death in the Middle Ages*, edited by Herman Braet and Werner Verbeke, 88–106. Leuven: Leuven University Press, 1983.

Barnhouse, Lucy. "Disordered Women? The Hospital Sisters of Mainz and Their Late Medieval Identities." *Medieval Feminist Forum* 55, no. 2 (2020): 60–97.

Bärsch, Jürgen. "Totenliturgie im spätmittelalterlichen Frauenstift Essen: Die exequiae mortuorum nach dem Liber ordinarius." In *Unitas in pluralitate: Libri ordinarii als Quelle für die Liturgiegeschichte*, edited by Charles Caspers and Louis van Tongeren, 327–356. Liturgiewissenschaftliche Quellen und Forschungen 103. Münster: Aschendorff Verlag, 2015.

Bates, Stephen. "Preparations for a Christian Death: The Later Middle Ages." In *A Companion to Death, Burial, and Remembrance in Late Medieval and Early Modern Europe, c. 1300–1700*, edited by Philip Booth and Elizabeth C. Tingle, 72–105. Leiden: Brill, 2021.

Beach, Alison I. *Women as Scribes: Book Production and Monastic Reform in Twelfth-Century Bavaria.* Cambridge: Cambridge University Press, 2004.

Bell, David. *What Nuns Read: Books and Libraries in Medieval English Libraries.* Kalamazoo, MI: Cistercian Publications, 1995.

Biay, Sébastian. "Building a Church with Music: The Plainchant Capitals at Cluny, c. 1100." In *Resounding Images: Medieval Intersections of Art, Music, and Sound*, edited by Susan Boynton and Diane J. Reilly, 221–236. Turnhout: Brepols, 2015.

Biay, Sébastian. "Les chapiteaux de rond-point de la troisième église abbatiale de Cluny (fin XIe–début XIIe siècle), étude iconographique." PhD diss., Université de Poitiers, 2011.

Biblioteca Vaticana. "DigiVatLib: Manoscritto Arch.Cap.S.Pietro.F.11.pt.A." Available at https://digi.vatlib.it/view/MSS_Arch.Cap.S.Pietro.F.11.pt.A.

Bibliothèque nationale de France. "Gallica: Pontificale Senonense." Available at https://gallica.bnf.fr/ark:/12148/btv1b8432295p.r=934?rk=21459;2.

Binski, Paul. *Medieval Death: Ritual and Representation.* Ithaca, NY: Cornell University Press, 1996.

Blair, John, and Richard Sharpe, eds. *Pastoral Care before the Parish.* Leicester: Leicester University Press, 1992.

Boe, John. "Votive-Mass Chants in Florence, Biblioteca Riccardiana, MSS 299 and 300 and Vatican City, Biblioteca Apostolica Vaticana, Archivio San Pietro F 11: A Source Study." In *Western Plainchant in the First Millennium: Studies in the Medieval Liturgy and Its Music*, edited by Sean Gallagher, James Haar, John Nádas, and Timothy Striplin, 259–316. London: Routledge, 2017.

Booth, Philip, and Elizabeth C. Tingle, eds. *A Companion to Death, Burial, and Remembrance in Late Medieval and Early Modern Europe, c. 1300–1700.* Brill's Companions to the Christian Tradition 94. Leiden: Brill, 2021.

Boretius, A., ed. *Capitularia Regum Francorum*, vol. 1. Monumenta Germaniae Historica, Legum Sectio II. Hannover: Impensis Bibliopolii Hahn, 1883.

Boudeau, Océane. "Manuscrits notés en neumes en Occident (MANNO): Paris, Bibliothèque nationale de France Latin 934." Accessed July 9, 2023, at https://manno.saprat.fr/sites/default/files/manno/notice/Latin%20934_1.pdf.

Bourdillon, Anne F. C. *The Order of Minoresses in England.* Manchester: The University Press, 1926.

Boynton, Susan. "Boy Singers in Medieval Monasteries and Cathedrals." In *Young Choristers*, edited by Susan Boynton and Eric Rice, 37–48. Woodbridge: Boydell Press, 2008.

Boynton, Susan. "A Monastic Death Ritual from the Imperial Abbey of Farfa." *Traditio* 64 (2009): 57–84.

Boynton, Susan. "Monastic Liturgy, 1100–1500: Continuity and Performance." In *The Cambridge History of Medieval Monasticism in the Latin West*, edited by Alison I. Beach and Isabelle Cochelin, 958–974. Cambridge: Cambridge University Press, 2020.

Boynton, Susan. *Shaping a Monastic Identity: Liturgy & History at the Imperial Abbey of Farfa, 1000–1125.* Ithaca, NY: Cornell University Press, 2006.

Bracaloni, Leone. *Il primo rituale Francescano nel breviario di S. Chiara.* Quaracchi: Collegio di S. Bonaventurae, 1923.

Braet, Herman, and Werner Verbeke, eds. *Death in the Middle Ages.* Leuven: Leuven University Press, 1983.

Brenner, Elma. "Between Palliative Care and Curing the Soul: Medical and Religious Responses to Leprosy in France and England, c. 1100–c. 1500." In *Medicine, Religion and Gender in Medieval Culture*, edited by Naoë Kukita Yoshikawa, 221–236. Gender in the Middle Ages 11. Cambridge: D. S. Brewer, 2015.

Brenner, Elma. "The Medical Role of Monasteries in the Latin West, c. 1050–1300." In *The Cambridge History of Medieval Monasticism in the Latin West*, edited by Alison I. Beach and Isabelle Cochelin, 865–881. Cambridge: Cambridge University Press, 2020.

Brodman, James W. "Religion and Discipline in the Hospitals of Thirteenth-century France." In *The Medieval Hospital and Medical Practice*, edited by Barbara S. Bowers, 123–132. AVISTA Studies in History of Medieval Technology, Science and Art 3. Farnham: Ashgate, 2007.

Brommer, Peter, ed. *Capitula episcoporum I*. Monumenta Germaniae Historia. Hannover: Hahnsche Buchhandlung, 1984.

Brown, Peter. *The Cult of the Saints: Its Rise and Function in Latin Christianity*. Chicago: University of Chicago Press, 1981.

Brown, Peter. "The Decline of the Empire of God: Amnesty, Penance, and the Afterlife from Late Antiquity to the Middle Ages." In *Last Things: Death and the Apocalypse in the Middle Ages*, edited by Caroline Walker Bynum and Paul Freedman, 41–59. Philadelphia: University of Pennsylvania Press, 2000.

Brown, Peter. *The Ransom of the Soul: Afterlife and Wealth in Early Western Christianity*. Cambridge, MA: Harvard University Press, 2015.

Brown, Rachel Fulton. "Prayer." In *The Oxford Handbook of Christian Monasticism*, edited by Bernice M. Kaczynski, 316–332. Oxford: Oxford University Press, 2020.

Bruggisser-Lanker, Therese. *Musik und Tod im Mittelalter*. Göttingen: Vandenhoeck & Ruprecht, 2010.

Buc, Philippe. *The Dangers of Ritual: Between Early Medieval Texts and Social Scientific Theory*. Princeton, NJ: Princeton University Press, 2001.

Bugyis, Katie Ann-Marie. *The Care of Nuns: The Ministries of Benedictine Women in England During the Central Middle Ages*. New York: Oxford University Press, 2019.

Bugyis, Katie Ann-Marie. "Female Monastic Cantors and Sacristans in Central Medieval England: Four Sketches." In *Medieval Cantors and Their Craft: Music, Liturgy and the Shaping of History, 800–1500*, edited by Katie Ann-Marie Bugyis, A. B. Kraebel, and Margot E. Fassler, 151–169. Woodbridge: York Medieval Press, 2017.

Bullough, Donald. "Burial, Community and Belief in the Early Medieval West." In *Ideal and Reality in Frankish and Anglo-Saxon Society*, edited by P. Wormald, D. Bullough, and R. Collins, 177–201. Oxford: Basil Blackwell, 1983.

Bullough, Donald. "The Carolingian Liturgical Experience." In *Continuity and Change in Christian Worship: Papers Read at the 1997 Summer Meeting and the 1998 Winter Meeting of the Ecclesiastical History Society*, edited by R. N. Swanson, 29–64. Studies in Church History 35. Woodbridge, Suffolk: Published for the Ecclesiastical History Society by the Boydell Press, 1999.

Burns, J. Patout, Jr., and Robin M. Jensen. *Christianity in Roman Africa: The Development of Its Practices and Beliefs*. Grand Rapids, MI: William B. Eerdmans, 2014.

Bynum, Caroline Walker. *The Resurrection of the Body in Western Christianity, 200–1336*. New York: Columbia University Press, 2019.

Bynum, Caroline Walker, and Paul Freedman, eds. *Last Things: Death and the Apocalypse in the Middle Ages*. Philadelphia: University of Pennsylvania Press, 2000.

Caesarius. Sancti *Caesarii Episcopi Arelatensis opera omnia*. Edited by D. Germani Morin. N.p.: Marietoli, 1942.
Campbell, Anna. "Franciscan Nuns in England, the Minoress Foundations and Their Patrons, 1281–1367." In *The English Province of the Franciscans (1224–c. 1350)*, edited by Michael Robson, 426–447. Leiden: Koninklijke Brill, 2017.
Cannon, Christopher. "What Did the Medieval Laity Hear When They Heard Latin?" Paper presented at the national conference of the Medieval Academy of America, Virtual Version, March 27–29, 2020.
CAO. See Hesbert.
Carruthers, Mary. *The Experience of Beauty in the Middle Ages*. Oxford: Oxford University Press, 2013.
Chailley, Jacques. "Les huit tons de la musique et l'éthos des modes aux chapiteaux de Cluny." *Acta musicologica* 57 (1985): 73–94.
Chavasse, Antoine. *Étude sur l'onction des infirmes dans l'Église latine du IIIe au XIe siècle*. Lyon: Librairie du Sacré-Cœur, 1942.
Chavasse, Antoine. *La Sacramentaire Gélasien (Vaticanus Reginensis 316): sacramentaire presbytéral en usage dans les titres romains au VIIe siècle*. Tournai: Desclée, 1958.
Chinca, Mark. *Meditating Death in Medieval and Early Modern Devotional Writing: From Bonaventure to Luther*. Oxford Studies in Medieval Literature and Culture. Oxford: Oxford University Press, 2020.
Chitwood, Zachary. "Dying, Death and Burial in the Christian Orthodox Tradition: Byzantium and the Greek Churches, ca. 1300–1700." In *A Companion to Death, Burial, and Remembrance in Late Medieval and Early Modern Europe, c. 1300–1700*, edited by Philip Booth and Elizabeth C. Tingle, 199–224. Leiden: Brill, 2021.
CLLA. See Gamber.
Comper, Frances M. M. *The Book of the Craft of Dying*. London: Longmans, Green, and Co., 1917.
Courtenay, William J. *Rituals for the Dead: Religion and Community in the Medieval University of Paris*. Notre Dame, IN: University of Notre Dame Press, 2018.
Cutter, Mary Ann. *Death: A Reader*. Notre Dame, IN: University of Notre Dame Press, 2019.
Cutter, Paul F. *Musical Sources of the Old-Roman Mass: An Inventory of MS Rome, St. Cecilia Gradual 1071; MS Rome, Vaticanum latinum 5319; MSS Rome, San Pietro F 22 and F 11*. Musicological Studies & Documents 36. Neuhausen-Stuttgart: American Institute of Musicology, Hänssler Verlag, 1979.
Cyrus, Cynthia J. *The Scribes for Women's Convents in Late Medieval Germany*. Toronto: University of Toronto Press, 2009.
Daley, Brian E., and Paul R. Kolbet. *The Harp of Prophecy: Early Christian Interpretation of the Psalms*. Notre Dame, IN: University of Notre Dame Press, 2014.
Daniell, Christopher. *Death and Burial in Medieval England 1066–1550*. London: Routledge, 1997.
Dante Alighieri. "Digital Dante: The Divine Comedy; Purgatorio." Edited by Teodolinda Barolini et al. Columbia University and Columbia University Libraries. Accessed September 15, 2020, at https://digitaldante.columbia.edu/dante/divine-comedy/.
Davies, Jon. *Death, Burial and Rebirth in the Religions of Antiquity*. London: Routledge, 1999.
Davis, Adam J. *The Medieval Economy of Salvation: Charity, Commerce, and the Rise of the Hospital*. Ithaca, NY: Cornell University Press, 2019.

de Clercq, Carlo. "Ordines unctionis infirmi des IXe et Xe siècles." *Ephemerides liturgicae* 44 (1930): 100–122.

De Ricci, Seymour. *Census of Medieval and Renaissance Manuscripts in the United States and Canada*. With the assistance of W. J. Wilson. New York: H. W. Wilson, 1935–1940.

Deshusses, Jean. "Le 'supplément' au sacramentaire grégorien: Alcuin ou Saint Benoît d'Aniane?" *Archiv für Liturgiewissenschaft* 9 (1965): 48–71.

Deshusses, Jean, ed. *Le sacramentaire grégorien*. 3 vols. Spicilegium Friburgense 16. Fribourg (CH): Éditions universitaires Fribourg Suisse, 1971–1982.

DiCenso, Daniel Joseph. "Moved by Music: Problems in Approaching Emotional Expression in Gregorian Chant." In *Emotion and Medieval Textual Media*, edited by Mary C. Flannery, 19–50. Turnhout: Brepols, 2018.

DiCenso, Daniel Joseph. "Sacramentary-Antiphoners as Sources of Gregorian Chant in the Eighth and Ninth Centuries." PhD diss., University of Cambridge, 2011.

Donohue, James Michael. "The Rite for the Commendation of the Dying in the 1983 *Pastoral Care of the Sick: Rites of Anointing and Viaticum*: A Study through a Comparison with Its Counterparts in the 1614 *Rituale Romanum* and in the 1972 editio typica of *Ordo unctionis infirmorum eorumque pastoralis curae*." PhD diss., Catholic University of America, 2000.

Driscoll, Michael. "Per Sora Nostra Morte Corporale: The Role of Medieval Women in Death and Burial Practices." *Liturgical Ministry* 10 (Winter 2001): 14–22.

Driscoll, Michael. "Reconstructing Liturgical History before the libri ordinarii: The Role of Medieval Women in Death and Burial Practices." In *Unitas in pluralitate: Libri ordinarii als Quelle für die Liturgiegeschichte*, edited by Charles Caspers and Louis van Tongeren, 299–326. Liturgiewissenschaftliche Quellen und Forschungen 103. Münster: Aschendorff Verlag, 2015.

Driscoll, Michael. "The Seven Penitential Psalms: Their Designation and Usages from the Middle Ages Onwards." *Ecclesia orans* 17 (2000): 153–201.

Droese, Janine. *Die Musik der Engel in ihrer Bedeutung für Musik und Musikanschauung des 13.–16. Jahrhunderts*. Hildesheim: Olms, 2021.

Duclow, Donald F. "Dying Well: The Ars moriendi and the Dormition of the Virgin." In *Death and Dying in the Middle Ages*, edited by Edelgard E. DuBruck and Barbara I. Gusick, 379–430. New York: Peter Lang, 1999.

Dumas, Antione, ed. *Liber sacramentorum Gellonensis*. Corpus Christianorum Series Latina 159, 159A. Turnhout: Brepols, 1981.

Dyer, Joseph. "Boy Singers of the Roman Schola Cantorum." In *Young Choristers*, edited by Susan Boynton and Eric Rice, 19–36. Woodbridge: Boydell Press, 2008.

Dyer, Joseph. "The Schola Cantorum and Its Roman Milieu in the Early Middle Ages." In *De musica et cantu: Studien zur Geschichte der Kirchenmusik und der Oper: Helmut Hucke zum 60. Geburtstag*, edited by P. Cahn and A.-K. Heimer, 19–40. Hildesheim: Olms, 1993.

Dyer, Joseph. "Sources of Romano-Frankish Liturgy and Music." In *The Cambridge History of Medieval Music*, edited by Mark Everist and Thomas Forrest Kelly, 92–122. The Cambridge History of Music. Cambridge: Cambridge University Press, 2018.

Dyer, Joseph, Kenneth Levy, and Dimitri Conomos. "Liturgy and Liturgical Books." In *Grove Music Online*. 2001. https://www-oxfordmusiconline-com.proxy.library.nd.edu/grovemusic/.

Effros, Bonnie. *Caring for Body and Soul: Burial and the Afterlife in the Merovingian World*. University Park: Pennsylvania State University Press, 2002.

Engels, Stefan. "Dies irae, dies illa." In *Krisen, Kriege, Katastrophen*, edited by Christain Rohr, Ursula Bieber, and Katharina Zeppezauer-Wachauer, 379–460. Heidelberg: Universitätsverlag, 2018.

Engels, Stefan. "The Office of the Cantor in Early Western Monastic Rules and Customaries: A Preliminary Investigation." *Early Music History* 5, no. 1 (1985): 29–51.

Fassler, Margot E. "Women and Their Sequences: An Overview and a Case Study." *Speculum* 94, no. 3 (2019): 625–673.

Feld, Helmut. *Franziskus von Assisi*. München: C. H. Beck, 2001.

Feld, Helmut. *Franziskus von Assisi und seine Bewegung*. Darmstadt: Wissenschaftliche Buchgesellschaft, 1994.

Férotin, Marius, ed. *Le liber ordinum en usage dans l'église wisigothique et mozarabe d'Espagne du cinquième au onzième siècle*. Reprint edition by Anthony Ward and Cuthbert Johnson. Bibliotheca "Ephemerides liturgicae" Subsidia 83. Rome: Centro Liturgico Vincenziano Edizioni Liturgiche, 1996.

Francis. *Francis of Assisi: Early Documents*. Edited by Regis J. Armstrong, J. A. Wayne Hellmann, and William J. Short. Hyde Park, NY: New City Press, 2002.

Frank, Hieronymus. "Der älteste erhaltene Ordo defunctorum der römischen Liturgie und sein Fortleben in Totenagenden des frühen Mittelalters." *Archiv für Liturgiewissenschaft* 7 (1962): 360–415.

Freedman, Paul. "Rural Society." In *The New Cambridge Medieval History* 6. c. 1300–c. 1415, edited by Michael Jones, 82–101. Cambridge: Cambridge University Press, 2000.

Freestone, W. H. *The Sacrament Reserved*. London: A. R. Mowbray & Co., 1917.

Frere, Walter Howard. *Antiphonale Sarisburiense: A Reproduction in Facsimile of a Manuscript of the Thirteenth Century*. London: Farnborough Gregg, 1901–1924.

Gamber, Klaus. *Codices liturgici latini antiquiores* [CLLA]. Spicilegii Friburgensis Subsidia 1, Pars secunda. Freiburg, Switzerland: Universitätsverlag Freiburg Schweiz, 1968.

Geary, Patrick J. *Living with the Dead in the Middle Ages*. Ithaca: Cornell University Press, 1994.

Geary, Patrick J. *Phantoms of Remembrance: Memory and Oblivion at the End of the First Millennium*. Princeton, NJ: Princeton University Press, 1994.

Gilchrist, Roberta. "Christian Bodies and Souls: The Archeology of Life and Death in Later Medieval Hospitals." In *Death in Towns: Urban Responses to the Dying and the Dead, 100–1600*, edited by Steven Bassett, 101–118. Leicester: Leicester University Press, 1992.

Gleeson, Philip. "Dominican Liturgical Manuscripts from before 1254." *Archivum Fratrum Praedicatorum* XLII (1972): 81–135.

Gordon, Bruce, and Peter Marshall, eds. *The Place of the Dead: Death and Remembrance in Late Medieval and Early Modern Europe*. Cambridge: Cambridge University Press, 2000.

Goullet, Monique, Guy Lobrichon, and Éric Palazzo, eds. *Le pontifical de la curie romaine au XIIIe siècle*. Paris: Les Éditions du Cerf, 2004.

Grand-Saint-Bernard, Congrégation du. "Patrimoine culturel MS 3 (ancien 10091)." Accessed September 22, 2020, at https://gsbernard.ch/6/64/643-1/man03/index.html.

Gragnolati, Manuele. "From Decay to Splendor: Body and Pain in Bonvesin da la Riva's Book of the Three Scriptures." In *Last Things: Death and the Apocalypse in the Middle Ages*, edited by Caroline Walker Bynum and Paul Freedman, 83–98. Philadelphia: University of Pennsylvania Press, 2000.Grasso, Maria R. "The Ambiguity in Medieval Depictions of Abraham's Bosom in the Areas and Spaces of the Christian Afterlife." In *Place and Space in the Medieval World*, edited by Meg Boulton, Jane Hawkes, and Heidi Stoner, 103–113. Milton: Taylor & Francis, 2018.

Gray, Madeleine. "Deathbed and Burial Rituals in Late Medieval Catholic Europe." In *A Companion to Death, Burial, and Remembrance in Late Medieval and Early Modern Europe, c. 1300–1700*, edited by Philip Booth and Elizabeth C. Tingle, 106–131. Leiden: Brill, 2021.

Greene, Thomas Anthony A. "Softening the Heart, Eliciting Desire: Experiencing Music in a Carolingian Monastery." In *Emotions, Communities, and Difference in Medieval Europe: Essays in Honor of Barbara H. Rosenwein*, edited by Maureen C. Miller, Barbara H. Rosenwein, and Edward Wheatley, 46–58. New York: Routledge, 2017.

Grier, James. "Musical and Liturgical Practice." In *The Oxford Handbook of Christian Monasticism*, edited by Bernice M. Kaczynski, 333–348. Oxford: Oxford University Press, 2020.

Guidera, Christine. "The Role of the Beguines in Caring for the Ill, the Dying, and the Dead." In *Death and Dying in the Middle Ages*, edited by Edelgard E. DuBruck and Barbara I. Gusick, 51–72. New York: Peter Lang, 1999.

Gy, Pierre-Marie. "Collectaire, rituel, processional." *Revue des sciences philosophiques et théologiques* 44, no. 3 (July 1960): 441–469.

Haas, Max. *Mündliche Überlieferung und altrömischer Choral: Historische und analytische computergestützte Untersuchungen*. Bern: P. Lang, 1997.

Hadley, D. M. *Death in Medieval England: An Archaeology*. Stroud: Arcadia Publishing, 2001.

Hallinger, Kassius, ed. *Initia consuetudinis Benedictinae: Consuetudines saeculi octavi et noni*. Corpus consuetudinum monasticarum 1. Siegburg: F. Schmitt, 1963.

Hammerstein, Reinhold. *Die Musik der Engel: Untersuchungen zur Musikanschauung des Mittelalters*. Bern: Francke, 1962.

Hänggi, Anton, and Anfons Schönherr, eds., *Sacramentarium Rhenaugiense*. Freiburg, Switzerland: Freiburg Schweiz Universitätsverlag, 1970.

Harrison, Anna. "Community among the Saintly Dead: Bernard of Clairvaux's Sermons for the Feast of All Saints." In *Last Things: Death and the Apocalypse in the Middle Ages*, edited by Caroline Walker Bynum and Paul Freedman, 191–204. Philadelphia: University of Pennsylvania Press, 2000.

Hart, David Bentley. *The New Testament*. New Haven, CT: Yale University Press, 2017.

Hartnell, Jack. *Medieval Bodies: Life, Death, and Art in the Middle Ages*. London: Profile Books, 2018.

Harvey, Barbara F. *Living and Dying in England, 1100–1540: The Monastic Experience*. Oxford: Oxford University Press, 1993.

Haug, Andreas. "Singing from the Book: The End of Sacrifice and the Rise of Chant in the Fourth Century." *Musical Quarterly* 104, no. 3–4 (2021): 370–391.

Heiming, Odilo, ed. *Liber sacramentorum augustodunensis*. Turnhout: Brepols, 1984.

Helsen, Katherine Eve. "The Great Responsories of the Divine Office: Aspects of Structure and Transmission." PhD diss., University of Regensburg, 2008.

Helsen, Katherine Eve. "The Use of Melodic Formulas in Responsories: Constancy and Variability in the Manuscript Tradition." *Plainsong and Medieval Music* 18, no. 1 (2009): 61–75.

Hen, Yitzhak. "Knowledge of Canon Law among Rural Priests: The Evidence of Two Carolingian Manuscripts from around 800." *Journal of Theological Studies* 50, no. 1 (1999): 117–134.

Hen, Yitzhak. *The Royal Patronage of Liturgy in Frankish Gaul to the Death of Charles the Bald (877)*. London: Boydell Press, 2001.

Hen, Yitzhak. "When Liturgy Gets out of Hand." In *Writing the Early Medieval West: Studies in honour of Rosamond McKitterick*, edited by Elina Screen and Charles West, 203–212. Cambridge: Cambridge University Press, 2018.

Hendrix, Julian. "Liturgy for the Dead and the Confraternity of Reichenau and St Gall, 800–950." PhD diss., Cambridge University, 2007.

Hesbert, René Jean. *Corpus Antiphonalium Officii* [CAO]. Rome: Herder, 1963–1979.

Hicks, Andrew J. *Composing the World: Harmony in the Medieval Platonic Cosmos*. Critical Conjectures in Music and Sound 1. New York: Oxford University Press, 2017.

Hicks, Andrew J. "The Regulative Power of the Harmony of the Spheres in Medieval Latin, Arabic, and Persian Sources." In *The Routledge Companion to Music, Mind and Well-Being*, edited by Penelope Gouk, James Gordon Kennaway, Jacomien Prins, and Wiebke Thormählen, 33–45. New York: Routledge, 2019.

Hild, Elaine Stratton. "Rites for the Sick and Dying in Sources from Klosterneuburg." *De musica disserenda* 14, no. 2 (2018): 7–24.

Hild, Elaine Stratton. "The Role of Music in a Franciscan Liturgy for the End of Life as Evidenced in Manuscript Newberry 24." In *Death and Disease in the Medieval and Early Modern World: Perspectives from Across the Mediterranean and Beyond*, edited by Lori Jones and Nükhet Varlık, 151–175. Woodbridge: York Medieval Press and Boydell & Brewer Ltd, 2022.

Hiley, David. *Western Plainchant: A Handbook*. Oxford: Clarendon Press, 1993.

Hirbodian, Sigrid. "Religious Women: Secular Canonesses and Beguines." In *The Oxford Handbook of Christian Monasticism*, edited by Bernice M. Kaczynski, 285–299. Oxford: Oxford University Press, 2020.

Hochner, Nicole. "On Social Rhythm: A Renewed Assessment of Van Gennep's Rites of Passage." *Journal of Classical Sociology* 18, no. 4 (November 2018): 299–312.

Horden, Peregrine. "A Non-Natural Environment: Medicine without Doctors and the Medieval European Hospital." In *The Medieval Hospital and Medical Practice*, edited by Barbara S. Bowers, 133–147. AVISTA Studies in History of Medieval Technology, Science and Art 3. Farnham: Ashgate, 2007.

Horden, Peregrine. "Religion as Medicine: Music in Medieval Hospitals." In *Religion and Medicine in the Middle Ages*, edited by Peter Biller and Joseph Ziegler, 135–153. Rochester, NY: York Medieval Press, 2001.

Horden, Peregrine. "Sickness and Healing." In *The Oxford Handbook of Christian Monasticism*, edited by Bernice M. Kaczynski, 403–417. Oxford: Oxford University Press, 2020.

Hughes, Andrew. A. *Medieval Manuscripts for Mass and Office: A Guide to Their Organization and Terminology*. Toronto: University of Toronto Press, 2004.

Huglo, Michel. *Les anciens répertoires de plain-chant*. Aldershot: Ashgate Variorum, 2005.

Huglo, Michel. "Le chant 'vieux-romain': Liste des manuscrits et témoins indirects." *Sacris Erudiri* 6 (1954): 96–124.

Huglo, Michel. "Les livres de chant notés à Cluny: Une survie à Solesmes?" *Revue Mabillon* 22 (=83) (2011): 39–51.

Huglo, Michel. "Remarques sur les mélodies des répons de l'Office des Morts." *Nordisk Kollokvium IV i Latinsk Liturgiforskning* 4 (1978): 118–125.

Hugon, Albano. "Orsières." In *Historische Lexikon der Schweiz*. November 3, 2009, accessed October 14, 2020, at https://hls-dhs-dss.ch/de/.

Hürlimann, Gebhard. *Das Rheinauer Rituale (Zürich Rh 114, Anfang 12. Jh.)*. Spicilegium Friburgense 5. Freiburg (CH): Universitätsverlag Freiburg, Switzerland: 1959.

Ibos-Augé, Anne. "Vernacular Song II: Romance." In *The Cambridge History of Medieval Music*, edited by Mark Everist and Thomas Forrest Kelly, 428–450. Cambridge: Cambridge University Press, 2018.

Ivanova, Velia. "Clarissan Death in Brussels: A Burial Procession in Plimpton MS 034." Columbia University. Accessed October 19, 2020, at https://chantmanuscripts.omeka.net/exhibits/show/burial-procession.

Jeffery, Peter. "The Early Liturgy of Saint Peter's and the Roman Liturgical Year." In *Old Saint Peter's, Rome*, edited by Rosamond McKitterick, John Osborne, Carol M. Richardson, and Joanna Story, 157–176. Cambridge: Cambridge University Press, 2013.

Jones, Claire Taylor. *Fixing the Liturgy: Friars, Sisters, and the Dominican Rite, 1256–1516*. Philadelphia: University of Pennsylvania Press, 2024.

Jones, Claire Taylor. *Ruling the Spirit: Women, Liturgy, and Dominican Reform in Late Medieval Germany*. Philadelphia: University of Pennsylvania Press, 2018.

Kaczynski, Bernice M., ed. *The Oxford Handbook of Christian Monasticism*. Oxford: Oxford University Press, 2020.

Kauffman, Christopher J. *Ministry and Meaning: A Religious History of Catholic Health Care in the United States*. New York: Crossroad, 1995.

Keefe, Susan. *A Catalogue of Works Pertaining to the Explanation of the Creed in Carolingian Manuscripts*. Instrumenta Patristica et Mediaevalia 63. Turnhout: Brepols, 2012.

Keefe, Susan. *Water and the Word: Baptism and the Education of the Clergy in the Carolingian Empire*. 2 vols. Publications in Medieval Studies. Notre Dame, IN: University of Notre Dame, 2002.

Kelly, Thomas Forrest. "Old Roman Chant and the Responsories of Noah: New Evidence from Sutri." *Early Music History 26* (2007): 91–120.

Kelly, Thomas Forrest, ed., *Chant and Its Origins*. Farnham, Surrey: Ashgate, 2009.

Kelly, Thomas Forrest, and Matthew Peattie, eds. *The Music of the Beneventan Rite*. Monvmenta monodica medii aevi 9. Kassel: Bärenreiter, 2016.

Ker, N. R., and A. J. Piper. *Medieval Manuscripts in British Libraries*. Oxford: Clarendon Press, 1992.

Korpiola, Mia, and Anu Lahtinen, eds. *Cultures of Death and Dying in Medieval and Early Modern Europe: An Introduction*. Collegium 18. Helsinki: Helsinki Collegium for Advanced Studies, 2015.

Kurt, Andrew. "Lay Piety in Visigothic Iberia: Liturgical and Paraliturgical Forms." *Journal of Medieval Iberian Studies* 8, no. 1 (2016): 1–37.

Küster, Konrad. "Death and the Lutheran Idea of Becoming a Heavenly Musician." In *Preparing for Death, Remembering the Dead*, edited by Jon Øygarden Flæten and Tarald Rasmussen, 351–359. Göttingen: Vandenhoeck & Ruprecht, 2015.

Kyll, Nikolaus. *Tod, Grab, Begräbnisplatz, Totenfeier*. Bonn: Ludwig Röhrscheid, 1972.

Lampard, John S. *Go Forth, Christian Soul: The Biography of a Prayer*. Peterborough: Epworth, 2005.

Lauer, Philippe. *Catalogue général des manuscrits latins*. Paris: Bibliothèque nationale, 1939.

Legg, J. Wickham, ed. *The Sarum Missal: Edited from Three Early Manuscripts*. Oxford: Clarendon Press, 1916.

Le Goff, Jacques. *La naissance du purgatoire*. Paris: Gallimard, 1981. Translated as *The Birth of Purgatory* by Arthur Goldhammer. London: Scolar Press, 1984.

Le Goff, Jacques. *Un Moyen Âge en images*. Paris: Hazan, 2000.

Leigh-Choate, Tova. "Singing for Their Supper: Chant in the Medieval Refectory." Paper presented at the international conference of Cantus Planus, Dublin, August 2–7, 2016.

Leisibach, Josef. "Grosser St. Bernhard." In *Scriptoria Medii Aevi Helvetica: Schreibstätten der Diözese Sitten*, edited by Albert Bruckner, 133–157. Denkmäler Schweizerischer Schreibkunst des Mittelalters 13. Genf: Roto-Sadag, 1973.

Leisibach, Josef, and François Huot. *Die liturgischen Handschriften des Kantons Wallis (ohne Kapitelsarchiv Sitten)*. Spicilegii Friburgensis subsidia 18; Iter Helveticum 4. Freiburg, Switzerland: Universitätsbibliothek, 1984.

Leroquais, Victor. *Les pontificaux manuscrits des bibliothèques publiques de France*. Ligugé: Bibliothèque de l'abbaye Saint-Martin Ligugé, 1937.

Lester, Anne E. *Creating Cistercian Nuns: The Women's Religious Movement and Its Reform in Thirteenth-Century Champagne*. Ithaca, NY: Cornell University Press, 2011.

Macrobius, Ambrosius Aurelius Theodosius. *Commentary on the Dream of Scipio*. Translated by William Harris Stahl. New York: Columbia University Press, 1990.

Madigan, Kevin. *Medieval Christianity: A New History*. New Haven, CT: Yale University Press, 2015.

Makowski, Elizabeth M. *English Nuns and the Law in the Middle Ages: Cloistered Nuns and Their Lawyers, 1293–1540*. Woodbridge: The Boydell Press, 2011.

Maloy, Rebecca. *Inside the Offertory: Aspects of Chronology and Transmission*. Oxford: Oxford University Press, 2011.

Manz, Georg. *Ein St. Galler Sakramentar-Fragment (Cod. Sangall. No. 350); Als Nachtrag zum fränkischen Sakramentarium Gelasianum (Cod. Sangall. No. 348)*. St. Galler Sakramentar-Forschungen 2. Liturgiegeschichtliche Quellen und Forschungen 31. Münster Westfalen: Verlag der aschendorffschen Verlagsbuchhandlung, 1939.

Marchesin, Isabelle. "Les chapiteaux de la musique de Cluny: une figuration du lien musica." In *Les représentations de la musique au Moyen Âge*, edited by Martine Clouzot, 84–91. Paris: Cité de la Musique Editions, 2005.

McCall, Richard D. *Do This: Liturgy as Performance*. Notre Dame, IN: University of Notre Dame Press, 2007.

McKitterick, Rosamond. *The Frankish Church and the Carolingian Reforms, 789–895*. London: Royal Historical Society, 1977.

McKitterick, Rosamond. *The New Cambridge Medieval History*. Cambridge: Cambridge University Press, 1995.

McKitterick, Rosamond. "Nuns' Scriptoria in England and Francia in the Eighth Century." *Francia* 19, no. 1 (1992): 1–35.

McKitterick, Rosamond. *Rome and the Invention of the Papacy: The Liber Pontificalis*. Cambridge: Cambridge University Press, 2020.

McKitterick, Rosamond, John Osborne, Carol M. Richardson, and Joanna Story, eds. *Old Saint Peter's, Rome*. Cambridge: Cambridge University Press, 2013.

McLeish, Tom. *The Poetry and Music of Science: Comparing Creativity in Science and Art*. Oxford: Oxford University Press, 2019.

Meyer, Kathi. "The Eight Gregorian Modes on the Cluny Capitals." *The Art Bulletin* 34 (1952): 75–94.

Migne, Jacques-Paul, ed. *Patrologiae cursus completus, Series latina*. Paris: Migne, 1844–1891.

Mitchell, Andrew W. "The Chant of the Earliest Franciscan Office." PhD diss., University of Western Ontario, 2003.

Mohlberg, Leo Cunibert, ed. *Liber sacramentorum romanae aeclesiae ordinis anni circuli (Cod. Vat. Reg. lat. 316/ Paris Bibl. Nat. 7193, 41/56; Sacramentarium Gelasianum).* Rome: Casa editrice Herder, 1960.

Montford, Angela. *Health, Sickness, Medicine and the Friars in the Thirteenth and Fourteenth Centuries.* Aldershot: Ashgate, 2004.

Moreira, Isabel. *Heaven's Purge: Purgatory in Late Antiquity.* New York: Oxford University Press, 2010.

Moreira, Isabel. "Visions and the Afterlife." In *The Oxford Handbook of the Merovingian World*, edited by Bonnie Effros and Isabel Moreira, 988–1011. New York: Oxford University Press, 2020.

Moreton, Bernard. *The Eighth-Century Gelasian Sacramentary: A Study in Tradition.* Oxford: Oxford University Press, 1976.

Morgan, Nigel J. "The Liturgical Manuscripts of the English Franciscans c. 1250–c. 1350." In *The English Province of the Franciscans (1224–c. 1350)*, edited by Michael J. P. Robson, 214–245. Leiden: Brill, 2017.

Mowbray, Donald. *Pain and Suffering in Medieval Theology: Academic Debates at the University of Paris in the Thirteenth Century.* Boydell: Woodbridge, 2009.

Mulchahey, M. Michèle. "Education in Dante's Florence Revisited: Remigio De' Girolami and the Schools of Santa Maria Novella." In *Medieval Education*, edited by Ronald B. Begley and Joseph W. Koterski, 143–181. New York: Fordham University Press, 2005.

Munier, C., ed. *Concilium Hipponense (Concilia Africae a. 345–a. 525, c. 4).* Turnhout: Brepols, 1974.

Murray, Placid. "The Liturgical History of Extreme Unction." In *Studies in Pastoral Liturgy II*, edited by Vincent Ryan, 18–35. Dublin: The Furrow Trust, 1963.

Muschiol, Gisela. "Gender and Monastic Liturgy in the Latin West (High and Late Middle Ages)." In *The Cambridge History of Medieval Monasticism in the Latin West*, edited by Alison I. Beach and Isabelle Cochelin, 803–815. Cambridge: Cambridge University Press, 2020.

Nardini, Luisa. "Allusioni liturgico-musicali in Dante attraverso un'analisi del manoscritto 13 dell'Harry Ransom Center." In *Nel 750° anniversario della nascita di Dante Alighieri: Letteratura e Musica del Duecento e del Trecento. Atti del Convegno Internazionale Certaldo Alto, 17–18 Dicembre 2015*, edited by Paola Benigni, Stefano Campagnolo, Rino Caputo, Stefania Cori, and Agostino Ziino, 131–139. Gesualdo: Fondazione Carlo Gesualdo, 2016.

Nardini, Luisa. *Chants, Hypertext & Prosulas: Re-texting the Proper of the Mass in Beneventan Manuscripts.* Oxford: Oxford University Press, 2021.

Nardini, Luisa. "The Masses for the Dead in Beneventan Manuscripts: Issues of Formulary Organization and Chant Manipulation." In *Proceedings of the 17th Meeting of the International Musicological Society—Cantus Planus Study Group, Venice (Italy), July–August 2014*, edited by James Borders, 481–494. Venice: Fondazione Levi, 2021.

Natvig, Mary. "Rich Clares, Poor Clares: Celebrating the Divine Office." *Women and Music: A Journal of Gender and Culture* 4 (2000): 59–70.

Nowacki, Edward. "Studies on the Office Antiphons of the Old Roman Manuscripts." PhD diss., Brandeis University, 1980.

O'Connor, Mary Catharine. *The Art of Dying Well: The Development of the Ars moriendi.* New York: Columbia University Press, 1942.

O'Regan, Cyril. "Theology, Art, and Beauty." In *The Many Faces of Beauty*, edited by Vittorio Hösle, 445–471. Notre Dame, IN: Notre Dame University Press, 2013.

Osborne, John. "Plus Caesare Petrus: The Vatican Obelisk and the Approach to Saint Peter's." In *Old Saint Peter's, Rome*, edited by Rosamond McKitterick, John Osborne, Carol M. Richardson, and Joanna Story, 274–286. Cambridge: Cambridge University Press, 2013.

Osten-Hoschek, Andrea. *Reform und Liturgie im Nürnberger Katharinenkloster: Die Sterbe- und Begräbnisliturgie des 15. Jahrhunderts; Edition und Kommentar*. Quellen und Forschungen zur Geschichte des Dominikanerordens—Neue Folge 27. Berlin: De Gruyter, 2023.

Ottosen, Knud. "Liturgy as a Theological Place: Possibilities and Limitations in Interpreting Liturgical Texts as Seen for Instance in the Office of the Dead." In *Liturgy and the Arts in the Middle Ages*, edited by Eva Louise Lillie and Nils Holger Petersen, 168–180. Copenhagen: Museum Tusculanum Press University of Copenhagen, 1996.

Ottosen, Knud. *The Responsories and Versicles of the Latin Office of the Dead*. Aarhus, Denmark: Aarhus University Press, 1993. Available online as an interactive databank: Universität Regensburg, "Cantus planus: Responsories of the Latin Office of the Dead," https://www-app.uni-regensburg.de/Fakultaeten/PKGG/Musikwissenschaft/Cantus/Ottosen/index.html.

Page, William, ed. "Friaries: The Minoresses without Aldgate." In *A History of the County of London*, Vol. 1: *London within the Bars, Westminster and Southwark*, 516–519. London: Victoria County History, 1909. Accessed November 5, 2020, through *British History Online*, http://www.british-history.ac.uk/vch/london/vol1/pp516-519.

Paxton, Frederick S. "Birth and Death." In *The Cambridge History of Christianity*, Vol. 3: *Early Medieval Christianities*, edited by Thomas F. X. Noble and Julia M. H. Smith, 383–398. Cambridge: Cambridge University Press, 2008.

Paxton, Frederick S. "Bonus Liber: A Late Carolingian Clerical Manual from Lorsch." In *The Two Laws: Studies in Medieval Legal History Dedicated to Stephan Kuttner*, edited by Laurent Mayali and Stephanie A. J. Tibbetts, 1–30. Washington, DC: Catholic University of America Press, 1990.

Paxton, Frederick S. *Christianizing Death: The Creation of a Ritual Process in Early Medieval Europe*. Ithaca, NY: Cornell University Press, 1990.

Paxton, Frederick S. "Death by Customary at Eleventh-Century Cluny." In *From Dead of Night to End of Day: The Medieval Customs of Cluny*, ed. S. Boynton and I. Cochelin, 297–318. Turnhout: Brepols, 2005.

Paxton, Frederick S. *The Death Ritual at Cluny in the Central Middle Ages*. Disciplina Monastica 9. Turnhout: Brepols, 2013.

Paxton, Frederick S. "The Early Growth of the Medieval Economy of Salvation in Latin Christianity." In *Death in Jewish Life: Burial and Mourning Customs among the Jews of Europe and Nearby Communities*, edited by Stefan Reif and Andreas Lehnardt, 17–41. Berlin: De Gruyter, 2014.

Paxton, Frederick S. "Performing Death and Dying at Cluny in the High Middle Ages." In *Practicing Catholic: Ritual, Body, and Contestation in Catholic Faith*, edited by Bruce T. Morrill, Joanna E. Ziegler, and Susan Rodgers, 43–52. New York: Palgrave Macmillan, 2006.

Paxton, Frederick S. "Sickness, Death, Burial." In *Brill Handbook of Medieval Latin Liturgy*, edited by Daniel DiCenso and Andrew Irving. Leiden: Brill, forthcoming.

Paxton, Frederick S. "*Signa Mortifera*: Death and Prognostication in Early Medieval Monastic Medicine." *Bulletin of the History of Medicine* 67 (1993): 631–650.

Pentcheva, Bissera V. "Performative Liturgies and Cosmic Sound in the Exultet Liturgy of Southern Italy." *Speculum* 95, no. 2 (April 2020): 396–466.

Pfisterer, Andreas. *Cantilena Romana: Untersuchungen zur Überlieferung des gregorianischen Chorals*. Paderborn: Ferdinand Schöningh, 2002.

Pfisterer, Andreas. "Origins and Transmission of Franco-Roman Chant." In *The Cambridge History of Medieval Music*, edited by Mark Everist and Thomas Forrest Kelly, 69–91. Cambridge: Cambridge University Press, 2018.

Pfisterer, Andreas. "Skizzen zu einer gregorianischen Formenlehre." *Archiv für Musikwissenschaft* 63, no. 2 (2006): 145–161.

Phillips-Robins, Helena. *Liturgical Song and Practice in Dante's Commedia*. Notre Dame, IN: University of Notre Dame Press, 2021.

Pieragostini, Renata. "The Healing Power of Music? Documentary Evidence from Late-Fourteenth-Century Bologna." *Speculum* 96, no. 1 (2021): 156–176.

Plato. *Timaeus and Critias*. Translated by Desmond Lee. London: Penguin Books, 1977[repr. ed.].

Power, Eileen. *English Medieval Nunneries, c. 1275–1525*. Cambridge: Cambridge University Press, 1922.

Probst, Christian. "Das Hospitalwesen im hohen und späten Mittelalter und die geistliche und gesellschaftliche Stellung des Kranken." In *Medizin im mittelalterlichen Abendland*, edited by Gerhard Baader and Gundolf Keil, 260–274. Wege der Forschung 363. Darmstadt: Wissenschaftliche Buchgesellschaft, 1982.

Quaglia, Lucien. "Les origines de l'hospice du Grand-Saint-Bernard." *Publication du Centre européen d'études bourguignonnes (XIVe–XVIe s)* 15 (1973): 31–36.

Radle, Gabriel. "The Veiling of Women in Byzantium: Liturgy, Hair, and Identity in a Medieval Rite of Passage." *Speculum* 94, no. 4 (2019): 1070–1115.

Ranft, Patricia. *Women and the Religious Life in Pre-Modern Europe*. New York: St. Martin's Press, 1996.

Rankin, Susan. *Writing Sounds in Carolingian Europe: The Invention of Musical Notation*. Cambridge: Cambridge University Press, 2018.

Rastall, Richard. *The Heaven Singing: Music in Early English Religious Drama I*. Cambridge: D. S. Brewer, 1996.

Rastall, Richard. *Minstrels Playing: Music in Early English Religious Drama II*. Cambridge: D.S. Brewer, 2001.

Rittgers, Ronald K. *The Reformation of Suffering: Pastoral Theology and Lay Piety in Late Medieval and Early Modern Germany*. Oxford: Oxford University Press, 2012.

Robertson, Anne Walters. *The Service-Books of the Royal Abbey of Saint-Denis: Images of Ritual and Music in the Middle Ages*. Oxford: Clarendon Press, 1991.

Robson, Michael J. P., ed. *The Cambridge Companion to Francis of Assisi*. Cambridge: Cambridge University Press, 2012.

Robson, Michael, and Patrick Zutshi. The Franciscan Order in the Medieval English Province and Beyond. Church, Faith and Culture in the Medieval West. Amsterdam: Amsterdam University Press, 2018.

Rowell, Geoffrey. *The Liturgy of Christian Burial: An Introductory Survey of the Historical Development of Christian Burial Rites*. London: S.P.C.K for the Alcuin Club, 1977.

Rubin, Miri. "Imagining Medieval Hospitals: Considerations on the Cultural Meaning of Institutional Change." In *Medicine and Charity before the Welfare State*, edited by Jonathan Barry, 14–25. Studies in the Social History of Medicine. London: Routledge, 1994.

Rush, Alfred C. *Death and Burial in Christian Antiquity*. Washington, DC: Catholic University of America Press, 1941.

Rutherford, Richard. *The Death of a Christian: The Rite of Funerals*. New York: Pueblo Publishing, 1980.

Rutherford, Richard. "Psalm 113 (114–115) and Christian Burial." In *Studia Patristica* 12, edited by Elizabeth A. Livingstone, 391–395. Texte und Untersuchungen zur Geschichte der altchristlichen Literatur 116. Berlin: Akademie Verlag, 1975.

Saenger, Paul. *A Catalogue of the Pre-1500 Western Manuscript Books at the Newberry Library*. Chicago: University of Chicago Press, 1989.

Salisbury, Matthew Cheung. *The Secular Liturgical Office in Late Medieval England*. Turnhout: Brepols, 2015.

Salmon, Pierre. *Les manuscrits liturgiques latins de la Bibliothèque vaticane*. Vatican City: Biblioteca Apostolica Vaticana, 1968–1972.

Salmon, Pierre. *L'Office divin au Moyen Age: Histoire de la formation du bréviaire du IXe au XVIe siècle*. Lex orandi 43. Paris: Les Éditions du Cerf, 1967.

Schell, Sarah. "The Office of the Dead in England: Image and Music in the Book of Hours and Related Texts, c. 1250–c. 1500." PhD diss., University of St Andrews, 2011.

Schmitt, Jean-Claude. *Les revenants: Les vivants et les morts dans la société medievale*. Paris: Gallimora, 1994. Translated as *Ghosts in the Middle Ages: The Living and the Dead in Medieval Society* by Teresa Lavender Fagan. Chicago: University of Chicago Press, 1998.

Schmitz-Esser, Romedio. *The Corpse in the Middle Ages: Embalming, Cremating, and the Cultural Construction of the Dead Body*. Translated by Albrecht Classen and Caroin Radtke. Turnhout: Harvey Miller Publishers, 2020.

Schmucki, Oktavian. "Spiritualität, Askese und Krankheiten nach den Schriften des Franziskus von Assisi." In *Franziskus von Assisi: Das Bild des Heiligen aus neuer Sicht*, edited by Dieter R. Bauer, Helmut Feld, and Ulrich Köpf, 71–96. Köln: Böhlau Verlag, 2005.

Scillia, Charles E. "Meaning and the Cluny Capitals; Music as Metaphor." *Gesta* 27 (1988): 133–148.

Seligman, Adam, Robert Weller, and Michael Puett. *Ritual and Its Consequences: An Essay on the Limits of Sincerity*. Oxford: Oxford University Press, 2008.

Seton, Walter W., ed. "The Rewle of Sustris Menouresses Enclosid." In *A Fifteenth-century Courtesy Book and Two Franciscan Rules*, edited by R. W. Chambers and Walter W. Seton, 63–125. Early English Text Society 148. London: Published for the Early English Text Society by Kegan Paul, Trench, Trübner and Humphrey Milford, Oxford University Press, 1914.

Short, William J. "The Rule and Life of the Friars Minor." In *The Cambridge Companion to Francis of Assisi*, edited by Michael J. P. Robson, 50–67. Cambridge: Cambridge University Press, 2011.

Sicard, Damien. "Christian Death." In *The Church at Prayer: An Introduction to the Liturgy; The Sacraments*, edited by Robert Cabié, Jean Evenou, et al., 221–240. Translated by Matthew J. O'Connell. Collegeville, MN: The Liturgical Press, 1988.

Sicard, Damien. *La liturgie de la mort dans l'église latine des origines à la réforme carolingienne*. Liturgiewissenschaftliche Quellen und Forschungen 63. Münster: Aschendorffsche Verlagsbuchhandlung, 1978.

Sicard, Damien. "La mort du chrétien et sa communauté." *La Maison-Dieu: Revue de pastorale liturgique* 144 (1980): 59–64.

Silberer, Leonie. *Klosterbaukunst der konventualen Franziskaner vom 13. Jahrhundert bis zur Reformation.* Petersberg: Michael Imhof Verlag, 2016.

Smith, D. Vance. *Arts of Dying: Literature and Finitude in Medieval England.* Chicago: University of Chicago Press, 2020.

Somfai, Anna. "The Eleventh-Century Shift in the Reception of Plato's Timaeus and Caldicius's Commentary." *Journal of the Warburg and Courtauld Institutes* 65, no. 1 (2002): 1–21.

Stahl, Harvey. "Heaven in View: The Place of the Elect in an Illuminated Book of Hours." In *Last Things: Death and the Apocalypse in the Middle Ages*, edited by Caroline Walker Bynum and Paul Freedman, 205–232. Philadelphia: University of Pennsylvania Press, 2000.

Staley, Lynn. "Pearl and the Contingencies of Love and Piety." In *Medieval Literature and Historical Inquiry: Essays in Honor of David Pearsall*, edited by David Aers, 83–114. Cambridge: D. S. Brewer, 2000.

Stornajolo, Cosimo. "*Inventarium codicum manuscriptorum Archivii Sancti Petri, tomus II, litterae E-H.*" Unpublished manuscript, early 20th century. Accessed July 9, 2023, at "DigiVatLib: Arch.Cap.S.Pietro.H.100," https://digi.vatlib.it/mss/detail/Arch.Cap.S.Pietro.H.100.

Taylor, Jeremy. *Holy Living and Dying.* London: Henry G. Bohn, 1850.

Tingle, Elizabeth. "Changing Western European Visions of Christian Afterlives, 1350–1700: Heaven, Hell, and Purgatory." In *A Companion to Death, Burial, and Remembrance in Late Medieval and Early Modern Europe, c. 1300–1700*, edited by Philip Booth and Elizabeth C. Tingle, 33–71. Leiden: Brill, 2021.

Tomlinson, Edward Murray. *A History of the Minories: London.* London: Smith, Elder, & Co., 1907.

Treitler, Leo. "Observations on the Transmission of Some Aquitanian Tropes." *Forum musicologicum* 3 (1982): 11–60.

Treitler, Leo. *With Voice and Pen: Coming to Know Medieval Song and How It Was Made.* Oxford: Oxford University Press, 2007.

Trembinski, Donna. "[Pro]passio Doloris: Early Dominican Conceptions of Christ's Physical Pain." *Journal of Ecclesiastical History* 59, no. 4 (2008): 630–656.

Tucker, Karen B. Westerfield. "Christian Rituals Surrounding Death." In *Life Cycles in Jewish and Christian Worship*, edited by Paul F. Bradshaw and Lawrence A. Hoffman, 196–213. Notre Dame, IN: University of Notre Dame Press, 1996.

Tufts University. "Perseus Digital Library: Latin Word Study Tool," Gregory R. Crane, editor in chief. Accessed April 4, 2020, at http://www.perseus.tufts.edu/hopper/morph?l=subvenite&la=la#lexicon.

University of Fribourg. "E-codices: Cod. Sang. 394." Accessed February 22, 2021, at e-codices.unifr.ch/en/list/one/csg/0349.

University of London School of Advanced Study, Institute for Historical Research. "Layers of London." Accessed November 5, 2020, at https://www.layersoflondon.org/map.

University of Oxford. "Medieval Libraries of Great Britain (MLGB3) 2015." Accessed November 5, 2020, at http://mlgb3.bodleian.ox.ac.uk/mlgb/book/3809/?search_term=585&field_to_search=shelfmark&page_size=500.

University of Oxford. "Medieval Manuscripts in Oxford Libraries: MS. Bodl. 585–Part 2 (2019)." Accessed November 5, 2020, at https://medieval.bodleian.ox.ac.uk/catalog/manuscript_1603.

Universität Regensburg. "Cantus planus: Responsories of the Latin Office of the Dead." Accessed February 22, 2021, at https://www-app.uni-regensburg.de/Fakultaeten/PKGG/Musikwissenschaft/Cantus/Ottosen/index.html.
University of Waterloo. "CANTUS: A Database for Latin Ecclesiastical Chant." Debra Lacoste, project manager. Accessed February 17, 2021, at https://cantus.uwaterloo.ca/.
University of Waterloo. "Cantus Index: Online Catalogue for Mass and Office Chants." Debra Lacoste, project manager. Accessed March 10, 2022, at http://cantusindex.org/home.
Van Dijk, Aurelian. "The Breviary of Saint Clare." *Franciscan Studies* 8, no. 1 (1948): 25–46.
Van Dijk, Stephen A. "The Breviary of St Francis." *Franciscan Studies* 9, no. 1 (March 1949): 13–25.
Van Dijk, S. J. P. "Some Manuscripts of the Earliest Franciscan Liturgy." *Franciscan Studies* 16, no. 1 (1956): 60–101.
Van Dijk, S. J. P. *Sources of the Modern Roman Liturgy: The Ordinals by Haymo of Faversham and related Documents.* 2 vols. Studia et Documenta Franciscana 1 and 2. Leiden: E. J. Brill, 1963.Van Dijk, S. J. P., and J. Hazelden Walker. *The Origins of the Modern Roman Liturgy: The Liturgy of the Papal Court and the Franciscan Order in the Thirteenth Century.* London: Darton, Longman & Todd, 1960.
Van Engen, John. "The Christian Middle Ages as an Historiographical Problem." *American Historical Review* 91, no. 3 (1986): 519–552.
Van Engen, John. "Dominic and the Brothers: *Vitae* as Life-forming *exempla* in the Order of Preachers." In *Christ among the Medieval Dominicans: Representations of Christ in the Texts and Images of the Order of Preachers*, edited by Kent Emery Jr. and Joseph Wawrykow, 7–25. Notre Dame, IN: University of Notre Dame Press, 1998.
Van Gennep, Arnold. *Les rites de passage; Étude systématique des rites de la porte et du seuil, de l'hospitalité, de l'adoption, de la grossesse et de l'accouchement, de la naissance, de l'enfance, de la puberté, de l'initiation, de l'ordination, du couronnement des fiançailles et du mariage, des funérailles, des saisons, etc.* Paris: É. Nourry, 1909. Translated as *The Rites of Passage.* Chicago: University of Chicago Press, 1960.
Van Rhijn, Carine. "Charlemagne and the Government of the Frankish Countryside." In *Law and Empire: Ideas, Practices, Actors*, edited by Jeroen Duindam, Jozef Frans, Jill Harries, Caroline Humfress, and Nimrod Hurvitz, 157–176. Leiden: Brill, 2013.
Van Rhijn, Carine. "The Local Church, Priests' Handbooks and Pastoral Care in the Carolingian Period." In *Chiese locali e chiese regionali nell'alto medioevo; Spoleto, 4–9 Aprile 2013*, 689–710. Atti Delle Settimane 61. Spoleto: Fondazione centro Italiano di studi sull'alto medioevo, 2014.
Vauchez, André. "The Church and the Laity." In *The New Cambridge Medieval History*, Vol. 5: *c. 1198–c. 1300*, edited by David Abulafia, 182–203. Cambridge: Cambridge University Press, 1999.
Vettori, Alessandro. "Religion." In *The Oxford Handbook of Dante*, edited by Manuele Gragnolati, Elena Lombardi, and Francesca Southerden, 302–317. Oxford: Oxford University Press, 2021.
Vogel, Cyrille. *Medieval Liturgy: An Introduction to the Sources.* Revised and translated by William G. Storey, Niels Krogh Rasmussen, and John K. Brooks-Leonard. Washington, DC: Pastoral Press, 1986.
Wagner, Peter. *Einführung in die gregorianischen Melodien: Ein Handbuch der Choralwissenschaft.* 3 vols. Hildesheim: Olms, 1962 [repr. ed.].

Ward, Jennifer C. *English Noblewomen in the Later Middle Ages*. London: Longman, 1992. Repr. ed. London: Routledge, 2014.

Watkins, Carl. "'Folklore' and 'Popular Religion' in Britain during the Middle Ages." *Folklore* 115, no. 2 (August 2004): 140–150.

Watt, Diane. *Women, Writing and Religion in England and Beyond, 650–1100*. London: Bloomsbury Academic, 2020.

Welch, Anna. *Liturgy, Books and Franciscan Identity in Medieval Umbria*. The Medieval Franciscans 12. Leiden: Brill, 2015.

Werminghoff, Albert, ed. *Concilia Aevi Karolini*. Monumenta Germaniae Historica, Concilia 2, 1. Hannover: Impensis Bibliopolii Hahniani, 1906.

Westwell, Arthur Robert. "The Dissemination and Reception of the Ordines Romani in the Carolingian Church, c. 750–900." PhD diss., University of Cambridge, 2018.

Whitehall, Walter Muir, Jr. "Gregorian Capitals from Cluny." *Speculum* 2 (1927): 385–395.

Whittle, Patrick J. "Franciscan Liturgical Practice and the Liturgy of Rome from Francis of Assisi to Haymo of Faversham: Reassessing Current Assumptions." PhD diss., Catholic University of America, 2022.

Wohlmuth, Josef, Gabriel Sunnus, and Johannes Uphus, eds. *Conciliorum oecumenicorum decreta*. Vol. 2. Paderborn: F. Schöningh, 1998.

Yardley, Anne Bagnall. "Clares in Procession: The Processional and Hours of the Franciscan Minoresses at Aldgate." *Women & Music: A Journal of Gender and Culture* 13 (2009): 1–23.

Yardley, Anne Bagnall. *Performing Piety: Musical Culture in Medieval English Nunneries*. New York: Palgrave Macmillan, 2006.

Index: Manuscripts Cited (with Abbreviations)

For the benefit of digital users, indexed terms that span two pages (e.g., 52–53) may, on occasion, appear on only one of those pages.

Tables are indicated by *t* following the page number

Alphabetized by manuscript location (city)

Albi, Bibliothèque municipale Rochegude 44
  Albi 44

Berlin, Staatsbibliothek zu Berlin – Preußischer Kulturbesitz, Ms. Phil. 1667
  Berlin 1667

Bourg-Saint-Pierre, Hospice du Grand-Saint-Bernard, ms. 3 (ancien 10091)
  GSB 3

Chicago, Newberry Library, Vault Manuscript 24
  Newberry 24

Cividale del Friuli, Museo Archeologico nazionale, Cod. CI
  Cividale 101

Cividale del Friuli, Museo Archeologico nazionale, Cod. CII
  Cividale 102

Dublin, Library of Trinity College IE TCD 60 (formerly MS A.1.15)
  Dublin 60

Ivrea, Biblioteca Capitolare d'Ivrea MS 31 (LXXXVI)
  Ivrea 31

Klosterneuburg, Augustiner-Chorherrenstift, Cod. 628
  Klosterneuburg 628

Klosterneuburg, Augustiner-Chorherrenstift, Cod. 629
  Klosterneuburg 629

Klosterneuburg, Augustiner-Chorherrenstift, Cod. 1022A
  Klosterneuburg 1022A

Klosterneuburg, Augustiner-Chorherrenstift, Cod. 1022B
  Klosterneuburg 1022B

Le Mans, Médiathèque Louis Aragon, Bibliothèque municipale 77
  Le Mans 77

Leningrad, Saltykov-Schredrin Public Library, Q.v.I.41
  Leningrad Q.v.I.41

München, Bayerische Staatsbibliothek Clm. 29164 I/1b Lit 27
  München 29164

New York, Pierpont Morgan Library MS G 57
  New York G 57

Oxford, Bodleian Library, MS 585, Part 2 (Summary Catalogue no. 2357)
  Bodleian 585

Paris, Bibliothèque nationale de France, lat. 934
  Paris 934

212 INDEX: MANUSCRIPTS CITED (WITH ABBREVIATIONS)

Paris, Bibliothèque nationale de France,
lat. 2290
Paris 2290
Paris, Bibliothèque nationale de France,
lat. 2291
Paris 2291
Paris, Bibliothèque nationale de France,
lat. 2984
Paris 2984
Paris, Bibliothèque nationale de France,
lat. 12050
Paris 12050
Paris, Bibliothèque nationale de France,
lat. 13875
Paris 13875

Reigate (Surrey), Parish Church of St Mary
Magdalene, Cranston Library, Ms.
2322
Cranston 2322
Reims, Bibliothèque de Reims,
Ms. 213
Reims 213

Sankt Gallen, Stiftsbibliothek, Cod. Sang.
349
St Gall 349

Stockholm, Kungliga biblioteket,
Holm. A 136
Stockholm A 136

Trier, Wissenschaftliche Bibliothek der
Stadt Trier, Hs. 1245/597 8'
Trier 1245/597

Vatican, Biblioteca Apostolica Vaticana,
Arch. Cap. S. Pietro B 79
SP B 79
Vatican, Biblioteca Apostolica
Vaticana, Arch. Cap. S. Pietro
F 11 pt. A
SP F 11
Vatican, Biblioteca Apostolica Vaticana,
Ott. lat. 312
Vatican 312
Vatican, Biblioteca Apostolica Vaticana,
Pal. lat. 485
Vatican 485
Vatican, Biblioteca Apostolica Vaticana,
Pal. lat. 550
Vatican 550

Zürich, Zentralbibliothek, Ms Rh 30
Rheinau 30

Alphabetized by abbreviation and indexed

Albi 44, 139*t*, 141*t*, 145, 147*t*

Berlin 1667, 24n.13, 60–61, 69n.23, 86,
139*t*, 141*t*, 142, 146–48, 152–53
Bodleian 585, 112n.6, 117n.13, 131–32,
134

Cividale 101, 70
Cividale 102, 70
Cranston 2322, 110–36

Dublin 60, 139*t*, 141*t*

GSB 3, 83–109

Ivrea 31, 86

Klosterneuburg 628, 5–6

Klosterneuburg 629, 5–6
Klosterneuburg 1022A, 5–6, 93–94, 96
Klosterneuburg 1022B, 5–6

Le Mans 77, 139*t*, 141*t*
Leningrad Q.v.I.41, 139*t*, 141*t*

München 29164, 139*t*, 141*t*, 147*t*

Newberry 24, 118–19, 118n.15, 123–24,
159n.38
New York G 57, 139*t*, 141*t*

Paris 934, iv
Paris 2290, 59n.1, 80n.41, 81n.43, 86n.12,
139*t*, 141*t*
Paris 2291, 139*t*, 141*t*
Paris 2984, 139*t*, 141*t*, 147*t*

INDEX: MANUSCRIPTS CITED (WITH ABBREVIATIONS)   213

Paris 12050, 139*t*, 141*t*
Paris 13875, 159n.41

Reims 213, 139*t*, 141*t*
Rheinau 30, 139*t*, 141*t*, 142

SP B 79, 14–15n.1, 147*t*, 154
SP F 11, 14–58

St Gall 349, 139*t*, 141*t*, 142–43
Stockholm A 136, 59n.1, 139*t*, 141*t*

Trier 1245/597, 139*t*, 141*t*, 145

Vatican 312, 2n.5, 60–61, 60n.2, 149
Vatican 485, 44n.20, 69n.23, 139*t*, 141*t*
Vatican 550, 86, 139*t*, 141*t*, 145, 146–48, 147*t*

Index: Chants and Other Items in Rituals (alphabetized by standardized incipit)

Bold typeface indicates music notation.
* indicates that the scribal work included only an incipit.
Tables are indicated by *t* following the page number.

Incipit	Genre	Biblical source	SP F 11	Pa 934	GSB 3	Cranston 2322
Ab auditione mala	versicle and response	Psalm 111:7	22-23, 176		98*, 185*	128, 131, 191
Absolve quaesumus domine	prayer		178			
Ad dominum cum tribularer	psalm	Psalm 119	44-47*, 179*	75-79*, 181*		117*, 189*
Ad te domine levavi	psalm	Psalm 24			187	
Anima eius in bonis	versicle and response	Psalm 24:13			99, 185	
Animam eius	antiphon		44-47, 58, 147*t*, 179			
A porta inferi	versicle and response		176	80*, 182*		125, 129-130, 190, 192
Ascendant ad te domine	prayer		177			
Beati immaculati	psalm	Psalm 118				117*, 189*
Beati quorum remissae	psalm	Psalm 31	17-20*, 176*			
Chorus angelorum	antiphon	cf. Luke 16:22		75-79, 148, 156, 158, 161n.46, 165, 181	96-97, 104, 148, 156, 158, 184	
Commendamus te omnipotenti deo eique te cuius es creatura	prayer		25n.14, 177			
Commendamus tibi domine animam famuli tui et precamur propter	prayer		25n.14, 177			115, 189
Commendamus tibi domine animam famuli tui in manibus patriarchum	prayer		23n.9, 177			
Commendo te omnipotenti deo	prayer					115-116, 188

216 INDEX: CHANTS AND OTHER ITEMS IN RITUALS

Incipit	Genre	Biblical source	SP F 11	Pa 934	GSB 3	Cranston 2322
Confitemini domino quoniam	psalm	Psalm 117		75*, 181*		117*, 189*
Convertere domine	antiphon	Psalm 6:5-6	34-36, 58, 147t, 154, 165, 178			
Credidi propter quod locutus	psalm	Psalm 115		75*, 181*	96-97, 184	
Delicta iuventutis	prayer					115, 189
De profundis	psalm	Psalm 129	17-20*, 47-49*, 176*, 179*		98*, 100*, 104*, 109*, 184*	
Deus cui omnia vivunt	prayer				93-94, 104, 109, 184	
Deus cui soli competit medicinam	prayer			178		
Deus misericors deus clemens	prayer					115, 188
Deus omnipotens qui dedit potestatem	prayer			178		
Deus qui humanarum animarum aeternis	prayer				102-103, 109, 186	
Deus vitae dator	prayer				101-105, 109, 186	
Dextera tua	antiphon	cf. Psalm 17:36	38-40, 147t, 179			
Dilexi quoniam	psalm	Psalm 114		75-79*, 181*	96-98, 184	
Dirige domine	antiphon	cf. Psalm 5:9	26-29, 58, 147t, 154, 178			
Diri vulneris novitate	prayer			79-80, 181		
Domine deus in multitudine	antiphon	cf. Psalm 5:8-9	32-34, 58, 147t, 178			
Domine exaudi orationem meam auribus percipe	psalm	Psalm 142	17-20*, 176*			
Domine exaudi orationem meam et clamor meus	psalm	Psalm 101	17-20*, 176*			
Domine exaudi orationem meam	versicle and response	Psalm 101:2	157, 176	80*, 157, 182*	100*, 157, 185*	125*, 129, 157, 190*, 192
Domine ne in furore tuo ... miserere	psalm	Psalm 6	17-20*, 176*			
Domine ne in furore tuo ... quoniam	psalm	Psalm 37	17-20*, 176*			

INDEX: CHANTS AND OTHER ITEMS IN RITUALS 217

Incipit	Genre	Biblical source	SP F 11	Pa 934	GSB 3	Cranston 2322
Dominus suscepit me	antiphon	cf. Psalm 117:13 cf. Psalm 26:13	40-42, 147t, 179			
Dominus vobiscum	versicle and response		176	80, 182	100*, 185*	
Erue domine animam eius	versicle and response		176			125, 127, 129-130, 190, 192
Et animas pauperum	versicle and response	Psalm 73:19			99, 185, 187n.f	129, 191
Et clamor meus ad te perveniat	versicle and response	Psalm 101:2	176			125*, 129*, 190*, 192*
Et lux perpetua	versicle and response	cf. IV Esdras 2:34-35				125*, 190*
Et ne nos see Pater noster						
Et semen	versicle and response	Psalm 24:13			99*, 185*	
Induc eum domine	antiphon	cf. Exodus 15:17	54-56, 147t, 154, 179			
In exitu Israhel	psalm	Psalm 113		69-74*, 165*, 181*	95, 106, 109, 184	
In finem	versicle and response	Psalm 73:19			99, 185	
In memoria aeterna erit iustus	capitulum / versicle and response	Psalm 111:7	176		98, 185	128, 130-131, 191
In paradisum deducant te	antiphon				102, 186	
Kyrie eleison			21*, 176*		92, 98-99, 102-103*, 104, 183, 184, 186*	124, **126-128**, 190, 191
Kyrie eleison	litany					114, 188
Laeto animo	antiphon	cf. Genesis 2:7	47-50, 58, 147t, 149n.16, 164, 179			
Libera me domine	responsory				187	
Miserere mei deus	psalm	Psalm 50	17-20*, 51-54*, 176*, 179*	182*	100-101*, 104*, 185*	

218   INDEX: CHANTS AND OTHER ITEMS IN RITUALS

Incipit	Genre	Biblical source	SP F 11	Pa 934	GSB 3	Cranston 2322
Misericordiam tuam domine sancte pater omnipotens	prayer			68, 181		
Nequando rapiat	antiphon	Psalm 7:3	35-37, 147t, 154, 164, 178			
Ne tradas bestiis	versicle and response	Psalm 73:19			99, 185	129, 191
Non intres in iudicium cum servo tuo	prayer				100-101, 105, 109, 185	
Non intres in iudicium	versicle and response	cf. Psalm 142:2		80*, 182*	99*, 185*	129-130, 191
O anima tibi dico	prayer		23, 177			
Omnipotens sempiterne deus conservator animarum	prayer		176			
Omnipotens sempiterne deus qui humano corpori animam	prayer		177	74-75, 181		
Partem beatae resurrectionis	prayer		177	80-81, 182		
Pater noster	prayer	Matthew 6	21-22*, 157*, 176*	80*, 157*, 182*	92-93*, 98-99*, 102-104*, 108*, 112*, 157*, 183*, 184*, 186*	125*, 127-128*, 157*, 190*, 191*
Pio recordationis (Piae recordationes)	prayer				93-94, 104, 109, 183	
Proficiscere anima Christiana	prayer		24, 177			115, 188
Quia non iustificabitur	versicle and response	Psalm 142:2			99*, 185*	129, 191
Qui cognoscis	antiphon	cf. Psalm 18:13	51-54, 58, 147t, 154, 179			
Redemisti me	antiphon	Psalm 30:6 Luke 23:46	42-44, 57-58, 147t, 154, 165, 179			
Requiem aeternam	responsory verse	cf. IV Esdras 2:34-35				118-124
Requiem aeternam	versicle and response	cf. IV Esdras 2:34-35		80*, 182*	96-97*, 100-101*, 184-185*, 187*	125, 127, 190

INDEX: CHANTS AND OTHER ITEMS IN RITUALS 219

Incipit	Genre	Biblical source	SP F 11	Pa 934	GSB 3	Cranston 2322
Requiesca[n]t in pace	versicle and response	cf. Psalm 4:9	176			125, 127, 129-130, 190, 192
Secundum magnam	antiphon	Psalm 50:3, 10	**29-32**, 58, 147*t*, 165, 178			
Secundum magnam see Miserere mei deus	psalm					
Sed libera see Pater noster						
Subvenite sancti dei	responsory			61n.6, **63-67**, 82, 148, 158-161, 165, 168-169, 180	**89-92**, 102-103*, 104-106, 108, 148, 158-161, 168-169, 183, 186*	**118-124**, 131*, 134, 148, 158-161, 168-169, 189*, 192*
Suscipe domine animam...quam de ergastulo	prayer				96, 184	129, 192
Suscipe domine servum tuum in bonum habitaculum libera	prayer			23-24, 177		
Suscipe domine ancillam tuam in locum	prayer					115-116, 189
Suscipiat eam [te] Christus	responsory verse	cf. Luke 16:22		**63-67**, 158, 168-169, 180	**89-92**, 104, 108, 158, 168-169, 183	**118-124**, 131*, 134-135, 158, 165, 168-169, 189*, 192*
Suscipiat te Christus	antiphon	cf. Luke 16:22	**54-56**, 147*t*, 148, 149n.16, 156, 158, 179	61, **69-74**, 104, 148, 158, 165, 181	95-96, 104, 148, 158, 184	
Te decet hymnus deus	psalm	Psalm 64			187	
Tibi domine commendamus animam famuli tui ut defunctus saeculo	prayer		178	67-68, 181		125-127, 190
Tu iussisti nasci	antiphon				187	

General Index

For the benefit of digital users, indexed terms that span two pages (e.g., 52–53) may, on occasion, appear on only one of those pages.

For specific chants, prayers, and psalms, please see Index: Chants and Other Items in Rituals

For specific manuscripts, please see Index: Manuscripts Cited (with Abbreviations)

Tables are indicated by *t* following the page number

Abraham, bosom of, 24–25, 44–47, 54–58, 63–67, 69–74, 75–79, 82, 89–92, 94–95, 104–6, 118–24, 156, 162–64, 165, 168–69
Andrieu, Michel, 2–3, 60–61, 60n.2, 139*t*, 141*t*, 148–51
angels, 20, 24–25, 54–56, 57, 63–67, 69–74, 75–79, 89–92, 94, 95, 96–98, 102–3, 104–6, 118–24, 162–64
antiphon, please. *See* vii
apostles, 20, 23–24
ascension, melodic, 12, 28–32, 34–36, 39, 40–41, 42–44, 51–54, 61, 63–67, 75–79, 82, 122, 165
ascension, of the soul, 12, 43–44, 61, 63–67, 75–79, 82, 122, 123, 161n.46, 165
Autun, 60–61, 86, 142

baptism, 14–15, 21–22, 74, 84–85, 86–87
Benedict of Aniane, 59–60, 67–68, 74, 79–82, 93n.22, 101, 141*t*, 143–45, 151

Calcidius, 169–70
cantrix, 5–6, 110–11, 117–18, 125–26, 134–35
chants. *See* vii
Cividale, 70
Cluny, 2–3, 21n.5, 70n.24, 78n.36, 80n.40, 85n.4, 93–94, 96, 98n.38, 101, 103, 117n.12, 158–61
comprehension, textual, 10–11, 12, 16–17, 34, 37, 41, 42, 48–50, 107

Council of Agde, 85
Council of Lyons, 163
Council of Nicea, 85

Dante, 60–61, 71–72
David (King), 51–54, 58, 100–1, 144–45
death, of the soul, 34–36
doxology, 44–50, 51–54, 69–74

exodus, of the Israelites, 54–56, 61, 69–74

Fulda, 139*t*, 141*t*, 144–45
funeral, 4–5, 17–18, 118, 132–33, 134–35, 155–56n.32, 156, 171

hell, 22, 79–81, 101, 124–31, 162–64
Hucusque, 60n.2, 67–68, 139*t*, 141*t*, 143–44

Isabelline Rule, 111–12

Jerusalem, heavenly, 24–25, 57
journey, of the soul, 16, 21, 23–25, 56, 57, 61, 64–67, 68, 69–74, 79, 81–82, 92, 103, 104–5, 162–63
See also migration
journey, of the Israelites. *See* 56

kingdom of God, 44–47, 58
Klosterneuburg, 5–6, 93–94, 96, 158–59

Lazarus, 24–25, 44–47, 75–79, 82, 92, 96–98, 165

GENERAL INDEX

libelli, 2–3, 5–6
lion, ravaging, 36–37

Macrobius, 171
manuscripts. *See* Index: Manuscripts Cited (with Abbreviations)
Mass liturgy, 4–6, 14–15, 25–26, 92–93, 110–11, 118, 126, 134–35, 142–43, 156, 163–64
migration, of the soul, 60, 63, 64–66, 92
military (use as a metaphor), 64, 81–82
Monte Cassino, 139*t*, 141*t*, 144–45

Nathan. *See* prophets, Nathan

Office liturgy, 4–6, 18, 25–26, 43, 73–74, 110–11, 111–12n.4, 112n.5, 144–45, 146–48, 154
Office of the Dead, 9–10, 14–15n.1, 69n.23, 76n.34, 81n.43, 138–48, 155–57, 163

patriarchs, 23–25, 94
Plato, 169–73
prayer. *See* vii
prophets, 23–24
    Nathan, 51, 144–45
psalm. *See* vii
psalms, penitential, 16, 17–20, 26, 57, 63, 81–82, 98, 104–6

purgatory, 9–10, 60, 81–82, 162–64, 168–69
    in Dante's *Divine Comedy*, 71

responsory. *See* vii
resurrection, 70, 71–72, 79–81, 142, 161n.46
ritual (book type), 5–6, 111n.3
Rituale of 1614, 3–4

Saint Clare, Second Order of, 111–12
Saints Cyrus and John (Via Biberatica), 14–15
Saint Peter's Basilica (Vatican), 14–15, 155–56
Satan, 25
Sicard, Damien, 2–3, 79, 148–55, 167–68
St-Amand, Abbey of, 59–60
St-Denis, Abbey of, 59–60, 61–62, 63, 68, 74, 86

Timaeus, 169–73
tonus peregrinus, 73–74
transport, of the body, 4–5, 105–6, 145

viaticum, 85–87, 133, 152–53, 169
vigil, with the body, 4–5, 61n.6, 105–6, 138, 146–48, 154–55, 156, 172

washing, of the body, 4–5, 17–18, 102–3, 128–31, 153–54, 160